Cornelius Francis Smarius

Points of Controversy

A Series of Lectures

Cornelius Francis Smarius

Points of Controversy
A Series of Lectures

ISBN/EAN: 9783744660327

Printed in Europe, USA, Canada, Australia, Japan

Cover: Foto ©Thomas Meinert / pixelio.de

More available books at **www.hansebooks.com**

POINTS OF CONTROVERSY,

SERIES OF LECTURES.

BY
REV. C. F. SMARIUS,
MISSIONARY OF THE SOCIETY OF JESUS.

THIRTY-THIRD THOUSAND.

New York:
JOHN GILMARY SHEA,
1870.

PREFACE.

The little volume which we present to the American public, in the form of doctrinal lectures, was written for no other purpose, than, with the assistance of Divine Grace, to convert souls to God. Our missionary experience has taught us, that though by no means necessary, a plain, simple work like the present, may prove useful to a great number of Catholics, Protestants, and Indifferentists in religion, who treat books as they do the fashions, dropping one to adopt another, almost every season. There is no lack of short controversial works in our Catholic Theological literature, and most of those that are before the public, have, doubtless, more intrinsic merit than our lectures. Yet zeal prompts us to add these to the stock, in the hope that they may find a few readers, to whom they may prove of some spiritual service. We shall consider ourselves amply rewarded for our labor, if they become instrumental in leading even one soul to abjure error and embrace the truth as it is in Christ Jesus.

Alas! how many millions of our fellow men, redeemed by the precious blood of the Saviour, are daily lost to the Church and to Heaven, who, if we exerted ourselves a little more in their behalf, might be rescued from darkness and the shadow of eternal death! How much could be done towards converting our countrymen, if we Catholics joined works of zeal and charity to fervent prayer! If we were untiring in our efforts to spread instruction and useful books, tracts, and pamphlets among them, as an antidote against the many slanderous publications which are put forth in hostility to us. How much sinful ignorance would be removed from among the children of the Church themselves, if, instead of subscribing to and purchasing the trivial and often pernicious romances and periodicals of the day, they were to buy and read a few good books of Catholic literature, and make them their delight and study.

Always willing to learn and improve by the wisdom and experience of others, we beg all those who will read these Lectures, to suggest to us, either publicly or privately, whatever additions or corrections they may deem necessary or useful, so that we may insert them in a second edition, or add them to the second volume, which, if this succeeds, we intend soon to publish.

In conclusion, we wish to place our little book under the protection and care of the ever Immaculate Virgin Mary, Mother of God, and Patroness of the infant Church in the United States of America, and we beg her to bless it, its author, and its readers.

CHURCH of the HOLY FAMILY,
    Chicago, Ill.

CONTENTS.

LECT.		PAGE
I.	INDIFFERENCE IN RELIGION............ ...	7
II.	THE BIBLE NOT THE RULE OF FAITH......	50
III.	THE CHURCH OF CHRIST	109
IV.	THE ROMAN CATHOLIC CHURCH, THE CHURCH OF CHRIST	170
V.	CONFESSION	243
VI.	ON PURGATORY AND INDULGENCES	296
VII.	ON THE REAL PRESENCE.................	342
VIII.	HONOR AND INVOCATION OF SAINTS, VENERATION OF IMAGES AND RELICS..........	411
IX.	ON THE HONOR AND INVOCATION OF THE BLESSED VIRGIN MARY.................	453

I.

INDIFFERENCE IN RELIGION.

"Without faith it is impossible to please God." Heb. xi. 6.

Infidelity and a general indifference to all religion are the characteristic traits of our age. The great and fierce battles of error against truth, that marked the years immediately following the so-called Reformation, have ceased, and have been succeeded by a false, delusive peace. A fatal lethargy has come over the minds and hearts of men, in which religion, virtue, duty, are looked upon as empty phantoms in a dream, leaving a momentary impression of their beauty, but soon to be forgotten in the more attractive and absorbing interests of daily life. While we boast of the triumphs of genius over matter, and point to a thousand inventions and discoveries that minister to our carnal wants, and carnal pleasures, we are silent on the fearful ravages which a total apathy to our higher and more lasting interests, has made in our midst. We have established lines of communication with the most distant nations of the earth, but we have ceased to commune with Heaven. Our merchant vessels are laden with the riches of every land, but the barque of our soul is without cargo or ballast, tossed to and fro by every wind of error and passion. Our schools and academies, our colleges and universities, impart the highest instruction in every branch of human knowledge, but the science of God and revelation, the science of the saints, is banished from the class-room, and the professor's chair. We are becoming a Godless people.

A chief cause of this moral degeneracy may be traced to the principle of private judgment introduced by Luther and Calvin, as the highest and only authority in religion and morality. Since the time of these Reformers, religion ceased to be the mistress, and became the slave of man. He was no longer bound to obey her, but she was bound to obey him. His reason was no longer subject to her divine authority, but she became subject to his prejudices and passions. The Scriptures, although cried up as the supreme authority, lost their objective value, and men no longer listened to the words, "Thus saith the Lord," but gave ear to the freaks and fancies of every upstart prophet and doctor, whose best reason for the faith that was in him, was, "I believe so;" "It is my impression;" "It is my opinion." Reason itself was soon dethroned, and feeling became the exponent of truth. Men judged of religion as they did or their breakfasts and dinners. This was true, and that was false, because they liked the one and disliked the other. They felt religion as they felt heat and cold, and behaved accordingly. New fashions of belief became as numerous as new fashions of dress. Every year, every month, produced a new one, which in its turn was succeeded by another still more recent. Oneness in faith and union of believers became impossibilities. Confessions and catechisms of doctrines, councils, and synods, reading recreant members out of church, excommunicating false teachers, and heterodox believers, could not stay the individualizing process of this principle. The most ignorant saw that such restraints upon their personal liberties were evident contradictions of the first principle introduced by the innovators. Had not every individual the same privilege as his neighbor to read the Bible, and interpret it as best he could, by the aid of his private judgment? Was the Spirit exclusive in his operations on the soul that wished to get religion from the common book of faith? What right had Luther to denounce the Anabaptists as heterodox? What right had Calvin to burn Servetus for opinions, which he also had conscientiously drawn from the pages of the inspired volume? A shoe-black was as much entitled as the learned doctor of Wittenberg, or the profound thinker of Geneva, to tell the world what he understood by the mystery of the Trinity, the incarnation of the Word, the predestination of the just and the wicked, and all the other dogmas of faith.

Toleration was the necessary result of the principle established. Not a mere toleration of opinion, preventing physical violence and persecution, leaving every one to worship God according to the dictates of his own conscience; but a toleration which approved all, even the most glaring contradictions in faith, as the working of one and the same Spirit of truth, who was given differently to different individuals, according to their religious capacities and wants. Free from all *external* restraint, bound no longer by councils, synods, confessions, or catechisms, individual religion became naturally invisible. It remained confined within the chambers of the mind. This gave rise to the idea of an invisible Church, and of course of an unseen faith, which although unknown to earth, was watched with peculiar interest in Heaven. But how was this invisible Church to be known even as invisible? That which cannot be seen by the eye of the body, nor the eye of the mind, must needs remain in impenetrable darkness. The common sense of the people was not slow in discovering the absurdity and the contradiction. But what was the remedy? There was none! Public authority was banished; individual faith had retired into privacy; the Bible truths were the property of each subjective understanding; apathy and indifference succeeded, as the natural consequences of a principle which dissolved all union among the members of the same faith, and all the obligations which spring from such a union. The educated, the talented among them, looked upon religion as a sham; and the vulgar, the illiterate, as a thing beyond the reach of their understanding. The Reformation ended in infidelity and indifference to all forms of faith and religion.

This is no unwarranted assertion of our own. Protestant writers bear ample testimony to its truth. Beckendorf writes that "there is no Church among his brethren, but merely parties; the old Church *is in ruins.*" Ball says: "The dissolution of the Protestant Church is certain;

the "Hallische Literatur Zeitung" declares that "there is no Protestant Church, but only Protestant churches;" "One sees Protestantism," says Professor Schwann, "but no Protestant Church;" Schlegel avers, that, of the greatest part of the Evangelical churches, it may be doubted whether they make any pretence to the name of Christian Church.

The "Gazette" of Berlin, in Prussia, wrote a few years ago: "It is easy to prove, yea, it has been proved more than once, that there is not one of all our pastors, who believes what another believes." "They are all laughed at as so many false prophets." (Ludke). "The people seeing their contradictions, treat their guides as imbeciles and impostors." (Fischer). "We unhesitatingly affirm," says Dr. Planck, "that there is not one theologian among us, who has not renounced some important point of faith, considered important by the Reformers." "The Antichristian spirit shows an open front; . . . the Bible is shamefully interpretted; . . . our universities increase the evil.' (John Müller). "Satan himself," says Ewald "has more faith than many of our Biblical interpreters, and Mohammed was much better than they." "The decadence of religion," exclaims Kirchaff, "in all Protestant countries, is but too evident." "Not the higher classes alone, but the people also," writes Bickel, "plunge daily more and more into religious indifferentism." "We are come to that pass," wrote the "Theological Journal," in 1830, "that if the middle classes are not yet despoiled of every moral habit, the religious spirit, at least, has completely forsaken them." "The Lutheran Church," says Frœseisen, "resembles, as to its different factions, a worm cut up into a thousand pieces, every one of which stirs so long as it retains the least particle of life, but ends by dying." (Discourse at Strasburg). The same infidelity and indifference have paralyzed the Calvinistic Church of Switzerland. Vernet's system of theology, which denies the divinity of Jesus Christ, is the standard work used in their university. "Believe anything you like of Jesus Christ," said he to his theological students, "but do not believe him to be God." (Sketch of Religious Discussions). No wonder that the people should re-echo the voice of such masters, and exclaim in the very streets, ' down with Jesus Christ."

Pass over to France,—you hear the same words of wailing from the lips of the Protestant leaders. "We had a Church," writes Edmond Schever, "we have now only churches. We were a Reformed Church, we are so no longer. Its name now adorns only a mutilated phantom." (Present State of the Reformed Church in France). The Foreign Aid Society's Report, read in 1841, as follows: "A few years ago, it was hardly possible to find twenty *pasteurs*, who confessed the doctrines of the Trinity and Atonement. At present, Protestantism in France is, for the most part, Socinianism."

The third volume of the "Scottish Christian Herald" (p. 51-54), informs us that "of Protestant ministers who, in Belgium, afford religious instruction to *thirteen* different congregations, there are only *four* who know the truth; the rest, being either Rationalists or Socinians, hate it with their whole hearts!"

Speaking of Sweden, Norway and Finland, Robert Haldane says, that, "Though the tide of infidelity reached these Northern countries more slowly, it's advent was none the less disastrous. The faith of the people was everywhere overturned by the preachers of humanity sent forth by the infidel University of Copenhagen. At present, one may travel through these countries, and, perhaps not find anything like the Gospel in *twenty* parishes." (R. Haldane's second review of the Conduct of the Directors of Brit. and For. Bible Society,

Edin., 1826-1861.) We all know what havoc indifferentism has made in England and our own country. Protestantism is no longer a protest against the religion of Rome, but against all religion. Positive dogmatism is no longer its attribute. It has lost the very few pieces of the seamless garment which it took along, at its first separation, and which it appeared willing to preserve, when it robbed the Catholic Church of some thousands of its nominal believers. Its ministers and doctors dare no longer preach or teach any article of faith, which the people are likely to disown, as uncongenial to their prejudices and feelings. Every minister who would be heard, must first feel the pulse of the audience to which he preaches the Gospel. Opposition to the sovereign will of the dear people in matters of faith and morals, is as sure to meet with contempt, as opposition in political matters. Every preacher is the creature of his congregation more thoroughly than every representative is the creature of his constituents. The awful truths, "He that believeth not shall be damned;" "Without Faith it is impossible to please God;" "One Faith, one Baptism," are heard no longer in the general assembly, or from the pulpit; but instead of them, the soft, flattering maxims, "Believe what you think fit;" "Suit yourselves;" "We shall all come right in the end."

Add to this intellectual apathy the no less general disregard of all moral obligation or restraint, which increases in proportion as faith loses its hold upon the people. Its causes also lie in the principles set down by the first Reformers. Disappointed pride generally seeks refuge in the gratification of the senses. The idolatry of the intellect is succeeded by the deification of the flesh. The worship of gods and demigods is followed by the worship of the passions. Often they go hand in hand together. The flesh is a powerful antagonist of the spirit, and fights as unrelentingly for its pretended rights as does the intellect. Hence the Reformers could not separate the one from the other. The same pens that wrote in favor of the rights of reason, as the judge of truth and falsehood, also wrote that man has lost his free will, and that it is impossible even for the just, to observe the commandments. Yea more, they made God the author of evil, the mover and impeller to sin: so that the vocation of Paul to the apostleship among the Gentiles, and the adultery of David, were alike the work of God.(Chemnitz, Loc. Theol. Ed. Leyser,

1615, p. 173. Zwingle, De Providentia, tom. i., c. vi. Calvin's Institutes, lib. iv., c. 18, § 2. Beza, Aphorism. xxii.). It is not difficult to see what an injurious influence such a doctrine must have had on the morality of the individual and of society. If, said the logical youth, my sins are not my own; if God is their author, why should I have faith any more than justice or purity? Yea, the conclusions derivable from these principles were carried further still. The Infidels, Spiritualists, and other Freethinkers of our day, have deduced from them: that there is no moral evil in the world; that all that is, is right; that physical evils are the only obstacles to man's happiness; that true virtue consists in obeying the voice of nature and the impulses of the heart.

Such is the lamentable condition to which many have come in our age and country. We ourselves have met several who had fallen into this deplorable abyss of mental and moral degradation. Can anything be done to remedy this evil? We must return to first principles, and from them deduce the obligations which have been disowned, the duties which have been neglected. This we shall endeavor to do in the following lectures.

There is a God; "the heavens and the earth are full of his glory." "The firmament on high is His beauty. . . . The sun, when he appeareth, showing forth at his rising, an admirable instrument, the work of the Most High. . . . Great is the Lord that made Him. . . . The glory of the stars is the beauty of heaven; the Lord enlightened the world on high. . . . By the words of the Holy One they shall stand in judgment, and shall never fail in their watches. Look upon the rainbow and bless Him that made it; it is very beautiful in its brightness. He encompasseth the heaven about, with the circle of its glory. The hands of the Most High have displayed it. . . . What shall we be able to do to glorify Him? For the Almighty Himself is above all His works." (Ecclus. xliii.)

"What shall we be able to do to glorify Him?" We shall fall down before Him and adore Him. This is our first, our reasonable, our necessary duty. If there is a God, and that God created us, as well as all things that exist, we are bound to acknowledge the relation in which we stand to Him. Now, we know and believe that it is not we ourselves who made ourselves, but that His hands have made us and formed us. God, then, is our first beginning. He it is who "formed the eye and planted the ear" (Ps. xciii. 9): He who "fashioned us wholly round about" (Job x. 8): He who "formed man of the slime of the earth, and breathed into his face the breath of life, and man became a living soul." (Gen. ii. 7). We are beholden to God for all that we are; and are therefore dependent on Him. Moreover, the same cause that made us, preserves our existence. Without His almighty power and infinite goodness, we should fall back into the nothing out of which He drew us. As our Creator and Preserver, His dominion over His creatures is absolute and universal. He has all and every right over the works of His own divine hands. His first right is, that a free but dependent creature should acknowledge this dependence on Him. If the heavens and the earth themselves, after their own way, confess His wonders (Ps. lxxxviii. 6); if from the earth the dragons, all the deeps, fire, hail, snow, ice, stormy winds, praise Him and fulfill His word (Ps. cxlviii. 7), how much more should man, who is created in His own image and likeness, praise and serve the Lord his God? If they, after their manner, adore and worship Him as their sovereign Lord, how much more should man?

As God is our first beginning, so is He also our last end. He proposeth to Himself an end worthy of Himself in creating the universe and man. That end could be no other than Himself. The infinite cannot subject itself to the finite, the limitless to the limited—the eternal to that which is passing—the immutable to the ever changing—the perfect to that which is essentially imperfect. Nor can man exist for the finite and limited creatures of time. Endowed with an intellect which is created for truth, and a heart which is made for good, man, although finite in nature, tends to the possession of infinite truth and infinite good, and by so doing recognizes the infinite truth and good, as worthy of a higher love than any limited truth and good. This is interior worship, and includes only acts peculiar to the mind and heart. But since the whole man, body and soul, depends on his Maker and his last end, he must acknowledge that double dependence by acts corresponding to the nature of his compound being. His body, then, must manifest, after its own way, its entire dependence on the God that made it, so that man must adore his Creator, by acts of external as well as internal worship. And as man is a social being, his external acts of worship mus necessarily come under the observation of the society of which he is a member.

God, to be worshipped as He deserves, must be known to the worshipper. How could man otherwise tend to God as his last end? We do not desire what is unknown to us. Our intellect, therefore, must study the nature of the Deity and His attributes, both to satisfy its infinite longings after the truth, and to furnish the will with the means by which it can reach the goal to which it tends, and for which it is created. Religion is that means; for its object is to make us acquainted with the nature of the Deity, the relations in which we stand to Him, and He to us, and consequently the obligations which flow from those relations.

Human reason can, absolutely speaking, know that there is a being, which is Eternal, Omnipotent, Supreme, Infinitely Perfect, and that man owes Him worship and adoration; and the human will can, absolutely speaking, practise the obligations, which flow from the knowledge of our relations to God,—yet all history and experience teach us that, in point of fact, the one, unaided by revelation, has never understood the full extent of these truths, nor the other, unassisted by grace, ever practised the obligations which these truths naturally entail. Scarcely was Adam banished from the delightful garden of Paradise, when those truths, which he beheld in all their beauty, and faithfully carried out in practice before his fall, were obscured in the minds of his children. The most absurd and contradictory notions of a Deity, and His attributes, began to prevail. The pure worship of the one true and living God was gradually abandoned, and idolatry and superstition succeeded in its stead. Not only the vulgar crowd, the illiterate multitude, but the most learned sages, the profoundest philosophers, the acutest lawgivers, the most prominent statesmen, orators and poets, lost sight of the true God, and indulged in the most ludicrous and revolting religious practices. Not one of them, from Confucius and Lao-Tsee, in China, to Cicero and Seneca, in Rome, was able to give the world a natural theology or moral philosophy which answered all the wants of mind and heart. The works of the best of them teem with errors and absurdities. Nor could they, on the hypothesis that they had taught the whole truth concerning God and man, and the relations which exist between them, have succeeded in acquainting the world at large, with what they th selves knew, or in enforcing the obligations which they deduced from that knowledge. To succeed in this, they should have had it in their power to communicate the talent necessary to fathom these truths and obligations, and the moral force to put them into practice. This they could not impart. Meanwhile, error asserted its right to dogmatize, and passion to be gratified and indulged. How could their most lucid demonstrations check the arrogance of the one, and the powerful impulses of the other, without the interposition of a higher influence? No wonder, therefore, that Plato exclaimed, "A teacher is necessary, but no one will teach us, unless a God lead the way."

That teacher came, that God appeared and showed us the way. He gave us a revelation from Heaven. That revelation is twofold. In the first place, it consists of those truths which reason alone could, strictly speaking, know without this special assistance, such as the existence of God, His eternity, providence, the immortality of the soul, the reward of virtue, and punishment due to vice. These truths are supernatural through revelation, not as to their objective verity, but as to the manner in which they are made known. Secondly, it comprises truths which transcend the natural powers of reason, and the revelation of which is supernatural as to their substance and their manner. Such, for example, is the truth that God is one in essence and three in person. Such truths, because they lie out of the natural capacity of human reason, are called mysteries. Since, then, there were truths which reason, unaided by revelation, could not possibly think of, much less understand, even after they were revealed as to their intrinsic nature or manner of existence, it was necessary that God should attest the fact of His having revealed such truths by unmistakable evidences, such evidences as would convince the reason of man that He truly revealed them.

These evidences He did give to man, and they consist of miracles and prophecies. A miracle is a sensible effect, at variance with the known laws of nature, and produced in confirmation of a certain doctrine. A prophecy is a certain prediction of an event which cannot possibly be foreseen in natural causes, and is uttered likewise in attestation of a certain truth.

Such miracles and prophecies transcending, as they do, all the known powers of created nature, can be the work of God alone. Whenever, therefore, they occur in confirmation of the truth of revelation, that revelation is thereby proved to be Divine, if there remains no solid reason to deny it after the revelation is made. But there can be no solid reason when the truth which the miracle attests is not evidently contradictory to any other well known truth of reason or of revelation, and when there is nothing in the manner of proposing the truth, nor in the end for which it is made, or in other circumstances, which could make it improbable.

Now, that such miracles have been wrought and prophecies uttered in attestation of the revelation made by God to man, is a well known fact of history.

The pages of the Old and New Testaments abound with miraculous facts and prophecies. The blind see, the lame walk, the dead rise from their graves, in confirmation of the doctrines which are there recorded. We are bound to accept revelations thus attested as the revelations of God Himself.

For, when God reveals any truth, whether of a speculative or practical nature, He must needs do so for an end. This end can be no other than His greater glory and our greater happiness. Both these motives oblige us to accept and believe His revelation. Has He not a perfect right to be known, to be reverenced, served, and adored as He pleases?

To withhold that tribute of our mind and heart, is to insult His sovereign dominion over our whole being. Zeal for our own happiness impels us to make use of those means which will most certainly and infallibly realize that happiness. But among these means none is more necessary than a correct knowledge of God, and of the duties which we owe Him as our first beginning and last end. Religion is the only adequate guide to this knowledge. Hence the necessity of admitting religion is as great as the necessity of attaining our happiness itself. Faith, therefore, in the doctrine of Divine revelation, is necessary unto our real well-being for time and for eternity.

But this revelation is essentially one in its nature. God is infinite and infallible Truth. He cannot be deceived Himself, nor can He deceive us in the revelation of His truths. All, then, are bound to believe the revelation made in the one only sense in which it was made. Different faiths in one and the same revelation are an evident contradiction.

It is not true, that all religions are equally acceptable to God. To predicate such absurdity of God is to blaspheme His name and to destroy His very nature. To believe God's word otherwise than as it lies in His divine mind, is to believe God to be different from, and contradictory to Himself. God is the truth: He cannot at the same time be error. God is one: He cannot possibly be divided. To admit that truth and error are the same in God is not only to place Him in contradiction with Himself, but to destroy His very nature. Error excludes truth. Put error in God and He will cease to be the Truth; He will cease to be God.

If all religions are the same, then God can be served by error and vice, as well as by truth and virtue. For these religions contradict each other, both in points of speculative and practical doctrines. What the one admits, the other denies. What the one prescribes as duty, the other forbids as sin. Can it be the same to God whether with the Socinian you deny the Trinity of persons, or with the Trinitarian admit the Triunity of God? Can it be the same to the Author of all truth, whether you believe, or whether you do not believe, that He has predestined some to be damned and others to be saved, without any regard whatsoever to their good or evil deeds? Is it the same, whether you believe in the necessity of regeneration by baptism, or absolutely deny its power to purify the soul? Is there no distinction between the doctrine of Luther—that faith alone will save a man—and the doctrine of those who preach the necessity of good works unto salvation? What kind of God do you make to yourselves? One who delights in all possible contradictions; who, like yourself, calls truth error, and error truth; virtue vice, and vice virtue? Truly, such a deity would be as absurd a being as Apis and Osiris among the Egyptians, Vishnou among the Hindoos, Zeus or Jupiter among the Greeks and Romans. God wishes to be worshipped in spirit and in truth, but He cannot be worshipped in truth, when the religion which commands the worship is false.

If all religions are equally acceptable to God, what will prevent you from embracing and rejecting the one after the other. To-day Jew, to-morrow Turk, the next day Greek, the fourth, Nestorian, the fifth, Armenian, the sixth, Eutychian, the seventh, Abyssinian, the eighth, Lutheran, next Calvinist, Anabaptist, Anglican, Methodist, Quaker, New Jerusalemite, Mormon, Spiritist; yea, what forbids you prostrating yourself under the wheels of the Juggernaut, instead of falling down before the Crucifix?

Nor is it true that as honesty is the best policy, so it is the best religion. Honesty, in your sense of the word, is the same as justice, but justice is a virtue which gives to every one his own. This virtue is not perfect, unless you give God His own. Hence, the Redeemer said: "Render unto Cæsar the things that are Cæsar's, and to God the things that are God's." (Matt. xxii. 21.) God has rights over you, and consequently, you have duties towards Him. To refuse compliance with those duties is to withhold from Him what is His due; it is to be unjust; to be dishonest.

From what has been said, you have learned, that religion alone can teach us the nature of those duties which we owe to God, and that the religion which teaches them is necessarily one. To know your duties, therefore, you must know that religion; and to accomplish them, you must follow its commands. Out of it, you cannot know them with certainty, because all religions out of it are necessarily made up of error; otherwise they would not be different from the one true religion. In following any of them, you follow the dictates of error, at least, to a certain extent, and God cannot accept the tribute of error with the same will with which He receives the homage of truth. You cannot, therefore, please God in any other than the one true religion, which He himself has revealed and established upon earth. And if the true religion is necessary to man's happiness, you cannot possibly be happy out of that one, only true religion.

You boast of your honesty as the best and only religion. But honesty is not the only virtue, injustice is not the only vice, in the code of morality. There are as many virtues and vices, as there are passions in the human breast. Every one of these virtues must be practised, every one of these vices must be avoided, in order to attain happiness. What sanction have you in the natural law, for the practice of the one and the avoidance of the other? Will you say that virtue is her own reward? True; but is the happiness which follows the consciousness of good, and the remorse which follows the consciousness of evil, a sufficient motive for all? Not only does conscience, left to itself, often entertain erroneous notions, concerning the duties which it is to perform, and the vices which it must avoid, but prejudice, interest, ambition, and a host of other passions, not unfrequently change and pervert all the principles of morality on which it should be based. To form conscience, to secure it against sophistry on the one hand, and passion on the other, you need religion, whose principles are the only safeguards against error and passion.

But, we are told, the sanction of virtue is in the social laws of nations. They are sufficient to make man an honest, upright, moral being, such as your religion requires him to be.

This objection is so directly at variance with common sense, and daily experience, that it scarcely deserves an answer. For, besides the well known fact, that no nation, ancient or modern, which attempted to draw up a code of laws for the government of its people, independently of religion, ever succeeded in making thoroughly just and reasonable laws, the sanction of them reaches at most only public crimes, and virtues. It punishes only those transgressions which lie on the surface of human depravity, and rewards only those virtues which find their way to public notice. What becomes, meanwhile, of the countless violations of law committed in secret? How do those laws reach the dishonest merchant, who, by a thousand ingenious methods, overreaches his neighbor in business? How do they affect the statesman and the magistrate, who, with honesty on their lips, practise the most outrageous frauds upon the people whom they govern? How do they prevent the private quarrels of the family? How do they check the private immorality of passionate youth, the secret infidelity of wedded love? These laws can indeed, to a certain extent, arrest the progress of public disorder; they can repress the fury of the madman, who would lift the incendiary torch, or unsheathe the sword of vengeance against his fellow-man; they can diminish highway robberies, and midnight thefts; but they cannot reach the heart or conscience of the crafty scoundrel, who plans his plots of mischief in the dark, and consummates the purpose of his villainy in the attics or cellars, where dwells the accomplice of his crimes.

These laws may throw the iron chain, or hang the heavy ball, upon the limbs of culprits; they may bury the transgressor in the gloomy cells of prisons and penitentiaries; they may even make a public example of him, by hanging him on a gibbet: but they cannot enforce the practice of those virtues which are the foundation stones of order, prosperity, and happiness, in the family and society.

They cannot teach the egotist, humanity; the drunkard, sobriety; the idle, industry; the miser, hospitality; the husband, chastity; the wife, fidelity: they cannot check those fearful scandals which are the ruin of the innocent, and the bane of morality.

Efficaciously to prevent the commission of

crime, and to inculcate the practice of virtue, the laws of religion must come to the aid of the laws of states and governments; the latter must be based on the former, and besides the terrors of human vengeance and the hopes or earthly rewards, religion must point out to the delinquent, punishments which end not with death, and rewards to the well-doer, which survive him in a better and happier world. The laws of religion alone can form a sound individual and social conscience, curb the restlessness of passion, and create respect for virtue. They alone can produce that moral heroism, which is willing to sacrifice all—father, mother, brother, sister, lands and estates, even life itself, if necessary, to assert the majesty of truth, or the dignity of virtue. They alone inspire that chivalry which makes a man conquer himself.

"All very well," says the man of business. "but let women do the praying, and we shall do the working. A man, after all, must live, his family must be provided for; we cannot leave these things to chance."

In other words, you wish to say that men have no need of religion; that it may be an amusement proper for the other sex, but that men, who are in the world, and have to work in it, discharge all their duties and satisfy their conscience, when they fulfill the obligations which spring from their professions or avocations in life. Do you really believe what you say? Is man's nature so different from woman's that he can claim a special exemption from duties and obligations which were imposed on all? Though head of the family over which he presides, has he no master to whom he owes submission and obedience? Though called upon by the votes of the people to govern states, kingdoms, or empires, is there none above him, who calls Himself the King of kings, and Lord of lords? Though generally more highly gifted in point of intellect, has his reason no need of a guide to prevent him from falling into error or into doubt? Are not his passions as strong, and his temptations to gratify them more numerous than those of woman? Does not the same judgment await him, and will he be less accountable for his evil deeds, merely because he had it in his power to commit them with greater impunity? Was not the same hell created for the adulterer as for the adulteress? Did not the prodigal need the conversion which was wrought in the Magdalen? Had not Zaccheus need of atoning for his injustice, the thief upon the cross for his robberies and murders? Why did St. Paul address the men of Athens, who worshipped an unknown God, and preach to them the existence of a God man, in whose name alone all that are to be, must be saved? Why did the God-man Himself denounce the hypocrisy of the Pharisee, and the Scribe, and the unbelief of all carnal Jews, if there is an exception made in favor of man?

True, you have your duties to fulfill with regard to your wife and children, your patrons, your customers, and your clients. But religion, far from preventing you from doing so, commands a scrupulous compliance with them. Nor do any of her doctrines or practices interfere with your domestic or social obligations. All she does is to regulate them, to give them the proper tendency, to point out the only real end for which they were imposed upon you. She stimulates activity, moderates excess, sympathizes with misfortune, removes the causes of despair, and opens the way to better hopes than those which spring from mere natural success in life. She teaches you how to sanctify labor, how to make every drop of sweat a pearl in the diadem of unfading glory.

The great misfortune of our age lies precisely in the inversion of the laws of order. We have forgotten that man liveth not by bread alone, that the Kingdom of God is not meat and drink; that to be true to ourselves we should first seek the Kingdom of God and His justice, and, that a kind Providence, which clothes the lily of the field, and feeds the little sparrow, will add all other things that are really necessary or useful to our happiness here below. We forget that money cannot supply the want of honesty, and that power does not preclude the necessity of submission and humility; that God cannot be bribed by the one, nor intimidated by the other; that He is no accepter of persons; that before Him we are all as if we were not, a handful of dust and ashes, a leaf which is borne away by the wind. We forget that we have no lasting resting place below, that we are seeking for a city which was not built by human hands; that our Eden was forfeited and that invisible cherubim guard the entrance against all regress into its delightful bowers. We forget the question of the Saviour, "What shall it profit a man if he gain the whole world, and lose his own soul? Or what shall a man give in exchange for his soul?" (Mark, viii. 36, 37.) We no longer realize the truth of David's exclamation: "What have I in heaven, and besides Thee, what do I desire upon earth?... It is good for me to adhere to my God, to put my hope in the Lord God." (Ps. lxxii. 25-28.) No, they are not truly happy, "whose sons are as new plants in their youth; their daughters decked out, adorned round about after the similitude of a temple: their storehouses full, flowing out of this into that. Their sheep fruitful in young, abounding in their goings forth: their oxen fat. But happy is that people whose God is the Lord." (Ps. cxliii. 12, 13, 14, 15.) Such are the people who believe true bliss and real happiness flow.

God is good. He hath loved us with an everlasting love. (Jer. xxxi. 3.) He willeth not the death of the sinner. (Ezech. xxxiii. 11.) He did not create me to be damned.

Yes; God is truly good and merciful; why then are you evil because He is good? He willeth not the death of a sinner; but why, then, do you refuse to be converted, and live. God is good, but He is also just. One attribute of the Divine Nature does not exclude nor contradict the other, for His attributes are one and the same thing with His divine essence. While His infinite goodness invites you to repentance, and offers you the precious gift of faith, without which it is impossible to be saved, His infinite justice, on the other hand, threatens obstinacy in sin, and wilful unbelief, with eternal destruction. He that will say on the last day to the just: "Come, ye blessed of My Father, possess the kingdom prepared for you from the foundation of the world," (Matt. xxv. 34): will also say to the wicked, "Depart from Me, ye cursed, into everlasting fire, which was prepared for the devil and his angels." (Ibid. 41.) You misconstrue the goodness of God. God is good, in creating you for an end which transcends all utterance and conception; for He Himself is to "be your reward exceeding great." (Gen. xv. 2.) He is good, in giving you the means to reach that end, in offering to all the gift of faith, in facilitating the observance of His commandments by His holy grace; in opening to all the channels of these graces through the sacraments. He is good, in furnishing all with the means of repentance and expiation for their sins, and of increase of holiness and perfection, when they have been justified, in giving them the means of bringing their temptations to a happy issue. In all these things God's goodness is most beautifully and touchingly visible. But you would have God's goodness,—conniving at impiety; sanctioning infidelity; encouraging scepticism; promoting indifferentism in religion! These things are inconsistent with God's nature, and He cannot approve or sanction them.

Doubtless God did not create you in order to damn you; he left that fearful power to yourself. Like a good father, He gave you the means to be saved, and told you, at the same time, that the abuse of them would lead to your own destruction. When your father sets you up in life with all the pecuniary means that are necessary to success,—when he tells you, moreover, in what undertaking you are sure to succeed, if you employ the proper means, and in what undertaking, if you abuse your natural gifts, you are sure to fail,—he has done his duty, and you alone are to blame if you miscarry in your choice. We are to judge ourselves, in order not to be judged by the Lord. Hence we read that Judas, who betrayed Christ, saw, before he terminated his wretched existence by suicide, that he was condemned. (Matt. xxvii.) His own reason and conscience convicted him of damnable guilt in the sight of his Maker. If the governor of a State offers life to a convict who is condemned to die, where rests the blame, if the latter insists on going to the gallows? God offers you life, if you will but comply with a few easy conditions which he attaches to the boon.

"But these conditions are too hard."

Have you ever endeavored to fulfill them? You cannot reasonably make this objection until you have tried the experiment. Do you deem it a legitimate excuse in the student to answer his master, "Oh, I cannot learn that lesson," as long as he has not made the attempt to do so? Can you excuse your servant for refusing to lift a certain weight, on his mere word, "I cannot," if he never once put his hand to it? You do not reason thus concerning the daily duties of life. Study, reflect, meditate, ask and pray, and you will find that the yoke which you dread is sweet, and the burden light. You will find that you can do all things in Him that strengtheneth you.

"I shall see to these matters hereafter."

When? When you are old and decrepit—when life's lease is out, and you are about to pay the forfeit of neglect of payment? Why not now? Time is short, eternity is long. Do you reason with regard to the things of time, as you do with regard to those of eternity? Do you say of your business matters, "I shall attend to them hereafter?" Do you defer your dinner till the next day, while the hungry appetite clamors for the food that is placed before you on the table? Do you say, "I shall make my bargain to-morrow," when to-day it is offered in the market? "O, ye sons of men, how long will ye be dull of heart?" (Ps. iv. 3.) "Watch ye, because you know not at what hour your Lord will come." (Matt. xxiv. 42.) Is not time given you to prepare for eternity? You delay not to purchase stocks, to accumulate capital, to add house to house, and acre to acre; why do you defer purchasing the precious pearl of the kingdom of Heaven? You have time to waste in attending clubs and meetings, in frequenting theatres and ball-rooms, in gaming and gambling, in eating and drinking; why can you not spend a moment in listening to the Word of God? in sating your hungry soul with the bread that came from Heaven? in drinking of the waters that spring up into life eternal? You have time to beautify your premises, to cultivate the fading flowers, to adorn your parlors and your sitting-rooms; can you not find a spare hour to adorn your heart with the beauty of virtue?

"There is good and evil in all religions; why should I be bound to connect myself with any?"

If you mean to say that the principles of all

religions are partly true and partly false, you are mistaken; for then there would be no religion at all. Religion comes from God, not from man, and nothing false or evil can come from God, who is the sovereign truth and good. If you mean to assert that even false religions have some principles which are good, you are right in the assertion, but wrong in the inference which you draw from it. A religion made up of sheer errors without any basis of truth, could scarcely be conceived, much less exist in the world. But it does not follow that a part of the truth is as good to you as the whole, any more than that a quarter of a dollar is as of much value to you as the whole, a maimed limb as good as a sound, a sick body as serviceable as a healthy one, or a little talent as valuable as prominent intellectual gifts or genius. We need the truth in its integrity, not in fragments only; we need the full blaze, not a mere glimpse or gleam. When God reveals, He wishes to be believed unreservedly. One word of His is as good as another, one command as binding as another. Christ is not divided; you cannot halt between Him and Belial, nor choose between light and darkness. In this instance, "Whosoever but offendeth in one point is become guilty of all." (James ii.

10.) If you wish to say that in all religions there are bad as well as good men, you must make a distinction. That there are good men in false religions in the sense that the false religion produces good men, is not true, any more than that a fig-tree bears grapes, or the vine figs, or fresh water yields salt. (James, iii. 12.) Men are better than their principles only when they abandon bad for good principles in their practice. That there are bad men in the true religion cannot be denied; but they are bad, despite, not in virtue of their religion. It is not the religion that should be blamed, but the men, who call themselves by her name, and cloak themselves with her garb. There are bad children in good families, and bad citizens under very good constitutions. Should the good children cease to be members of the family, disown the father that begot them and the mother that brought them forth, merely because they have brothers and sisters who neglect their filial duty? Should the honest citizen flee his state or country, because he lives in the midst of knaves and rogues? The religion of the Saviour did not lose any of its truth or beauty, because a weak Apostle denied his Master, and a wicked traitor defiled his soul by the crimes of hypocrisy, sacrilege, and suicide. The rays of the sun do not lose their light, because they fall upon substances impervious to their splendor. The art of healing cannot be set aside as useless, because its remedies do not cure every patient to whom they are applied. The true religion has to deal with men who have their freedom of choice and action. They can reject or abuse the blessings which it offers them. The offer is not the less good, because the recipient of the gift proves ungrateful. Truth and virtue are not convertible terms, they are not even correlative. The best lawyer at the bar may be the greatest rogue in his office, and the most learned and experienced judge, be a greater criminal than the culprit whom his sentence dooms to death. So the strongest believer may fall into sin.

Men can contradict the convictions of their mind, by the wickedness of their heart, and deny, in practice, what they know to be true in theory.

"My parents do not allow me to follow the convictions of my mind. If I became a member of the Church, they would disown me, disinherit me. My friends would forsake me, my companions would laugh at me."

Suppose all these consequences were to fol

low; should you on that account expose your immortal soul to eternal ruin? Have you not read in the Scriptures:

"Fear ye not them that kill the body and are not able to kill the soul; but rather fear Him, that can destroy both body and soul into hell. Are not two sparrows sold for a farthing? And not one of them shall fall on the ground without your Father. But the very hairs of your head are numbered. Fear not, therefore: better are you than many sparrows.

"Every one that shall confess Me before men, I will also confess him before My Father who is in Heaven.

"But he that shall deny Me before men, I will also deny him before My Father who is in Heaven.

"Do not think that I came to send peace upon earth; I came not to send peace, but the sword.

"For I came to set a man at variance with his father; and the daughter against her mother; and the daughter-in-law against her mother-in-law.

"And a man's enemies shall be they of his own household.

"He that loveth father or mother more than Me, is not worthy of Me; and he that loveth son or daughter more than Me, is not worthy of Me.

"And he that taketh not up his cross and followeth Me, is not worthy of Me. He that findeth his life, shall lose it; and he that shall lose his life for Me, shall find it." (Matt. x. 28–39.)

Again, have you not read: "If the world hate you, know ye that it hath hated Me before you. If you had been of the world, the world would love its own; but because you are not of the world, but I have chosen you out of the world, therefore the world hateth you. Remember My word that I said to you. The servant is not greater than the master. If they have persecuted Me, they will also persecute you." (John, xv. 18–20.) The difficulties which you are to encounter, the sufferings and persecutions, the sneers and scoffs which you will have to endure, are the best proof, that the religion which you would otherwise embrace is the religion of Christ, therefore the true, the only saving religion of the Gospels.

Did the Apostles shrink from the prison and the scourge? Did they on that account deny their faith, or even cease to preach in the name of Jesus? Let your answer to parents, friends, and relatives, be that of Peter and John to the princes, and ancients, and scribes, in Jerusalem: "If it be just in the sight of God to hear you rather than God, judge ye; for we cannot but speak the things which we have seen and heard." (Acts. iv. 19, 20.) Were your fears the fears of the martyrs, who rather than betray, by a single sign, their indifference to the religion which they had embraced, proclaimed its necessity unto salvation, from the pyre, the boiling cauldron, the wheel, and the gibbet? Were these the sentiments of the heroic confessors who were torn from home and friends, had their property confiscated, and were themselves cast into filthy dungeons, or banished into arid wastes and deserts? Shame upon your cowardice! If you are convinced of the truth, why do you blush to confess it before men, before God, and His angels? Do you hope to be saved by your persecuting parents, your sneering relations, or your scoffing friends? Will they give their souls in exchange for your own, when it shall have been damned because you refused to believe?

It is true, that you owe respect, honor, obedience, and love, to the secondary authors of your being; but it is also true that you must love God above all other things, with your whole heart, your whole mind, your whole soul, for this is the first and the greatest of all commandments. God has the first right to your honor, obedience, and love.

Moreover, do not your parents, relatives, and friends, tell you daily, that every man is free to worship God according to the dictates of his own conscience? Why then are you afraid to assert your rights, merely because, in contradiction with their own principles, you would be exposed to the shafts of their ridicule, and the cruelty of their persecutions? Remember that you are accountable to God for your own deeds, that every one shall bear his own burden, and that God will render to every one according to his works.

Look well into this matter. Your all depends upon the choice you make in religion. You need religion; without it you cannot serve your Maker, nor love Him as He deserves. Without it you cannot perfect your nature, nor attain the end for which you were created. Your soul is at stake. Heaven and hell are in the balance. There can be but one religion; for truth is one: then seek that one religion, and you shall find it. Above all, ask for the gift of faith, and it shall be given you. "For this cause bend your knees to the Father of our Lord Jesus Christ, that He would grant you, according to the riches of His glory, to be strengthened by His Spirit, with might unto the inward man, that Christ may dwell by faith in your hearts." (Eph. iii. 14, 16, 17.)

II.

THE BIBLE NOT THE RULE OF FAITH.

"Go ye into the whole world and preach the Gospel to every creature. He that believeth, and is baptized, shall be saved; but he that believeth not, shall be condemned." MARK, xvi. 15, 16.

WE have seen that Faith is necessary to salvation: that without it, it is impossible to please God. Therefore, they who die without faith shall be condemned. (Mark, xvi. 16.)

But it is clear, that not every kind of faith is sufficient unto salvation. We must have divine faith; the faith which Christ, the God-man, came to preach. That faith, like Christ Himself, is necessarily one. Christ cannot contradict Himself. He must needs teach one and the same truth, concerning one and the same article of faith. He cannot teach two opposite sets of doctrines, on one and the same subject. There is, therefore—there can be—but one true faith. If that one true faith is to save us, then we must have a means to get at it—an easy, a certain, a secure means. It must be an easy means—for *all* must believe—the ignorant, as well as the learned; the uninstructed barbarian, as well as the enlightened academician, or universitarian. It must be certain; for, faith is an act of the mind which excludes all doubt. He who doubts, does not believe; and he who believes, does not doubt. It must be secure; the very fear of the possibility of being deceived must be removed: for, if there is any ground to fear that the means which we employ for getting faith may lead us astray, then our faith may be an illusion, and no faith at all.

Now, what is this easy, certain and secure means of having that faith without which it is impossible to be saved? Our separated brethren tell us, it is the written word—the Bible, the whole Bible, and nothing but the Bible, interpreted by every one's private judgment.

This, we Roman Catholics deny, and we adduce the reasons of our denial.

In the first place, we say that if the Bible, or written word alone, was designed by Christ to be every man's rule of faith, then every man must be able to find out whether he has the Bible, the whole Bible, and nothing but the Bible. And if he is consistent, he must find it out by himself. He must settle this matter by his own private judgment. Evidently, the first act of faith is to be exercised regarding the Bible itself. Before you can believe any specific article of faith, on the authority of the Bible as the word of God, you must first be infallibly certain that the book, in which you find that specific article, is the word of God, and not the word of man. Before we accept any article of the Constitution of the United States, we must first be certain, that the book in which this or that article is found, is really and verily the genuine Constitution. Now, how shall the believer settle that question? Not by the Bible itself; for that would be begging the question. Suppose the Bible should assert its own authenticity, the question would still return: "But how do I know that the assertion of its own authenticity is itself authentic; how do I know that this assertion is God's own?" No book or written document proves its own authenticity. No last will, no paper, containing, for instance, a contract entered upon by buyer and seller, proves its own genuineness. Witnesses, living witnesses, credible witnesses, are the only sufficient evidence of their genuineness. So it is with the written word of God. Its authenticity, its genuineness, its inspiration, must be proved by living and credible witnesses. But where and who are those witnesses? Those who were present when the Bible was written, those who knew the penmen that wrote it, and those who handed it down as it was written, during the lapse of ages. Now, the Gospel bears the venerable age of nineteen centuries! Who were the witnesses, present at the time it was first written? The first Christians, of course; those who lived in the days of the Evangelists and sacred penmen themselves. But these Christians were Catholics. Protestantism was not born till 1517; sixteen centuries after the Bible had been written. Our separated brethren, then, must refer to Catholics, and Catholic tradition, or history, in order to settle the first question of their faith. But to do this would be to contradict themselves. For they look upon the Roman Catholic Church as the parent of all errors, so that whoever believes her testimony, believes a lie. They, moreover, assert that she has corrupted the word of God, that, contrary to the divine command, she has added to and taken away from the written word. How then will they settle the very first article of their faith, which should run as follows: "I firmly believe, as firmly as I believe my own existence, as firmly as I believe the existence of God, that the book which I hold in my hand, is the whole word of God, neither more nor less." Abandoning the ground of invoking the external evidence of the Church of Rome, in behalf of the inspiration and genuineness of the Bible, they appeal to the contents of the book, as irrefragable proof of its inspiration: "The sublime doctrines of faith and morality contained in the old and new Testaments, are themselves their own proof, are unmistakable evidence of their divine origin." This evidence, we suppose, is clear to all. Every one that reads can see, as well as you, whether what he reads is inspired or not, divine or human. If so, how comes it that so many even holy men, have differed among themselves, as to what books, chapters, and verses were or were not divinely inspired? For you know that the question of the canonicity of all the scriptures was not finally settled till the third council of Carthage, held in the fourth century. Yea, the very reformers who introduced the maxim, that the Bible, and the Bible alone, is every man's rule of faith, were not agreed upon this question. Luther cast serious doubts upon the inspiration of some books, and altogether rejected others, which you hold to be inspired.

Thus he writes:

"The books of Kings are more worthy of credit than the books of Chronicles." If they are both inspired, how can the one be more worthy of credit than the other?

Of the book of Job, he says: "Job spoke not as it stands written in his book; but had only such cogitations. It is merely the argument of a fable. It is probable that Solomon made and wrote this book." How can you make an act of divine faith on the contents of a book which is merely the argument of a fable?

"The book entitled Ecclesiastes, ought," he continues, "to have been more full. There is too much incoherent matter in it. It has neither boots nor spurs; but rides only in socks, as I myself did, when an inmate of the cloister. Solomon has not, therefore, written this book, which was made in the days of the Machabees, by Sirach. It is like a Talmud, compiled from many books, perhaps in Egypt, at the desire of King Evergetes. So have, also, the Proverbs of Solomon, been collected by others."

"The book of Esther," he exclaims, "I toss into the Elbe! I am such an enemy to the book of Esther, that I wish it did not exist;

for it judaizes too much, and has in it a great deal of heathenish naughtiness."

"Isaiah the prophet has borrowed his knowledge and his art from the Psalter."

"The history of Jonah is so monstrous, that it is absolutely incredible."

"That the Epistle to the Hebrews is not by St. Paul, nor by any other apostle at all, is shown by chapter ii., verse 3d. It is by an excellent, a learned man, a disciple of the Apostles. It should be no stumbling-block, if there be found in it, a mixture of wood, straw, and hay." But, how am I to make an act of divine faith on an epistle which was not written by any Apostle, but only one of their disciples? and how am I to discern the wood, the straw, and hay, from the pure gold and silver?

He called the Epistle of St. James "an epistle of straw," unworthy of an Apostle, and adds: "in the Revelation of St. John, too much is wanting to have me deem it Apostolical; I can discover no trace in it that it is established by the Spirit." (Edinburgh Review, No. 121.)

The same review from which we have drawn the above quotations, subjoins the following: "The most learned and intelligent of Protestant divines here, *almost all* doubted, or denied the canonicity of the book of Revelation. Calvin and Beza pronounced the book unintelligible, and prohibited the pastors of Geneva from all attempts at interpretation, for which they were applauded by Joseph Scaliger, and Isaac Casaubon. Joseph Scaliger, who also rejected the Epistle of St. James, did not believe the Apocalypse to be the writing of St. John, and allowed only two chapters to be comprehensible, while Dr. South scrupled not to pronounce it, a book that either found a man mad, or left him so."

If these learned men were puzzled, when they had to decide the question, what portions of the Bible are, and what others are not the inspired word of God, how much more difficult must such decision be for the people—for the masses? How impossible to the ignorant? And yet these must have faith—these must believe the whole Word of God, and nothing but the Word of God—as well as the ablest divines, the most learned theologians.

Nor will it do to say as Luther, and Calvin, and Wesley, seem to have said: that besides the external word, there is an internal word, which helps us to understand what is divinely inspired. For the question always returns: How are you sure that there is such an internal word? From the Scriptures? But that would be to reason in a vicious circle. You assert the internal word, on the evidence of the external, or written word; and the external word on the evidence of the internal word. You prove by the internal word, that the text of the external, or written word, must be regarded as asserting the existence of the internal word. How do you know that the internal word is not mistaken in the interpretation of the external word? Moreover, does the external word testify with certainty to the fact, that only such, and no other books of the Scriptures, are inspired? Suppose, for instance, that there were other books besides those which you have in your edition of the Bible, which others, led by the same internal word of the Spirit, deem divinely inspired, would not your spirit contradict their spirit, and would both spirits be the sufficient reason for you to reject, and for them to retain those books as inspired? If so, they cannot both be the Spirit of God, for He is the Spirit of truth, and does not contradict Himself. The same argument will apply to every chapter, verse, and word of the Scriptures. What evidence have you, from the internal word, that every chapter, verse, and word which you have in your edition, is inspired just as they read, and are printed? How, then, comes it, that there are so many readings of these same chapters, verses, and words? Have you never heard of the numerous varieties of readings in the different editions of the Bible, both in Hebrew, Greek Latin, English, and indeed, in all the languages into which the Bible is translated? If all have the internal word to settle so important a matter, how comes it that no uniformity has as yet been established in the reading of all these editions?

And have you any assurance that this internal word belongs to you, any more than to us? If the internal spirit be the only medium; infallibly to decide what is inspired and what is not inspired, in the Scripture, the fathers, doctors, and councils of the Church must have had the same guide in their decisions as you have—yet, their spirit decided differently from your own. One of these spirits, then, must necessarily be a spirit of error. It is for you to prove that yours is not that spirit.

Suppose, for argument's sake, that you discovered, by the aid of the internal word, the inspiration of the books you hold in your hand, what will you do with those books which are set down as containing certain facts—perhaps doctrines—not to be found in your edition? Thus, for instance, how do you know by your internal spirit, that the book of the Wars of the Lord, mentioned in Numbers (xxi. 14), the book of the Just (Jos. x. 13), the book of Nathan the prophet (1 Chron. xxix. 29), the book of Ahiah the Silonite, and of Addo the Seer against Jeroboam, and the books of Semeiah the prophet (2 Chron. ix. 29; xii. 15), were not inspired, and therefore, a part of the revealed Word of God, necessary to be believed?

In the beginning of the Church there were extant many writings, which, by some, were looked upon as inspired, and by others rejected as uninspired Scriptures: what says your internal spirit, or word, concerning them? How can your spirit pronounce without reading them—and some of them, such as those we have quoted from the Old Testament, can no longer be read, because they no longer exist? But, what says your spirit concerning those that were written since the beginning of Christianity? Do you place them in the hands of the people, just as you do the authorized version of King James? If not, why not? Should not every one of you be able to decide on their inspiration? And how can that decision be given without reading them?

Why do you reject, for instance, the Gospels of Matthias, of Peter the Apostle, of James, of Barnabas, of St. Thomas, of St. Bartholomew, of St. Andrew; the Acts of Peter, of Andrew, of Thomas, of Philip, of Thecla and Paul the Apostle; the books of the Nativity of Our Lord, and the Infancy of the Saviour?

Why reject the book called the Pastor or Shepherd, which Origen quotes as divinely inspired, which Ruffinus numbers among the books of the New Testament, and the Protestant Whiston calls "an inspired book which comes directly from our Saviour as does the Apocalypse?"

How will every man who is to be saved by reading the Bible alone, decide for himself, whether the book called the Foundation, another called the Treasure; the book of the children of Ada; the Centemetrum of Christ; the book of Cephas; the Revelations of St. Paul; the Revelations of St. Thomas the Apostle, of St. Stephen; the book of the Transitus of Mary; the Penitential Acts of Addo; the Testament of Job; the Penitence of Jannes and Mambres; the Praise of the Apostles; the Canons of the Apostles (once held, by some local Churches, on the same level as the four Gospels and the Acts of the

Apostles), are not, now, to be considered the inspired word of God? If the authority of the Church of Rome is sufficient evidence to you that they are not inspired, why is her authority not equally sufficient, when she tells you that others, which you now reject, such as the Machabees, are really inspired? Her authority is as reliable in the one as in the other instance.

No one, therefore, can be infallibly certain, without an infallible authority outside of the Bible, that he has the whole Bible, and nothing but the Bible; consequently, no one can say that he believes all the truths of faith.

If you appeal to the Bible itself as the witness of its sufficiency, it will tell you that it does not contain all that might and should be written. St. John, who was the last to write his Gospel, concluded his closing chapter by saying: "And there are also *many other things,* which Jesus did, which, if they were written, every one, the world itself, I think, would not be able to contain the books that should be written." (Jo. xxi. 25.) Where is St. Paul's epistle to the Laodiceans, which he commands the Colossians to read in their Church? (Coloss. iv. 16.) St. Paul tells the Corinthians "I wrote to you in the letter," etc. (i. Cor. v. 9.) Where is that epistle of St. Paul to the Corin thians? By what prophet was it written: "He shall be called a Nazarite." (Matt. ii. 23.) All these scriptures are lost. Hence, you must conclude that you have not, and cannot have, the whole word of God. And yet, according to you, nothing but the Bible, the *whole* Bible, is your rule of faith.

The difficulty does not end here. To make an act of divine faith on the Bible, it is further necessary to make, first, an act of divine faith on the correctness of the copy which you are reading. Now, what you read is generally a translation. Many of our separated brethren never for a moment reflect that the greater part of the Bible was originally written in Hebrew, some of it in Syro-Chaldaic, or Chaldean, and the rest in Greek. How will you determine the correctness of the translation which you hold in your hands? Not by comparing the copy with the originals; for that would suppose, first, that the originals did still exist, which is not the fact; and secondly, that the majority of the readers, or rather all, know the languages in which the originals were written. This cannot be supposed; for then translations would be useless. But, I am told, "Look at the title page;" it reads: "The Holy Bible, translated from the original Hebrew and

Greek;" and sometimes we find the slight addition: "Carefully compared and revised." Who will vouch for the truth of the fact there asserted? How does an ordinary mechanic or a laboring man (and they compose the majority of believers) know that the translator, or translators, had sufficient knowledge of these languages, to guarantee the correctness of the translation? Were they specially assisted by Heaven? Had they a sufficient knowledge, not only of the languages, but also of the doctrines of the work which they translated? Who does not know how difficult it is for any number of scholars, however learned, perfectly to agree on the meaning of certain idioms and allusions, national, personal or local, the real nature of which is lost to the world, because not consigned to history, or if consigned there, not sufficiently explained? Who does not know how many volumes of scriptural hermeneutics or biblical criticism have been written to clear up certain expressions in the Bible, which are obscure on account of the distance of time and place, and the antiquity of the people, among whom or of whom they were written? How can unlearned men settle such difficulties? They cannot do it from personal knowledge. Are they safe in relying upon the knowledge of fallible translators? Suppose the translators were mistaken in rendering the exact meaning of but one text which contains an article of faith, then the reader is equally mistaken in reading the inaccurate version. Then he is mistaken in his belief. But a mistaken faith is no faith at all. Therefore, such a reader could not have a salutary faith.

How stands the question of these translations according to the testimony of our separated brethren themselves? Luther was the first among the Reformers to translate the Bible into his native tongue. How did he succeed? Listen to Zwingle. Writing of Luther's version, he says: "Thou corruptest, O Luther, the word of God. Thou art known to be an open and notorious perverter of the Holy Scriptures. How much are we ashamed of thee now, whom we had once so much respected!"

Luther returns the compliment to Zwingle. He calls the translators of the Zwinglean Bible "a set of fools, antichrists, and impostors."

Of Castalio's translation, Beza, the Calvinist, says, that "it is sacrilegious, wicked, and down right pagan."

Molineux wrote of Calvin's translation, "Calvin makes the text of the Gospel leap up and down. He does violence to the letter, and makes additions to the texts."

The same author says of Beza's translation: "Beza actually changes the text;" and Castalio adds, that "it would require a large volume to mark down the multitude of errors, which swarm in Beza's translation."

Let us listen to the Anglican clergy of Lincoln, writing to King James, on the authorized version still in use: "Our translation takes away from the text, and adds to the text. It obscures and changes the meaning of the Holy Ghost."

This caused Mr. Burgess, a learned member of the Establishment, to write: "How shall I approve, under my hand, a translation which has so many omissions, and so many additions; which sometimes obscures, sometimes perverts the sense; being sometimes senseless, sometimes contrary ?"

How can any man rely upon such translations, as the word of God? Indeed, the question of a new translation, has been agitated among several of the sects, and preparations were in progress, some years since, to effect so desirable and necessary an object as soon as possible. We derive from these facts: First, the avowal that hitherto our separated brethren have not been able to make an act of Divine faith on their translated Bibles. Secondly that it will remain impossible for posterity to do so until they contrive another means by which they may infallibly secure the correctness of a new translation. However numerous and learned the new translators may be, they can never, without a higher authority than that which flows from literary knowledge, prove to the satisfaction of their readers, that they could not be, and therefore were not mistaken in their new version of the Scriptures. To do this requires an authority equal to the Scriptures themselves; an authority which is the divinely appointed guardian and interpreter of the whole Word of God. But such an authority they reject, and, if true to their principles, will continue to reject as long as they exist.

Testing this question still further by the rules of common sense, we affirm that, in order to make the reading of the Bible the only rule of faith, Christ must have foreseen that all should be able to get a copy of the Bible. But this He could not possibly foresee, since it was never to be a fact. Had Luther lived one century and a half earlier than he did, he would never have established his principle. For he would have been met on all sides by the question: How shall we get a copy of the Bible? Before the invention of the art of printing, all books had to be procured by the tedious and costly process of the stylus or pen. It is easy to conceive that the majority of mankind were necessarily deprived of the pleasure of reading many a book, which the printing-press has since multiplied almost indefinitely. To copy with the pen thirteen hundred chapters, containing over thirty thousand verses, was no easy task for any scribe or amanuensis. How many of these scribes it would require to place in the hands of one in a thousand men or women, a single copy of the Word of God, would be an interesting problem to solve. But how many must needs have been deprived of the book merely because they could not find such a scribe, or because they had not the means to pay him for his labor. We are serious when we assert that if our Bible-reading brethren could get at a copy only as did Christians before the fifteenth century, they would blush at the idea of making it the only rule of faith for all; yea, we dare assert that if they had to pay a scribe for copying the Scriptures, they would look twice at their purse before striking a bargain, and many would say, if my faith is to cost me so dear, I will have none of it. Yet during fifteen centuries of the Christian era, scarcely one in a thousand could obtain a copy of the Bible; and if it be true that without it they could not be saved, the majority of the Christian world, before the invention of printing, went to hell, and are lost without any real fault of their own. The supposition is impious. Christ, therefore, did not make the reading of the Bible the only rule of man's faith.

In the next place, Christ must have foreseen that all would be able to read their copy of the Bible. But He could no more see this, than the foregoing fact, for it was never to be. Education depends on circumstances. These are not equally favorable in all ages, and among all people. Before the art of printing, all education was, of necessity, mainly oral. The scholar had to hang on the lips of his masters for whatever knowledge he expected to acquire in the college, academy, or parish school. His only hope, besides this, was the rare privilege of looking at a manuscript in some collegiate or monastic library. You can easily conceive that the difficulty of acquiring even the first rudiments of learning, such as spelling and reading, must have deterred a great many from acquiring those accomplishments. If even, at this period of the world, with all the improvements and facilities which printed books afford, there are many who cannot read at all, how much more general must that ignorance have been during the centuries which preceded the great invention of Faust and Guttenberg. We have met hundreds, not of aliens only, but of men born on the soil of this Republic, who had to own that they could neither read nor write And when the cause was asked, one would answer, "I lived in the country, where there was no school nearer than ten miles, and of course I could not attend it. My parents were unable to afford a private tutor, and they themselves were uneducated, simple people." "I was left an orphan at an early age," would another say, "and had to hire out my services to make a living." Did Christ intend that all these should get their faith by reading? If not, then the principle does not hold—that the Bible alone is every man's rule of faith. We shall not speak of the millions and millions of barbarians, who never could read, and never will be able to read. Their incorrigible tendency to a nomadic life, their indolent habits, their very hatred of the polished and refined white-man, are all so many obstacles to civilization, whose mental rudiments begin with the learning of the alphabet and the primer.

But suppose even that all can read; have they sufficient intelligence to understand the Bible? Genius and talents are rare gifts, the privilege of one in a thousand. The majority of the race have but very limited intellect and judgment. To convince yourselves of the fact, you have only to make the experiment in a promiscuous multitude at a political, religious, or social meeting. Hand round your simplest village newspaper. How many will read it with any thing like intelligence? One will spell his way through a few short sentences; another will run comma into semicolon; and colon into full stop, without any connection of phrase or sense. Now suppose these same men stuttering and stumbling through thirteen hundred chapters and thirty thousand verses of a book, which contains the sublimest doctrines of faith and morality that were ever taught on earth. How do you expect them to analyze and synthetize, with a knowledge and care on which their very salvation depends, all the different texts and contexts that bear upon one and the same mystery of faith, or dogma of morality? How can you expect them to reconcile all apparent contradictions, all the seeming discrepancies that occur between Gospel and Gospel, Epistle and Epistle? To do this with any thing like success, would require the effort of a gigantic genius; and even such a one, according to Luther himself, would fail in the task. For, according to the Father of the Reformation, it would take a man a hundred years to become acquainted with only some portions of the Scriptures; and Claude, a French Calvinist minister, in the days of the great Bossuet, declared, that "Life is too short, and human strength too weak, to fathom the sense of the Bible,—that fathomless well of mysteries and of truth."

Add to this, that Christ foresaw that millions and millions would not have the time, even if they had the will, and the ability, so to read the Bible as to make it their only safe guide in matters of faith and morals. Man has social and domestic duties enjoined him by Heaven itself, which he must fulfil, if he wishes to escape punishment. How will he reconcile two evidently contradictory wills of the same Deity in his regard? There is the poor husbandman, who has a growing family relying on his labor and industry for their scanty support. In the sweat of his brow, he works from morning till night, from week to week, and year to year. Will you tell that man, after he comes home n the evening, worn out with the day's toil, that, instead of entertaining his wife with the pleasing details of his labor, and the prospect of an abundant crop; instead of calling his children to his knees, and caressing them, he must sit down to search the Scriptures? After he has attended meeting of a sabbath, will you deprive him of a refreshing walk with his wife and children, or a visit to a relative, friend or neighbor, whom he cannot possibly see at any other time? Will you tell that servant-girl of yours that, if ever she hopes to be saved, she must, after having waited upon your family, from five in the morning until ten or eleven o'clock at night, forego her few hours of sleep to enter upon the still more fatiguing labor of studying out the Word of God? Would she not reasonably demur, and complain of such an injunction? And yet, all these are the consequences which flow logically from the principle, that the written word alone was designed by Christ to be every man's rule of faith.

The fact is, very few among our separated brethren seem practically to believe in their own principle. Examining closely the conduct of the Bible Christians in any sect, how many will you find, who really read the Scripture, and read it as it should be read, assiduously, carefully, prayerfully, in order to make it a rule of faith and action?

How will a child eight or even ten years of age get the saving faith from the Bible? It is certain, that, ordinarily speaking, a child that has reached the age of seven or eight, is capable of distinguishing between virtue and vice, and the necessity of practising the one, and avoiding the other. Now, faith is the first and the most essential virtue for that child. Without faith it cannot please God, it cannot be saved. But it must come to faith by the exercise of its own private judgment. It must read the Bible, and interpret it for itself. Tell me by what process of reasoning will that child come to the knowledge of the following facts: first, that there is a Bible; secondly, what that Bible is; of how many books it is composed; whether all those books, and their chapters and verses and words, are all and every one from God and the pens of inspired writers; thirdly, whether the translation it is reading is genuine, correct, faultless. Next, how shall it go about interpreting the various doctrines which are therein contained? How shall it solve its own objections; clear up its own doubts? To say that the child can do all this without an authority extrinsic to the book which it is reading, is simply absurd. But what authority, extrinsic to the Bible, is sufficient to save that child from error? Is it parental authority? What Scripture teaches, that the parents of such a child are its Heaven-appointed teachers, in matters of faith and religion? Is it the minister of the village or town in which the child lives? Can he prove his appointment as a teacher, and can he say to the child: "He that hears me, hears Jesus Christ, and he that despises me, despises Christ?" Dare he obtrude his own opinions on the mind of the child? What guarantee does he give to the child, that he is not, that he cannot be, mistaken? Must he not, if he is consistent with his own principles, refuse to teach the child anything, since he holds it as a first principle that there is no sufficient authority in matters of faith, except the Bible as read and interpreted by every individual who has come to the years of discretion? Without an infallible guide that child cannot possibly believe, and must remain an infidel or a sceptic during a great portion of its life. But it may die, and if it die without the gift of faith, it shall be condemned.

What we say of children, may be said of the illiterate. They cannot possibly believe, if the Protestant rule of faith is admitted, and, consequently, they must perish for ever.

Our dissenting brethren cannot refer to authority as a substitute for the Bible; for, in so doing, they contradict their own principle, and do not advance one step further. For, the human authority on which they rely, instead of the divine authority of the Bible, cannot give the illiterate any more than a *human* faith, which is not sufficient unto salvation.

We now pass to another class of common-sense arguments on this all-important question. If Christ really intended that a written book should be the only authority and rule of faith unto all men, is it not natural to suppose that He Himself would have written it? And yet, our Divine Saviour never wrote a single line.

Our Saviour not only did not write Himself, but He never ordered His Apostles or disciples to write a word of all that He had taught them. He ordered them to go and preach the Gospel to every creature, to teach all nations whatsoever He had commanded them; but He never so much as insinuated a desire that they should record a single word of all that He had said to them. How do you explain this apparent contradiction?

If the Gospel was to be propagated by reading, rather than by hearing the Word of God some of the Apostles were very remiss in their duty. For it does not appear that, besides Saints Matthew, John, Peter, Paul, James, and Jude, any other Apostle ever wrote a line. Yea, those who did write can scarcely be exonerated from a serious neglect of their Master's will. St. Matthew, who was the first to write, waited some six years after the ascension of our Lord, before he placed his pen on papyrus, and thus deprived the Jews and Pagans of the only rule of faith, by which they were to be saved. The other Apostles and Evangelists delayed still longer; and St. John did not finish his Apocalypse until about sixty-four years had elapsed after the foundation of the Christian Church; nor did they write everything they had heard or witnessed, as we have already seen, from the last chapter of St. John. St. Paul does not seem to have written the whole Gospel which he had received from God; for, to the Thessalonians he writes: "Therefore, brethren, stand fast; and hold the traditions, which ye have learned, whether by word or by our epistle." (2 Thess. ii. 14.) Again: "We charge you, brethren, in the name of our Lord Jesus Christ, to withdraw yourselves from every brother walking disorderly, and not according to the tradition which they received from us." (Ibid. iii. 6.) What mean his expressions to the Corinthians: "and keep my ordinances as *I have delivered* them to you" (1 Cor. xi. 2); and "I have received of the Lord that which also *I delivered* unto you" (ibid. 23); "And the rest I will set in order, when I come"? (Ibid. 34.)

What mean the following words to Timothy? "Hold the form of sound words, which thou hast *heard* of me in faith" (2 Tim. i. 13); "And the things which thou hast *heard* from me by many witnesses, the same commit to faithful men, who shall be fit to teach others also" (ibid. ii. 2); "But continue thou in the things which thou hast *learned*, and which are *committed* to thee; knowing from whom thou hast *learned*?" (Ibid. iii. 14.) St. Paul, then, notwithstanding the many Epistles he had written, did not write all that was necessary to be taught and observed; nor does he refer those, whom he addressed, to his other epistles, or to the Gospels of the other Evangelists and Apostles, but to the traditions—the things which he had delivered to them—which had been entrusted to them, which they had learned from his lips.

The Christians, during the lifetime of the Apostles, did not, therefore, get their faith by the Bible alone. Nor did the millions and millions who succeeded them during the centuries which followed. If the Apostles had been taught by their Master, that the ordinary means of coming to the faith was to be the reading of the Bible, they certainly would have impressed this truth so forcibly upon the mind of their successors in the ministry, and upon the people, that we should have unmistakable evidences of this fact in the history of the Church and the writings of the Fathers. So far from having any evidences that a single tribe or nation was Christianized by reading the Bible, we find countless proofs that most, if not all of them, joined the Church without having ever read a letter of the Scriptures. To this St. Irenæus and other Fathers bear the clearest testimony. If the Scriptures had been the only touch-stone to test truth and heresy, the Church would never have condemned, as heretics, those who denied doctrines not clearly contained in the Scriptures. This, however, she did from the very beginning of Christianity. Thus, the baptism of children is, according to the showing of many separated Churches, not clearly proved from the Bible to be necessary unto salvation; and yet the council of Miletus condemned as heretics such as deny this doctrine. The Quarto-decimani were also condemned as heretics, because they would not believe that Easter should always be kept on the fourteenth day of the moon; a doctrine which it is not easy to prove from the Scriptures alone. Again, how could the early writers of the Church have held it a peculiarity of heretics to appeal always to the Scriptures for the doctrines which they advanced, or which they denied, if it was the very rule which Christ Himself had established, as the only test of truth and error? "Heretics," writes St. Ephrem, "wishing to give strength to their error, endeavored to extract passages from the Scriptures, by which to pervert the minds of those who may listen to them." (De Virtute, c. viii., 2.)

"Heresies," says the great St. Augustine, "and other certain pernicious doctrines, have not arisen except from the holy Scriptures being ill understood." (Tract xviii. n. i., in Joan.)

If the Scriptures were really intended to be the only rule of man's faith, they should evidently contain all the doctrines that are to be believed; yet how many doctrines are believed by our separated brethren, which cannot be clearly established by the Scriptures alone? Thus the Scriptures nowhere assert their own inspiration, nor the number of the books, nor the genuineness of all the texts. They do not state whether their contents have a literal or a figurative meaning, or when they should be understood literally or figuratively. They do not enumerate the precise points which are to be believed of necessity unto salvation. They do not teach the necessity of infant baptism, nor specify the change of the Sabbath to the Sunday. Where will you find in them, that those who were baptized in heresy, must not be rebaptized? or that baptism should be administered by immersion instead of by sprinkling? They do not clearly settle the order and subordination of the Pastors of the Church. Nor is it clear from them whether there should be bishops, or elders only. Finally, they do not establish distinctly the number of the sacraments, and their nature.

So on the other hand, there are many things clearly prescribed in the Scriptures, which our separated brethren observe no more than we. Who among them, except the Dunkers, wash the feet of the disciples before they take the Lord's Supper? Who of them abstains from any kind of meat, whether strangled or not;

and from blood-pudding, which were forbidden in the name of the Holy Ghost, by the Apostles to the first Christians? Who observes the moral precepts: "Go, then, and eat thy bread with joy, and drink thy wine with gladness because thy works please God. At all times *let thy garments be white,* and let not oil *depart from thy head.* Live joyfully with the wife whom thou lovest." (Eccl. ix. 7-9.) Who but the Quaker observes the following? "I say to you, not to swear at all." (Matt. v. 24.) "Call none your father upon earth, neither be ye called masters; for one is your Master— Christ." (Ibid. xxiii. 9, 10.) "If a man will contend with thee in judgment and take away thy coat, let go thy cloak also unto him." (Ibid. v. 40.) "Give to every one that asketh of thee; and from him that taketh away thy goods ask them not again." (Luke vi. 30.) "When thou makest a dinner or supper, call not thy friends nor thy brethren." (Ibid. xiv. 12.)

Faith is one. The means which Christ appointed to obtain that Faith must, of its nature, lead to unity. Has the Bible, as the only rule of faith, produced unity of belief among those who are so loud in its praises? No sooner did Luther proclaim his principle against the authority of the Church, and of Tradition, than he witnessed and deplored the sad but inevitable consequences which flowed from it. In 1526, Carlstadt, Zwingle, and Oecolampadius established their Sacramentarianism, or the figurative presence, in opposition to Luther's Real Presence. In 1527, Paccomannus and Rothman introduced their Anabaptism. The Lutherans, as Oecolampadius objected to them, were divided among themselves. There were Antinomians, Osiandrians, Majorists, Synergists, Stancarians, Amsdorfians, Flaccians, Substantiatians, Accidentarians, Adiaphorists, Musculans, and Ubiquists.

In 1538, John Calvin left his master, Zwingle and set up for himself. Luther wrote of him and his heresy: "I scarcely ever read of a more deformed heresy; divided, in its beginning, into so many heads, such a number of sects, *not one like another*, and such variety and disagreeing of opinion" (Op., tom. 7); in another place (Op., tom. 6), he says that "six or seven sects of them had risen in only two years, space."

Servetus claimed his right to interpret the Bible according to his understanding and the dictates of his conscience, but he was condemned to the flames by Calvin.

John Bockhold, a tailor of Leyden, declared that the King of Zion was at hand, that God had raised him up to establish twelve Judges over Israel. He took the government of Munster into his own hands, appointed twenty-six apostles to propagate his new scripture doctrine, but was surprised by death before he could accomplish his design. He had, however, time to obey the motions of his interior spirit, which told him to marry eleven wives, and to kill them after he had married them. (Brandt, tom. i., p. 46; Mosheim, vol. iv., p. 542.) Hermann is taught by the spirit to declare himself the Messiah, and to kill all the priests and magistrates in the world. (Brandt, p. 51.) David George proclaims himself the true Son of God. (Mosheim, vol. iv., p. 484.) Nicholas, his disciple, goes over to England, pronounces to the world that the feelings of Divine love constitute the essence of religion, and professes to remain in sin that grace may abound. (Ibid.) Venner is taught by the spirit that Jesus is the only lawful sovereign, and that neither he nor his followers would sheathe the sword till they had made Babylon (Monarchy) a hissing and a curse, not only in England but also in foreign countries. (See Milner's End of Controv., Letter vi.)

Menno founded the Mennonites, and Count Zinzendorf the Hernhutters.

The Anabaptists, in their turn, soon divided into a variety of sects.

The Adamites believed in the necessity of walking about in a state of nudity.

The Apostolics understood Christ's words literally, that whatever they had heard in secret, they should preach on the house-tops.

The Taciturns, on the contrary, refused all information, and the preaching of the Gospel.

The Perfect understood the words, "Wo to you that laugh, for you shall weep," in the strictest sense, and forbade any one the privilege of ever smiling.

The Innocents, or Impeccables, held, that man, after baptism, was sinless, and, therefore, need not say: "forgive us our trespasses," which words they accordingly ordered to be left out of the Lord's Prayer.

The Libertines disavowed all authority, temporal and spiritual.

The Sabbatarians contended, on Scriptura grounds, for the observance of the Sabbath, instead of the Sunday.

The Clancularians held, that man may dissemble his own faith, and profess that of others;

whilst the Manifestarians taught the contrary doctrine.

There were Weepers, who professed the necessity of tears; and Rejoicers, who taught that God loveth a cheerful giver.

The Abecedarians held the knowledge of reading as essential to salvation.

There were, also, Sanguinarians, who taught that the blood of Christians was an agreeable sacrifice to the Lord.

Arminians repudiated Calvin's absolute predestination to sin and damnation. And the Collegians, seeing the absurdity of establishing a Church in which there should be unity of faith, left every man free to believe what he pleases, without any regard to confessions of faith, catechisms, or decisions of synods.

But why should we weary our readers with an endless catalogue of so-called Churches, which have sprung up since the year 1517, all defending their own faith, with the Bible in hand, against their several antagonists. Let us sum up the various sects, which, according to a book now before us, entitled, "An Original History of the Religious Denominations, at Present Existing in the United States," unhappily divide our country. There we find Old and New Presbyterians; Associate, and Reformed, and Cumberland Presbyterians; Lutherans; Dutch Reformed; German Reformed Churches; Evangelical Lutherans; Baptists; Free-Will Baptists; Seventh Day Baptists; Baptist Brethren, German Seventh Day Baptists, and—as we have sometimes heard and read of—Hard and Soft Shell Baptists; Methodists,—The Methodist Society, The Methodist Episcopal, and Methodist Protestant Churches, The Reformed Methodist, and finally, the *true* Wesleyan Methodist Church. Here, too, we find Mennonites, and Reformed Mennonites; Shakers and Quakers; Seekers and Finders; Tunkers and Restorationists, Millenarians and New Jerusalemites; Schwenkfelders and Second Advent Men; United Brethren in Christ; Congregationalists, Universalists, Unitarians, Moravians, Christians, True Christians, Saints, and Latter-Day Saints. To these, in the new edition, the author will have to add, the Spiritualists, and Freelovers, besides others which have since arisen.

These divisions and subdivisions of sects, are the logical offspring of the principle laid down by the so-called father of the Reformation. Luther saw it in his own day. "Men," says he, "are now come to such a pitch of disorder, that they stand no longer in need of any teacher; every man now gives the law to himself."

Writing to the Christians of Antwerp, he says: "The devil has got among you; he daily sends me visitors to knock at my door. One will not hear of Baptism; another rejects the Sacrament of the Eucharist; a third teaches, that a new world will be created by God before the day of judgment; another, that Christ is not God; in short, one this, and another that; there are almost as many creeds as individuals. There is no booby, who, when he dreams, does not believe himself visited by God, and who does not claim the gift of prophecy. I am visited by these men, who claim to be favored by visions, of which they all know more than I do, and which they undertake to teach me. I would be glad if they were what they profess to be.

"No later than yesterday one came to me: 'Sir, I am sent by Almighty God, who created Heaven and earth;' and then he began to preach to me as a veritable idiot, that it was the order of God, that I should read the books of Moses for him. 'Ah, where did you find this commandment of God?' 'In the Gospel of St. John.' After he had spoken much, I said to him: 'Friend, come back to-morrow; for I cannot read for you, at one sitting, the books of Moses. 'Good-bye, master, the Heavenly Father, who shed His blood for us, will show us the right way, through His Son Jesus. Amen.'" Luther adds: "*While the papacy lasted, there were no such divisions or dissentions.*" ... "A spirit of confusion is among you;" and he concludes: "Begone, ye cohorts of devils—marked with the character of error. God is a Spirit of Peace, and not of dissensions." (Dr. Mart. Luther, Briefe, tom. iii., 60.)

Well did Munzer answer a Lutheran, who appealed to the Bible for the truth of what he advanced, "The Bible? Babel! For, never was there a book which produced greater confusion in the minds of men than the Bible, interpreted by every one's private reason."

"The unrestricted reading of the Bible," said the learned Protestant Archbishop Bramhall, "is more injurious to religion, than all the restraints of the Catholics." "These two words," writes the accomplished Selden, "*Search the Scriptures*, have undone the world." "The Bible, the Bible," says Bishop Hare, "is the religion of the Protestant; and so say all the heretics and schismatics that ever were." "Scripture," writes the renowned Hooker, "may be abused to any purpose." Thus it was made by the Presbyterians to prove, that whatever we do, if we be not directed by it, the same is sin. Thus the French Protestants would not pay their rents, pretending to scruple it, unless their landlords could bring a text to prove that they should pay them.

The results of interpreting the Bible by private judgment alone, in Germany, are thus graphically described in a sermon preached by the Rev. Mr. Rose, in the college of Cambridge, England, and dedicated to the Bishop of Chester. " From the state of Protestantism in Germany, a stronger and perhaps more important lesson is offered, on that subject which is said to form the *base* and the *boast* of Protestantism—the right of private judgment. The terrible evils resulting in the German Church from its exercise, are the strongest practical proof of the wisdom and necessity of restraining it. Among the German divines it is a favorite doctrine that it is impossible there could have been a miracle, and the words of Scripture are examined, and forced into any meaning but their own. By some the miracles are said to be that mythology, which must attend every religion, to gain the attention of the multitude; by some the common and well known ribaldry of the infidel is unsparingly used; by one or more, high in station in the Church, some artifice, and probably magnetism, has been, even within the last ten years, suggested; others go so far as to attack the whole body of the prophets as impostors, in most outrageous and revolting terms. This doctrine is taught by divines from the pulpit—by Professors from the chairs of theology. It is addressed to the old, to free them from ancient prejudices, and to the young, as the knowledge which can make them truly wise. This abdication of Christianity is not confined either to the Lutheran or the Calvinist profession, but extends its withering influence with baneful force over each. It is curious to observe in what way they get rid of all miracles. Professor Paulus, in his critical commentary assures us, that the man with the withered hand had only a luxation of the shoulder, which Jesus perceiving, pulled it into joint."

Professor Schultness explains the same miracles as follows:

"The man had a severe rheumatism; Christ observing that his blood was much moved, by the indignation with which he heard the question of the Pharisees, said to him in that favorable moment: 'Stretch out thine hand!

the man attempted to do it, and was healed because that extraordinary excitement had removed the impediment under which he labored. When Christ restored sight to the blind man, the poor fellow had such weakness in his eyelids, that he could not keep his eyes open. Christ, observing that he never made the attempt to open them, said to him: 'Thou shalt open thine eyes!' the confidence of the man was so great that, making the attempt with all his might, he opened his eyes. Christ never walked on the waves, but on the shore, or He swam behind the ship, or He walked through the shallows. The daughter of Jairus was not dead, because Christ Himself said: 'She sleepeth.' When Jesus said to Peter: 'Thou shalt catch a fish, and find in its mouth a piece of money;' the meaning is: before you can sell it for so much, you must open its mouth, and take out the hook. At Cana, in Galilee, Jesus gave a nuptial present of very fine wine, with which, for a joke, He filled the waterpots of stone. The paralytic was an idle fellow, who for thirty years had moved neither hand nor foot. Christ asked him ironically: 'Perhaps thou wouldst be whole?' This irony stirred him up; he forgot his hypocrisy."

It will not do to say that these are the abuse;

of the principle, and that abuses prove nothing against the truth of the principle. This observation would hold, if the principle itself did not logically lead to these abuses. When you tell the world that the Founder of Christianity left no other rule by which to come to true faith in Him, than the written word, to be read and interpreted by every man and woman, you lay down a principle which necessarily paves the way to all these disorders. It is useless to tell these men that they do not read the Scriptures prayerfully; that they do not ask for the Spirit, who is given to all those who ask; for the moment they reply that they have done all this, you cannot object to the conclusions which they draw from your own premises. And who is to judge between you and them, as to which of the two reads the Scripture as it should be read? They have as much right as you, to interpret the conditions and dispositions of mind and heart which must precede and accompany the reading. They have a perfect right to retort the argument on yourself, and there is no appeal to any court, which can decide between you, since you place the ultimate power of decision in the very book which you both interpret.

Just suppose that our Constitution were

placed in our hands, with this principle for our guidance in perusing it. Read this Constitution, interpret it for yourself. Whatever, upon careful study, you shall decide is its meaning, that *is the* meaning of the book. How many of us will read it in the same spirit, and find in it the same identical meaning? Perhaps not a thousand in ten or twenty millions will interpret every article and clause in the same sense. And yet the Constitution can have but one true sense and meaning in every one of its articles or clauses. How will you settle the difference? Not by the Constitution, for it is about it you differ; not by appealing anew to your convictions; for your minds are honestly made up, that you have the only true meaning of the document. An appeal to physical force is the only alternative that remains;—precisely what we are learning at so fearful an expense of money and men in the present lamentable war. And yet we have a supreme tribunal, whose judicial sentence we were taught was to be considered final, on all matters coming within the sphere of its extensive jurisdiction. Unity is an impossibility, where every one is sovereignly free to interpret for himself any doctrines or practical regulations, whether in the family, in the State, or in the

Church. There must needs be a living tribunal, from whose judgment there is no appeal.

But, it may be urged, do not the Scriptures themselves lay this religious obligation on every man? Why otherwise do we read?—"And these words which I command thee this day, shall be in thy heart: and thou shalt tell them to thy children; and thou shalt meditate upon them, sitting in thy house, and walking on thy journey, lying down and rising up. And thou shalt bind them as a sign on thy hand; and they shall be as frontlets between thy eyes. And thou shalt write them in the entry, and on the doors of thy house." (Deut. vi. 6-9.) Here is one of those passages of Holy Writ, whose meaning is open to diverse interpretations. That the words are not to be understood literally, is proved by the conduct of our adversaries themselves, for they surely do not do all that is prescribed by the texts. Then there is no question of reading the words, but of telling them orally to their children, of meditating upon them, etc. This they could do, by having them taught the decalogue, of which these texts make mention, and which Moses was commanded to teach the people. From Isaiah (liv. 13): "All thy children shall be taught of the Lord," they conclude that the

Bible shall be the rule of faith; but how this inference is logically contained in the premises we cannot see. Were not the Jews taught by the Lord in person, when He came to preach His Gospel? And did not Christ Himself apply that text to His own teaching in John vi. 45, saying: "It is written in the prophets *and they all shall be taught of God;*" subjoining immediately: "Every one that hath *heard* of the Father and hath *learned*, cometh to me!"

"After those days, saith the Lord, I will give My laws in their inward parts, and I will write it in their heart; and I will be their God, and they shall be My people. And they shall teach no more every man his neighbor, and every man his brother: for all shall know Me from the least of them even to the greatest." (Jer. xxxi. 33, 34.)

Orthodox and rationalist Protestants, in our day, interpret these texts to mean simply the greater facility, which believers in the New Dispensation will have, to know the law of God, and the wider diffusion of the doctrine of Monotheism, after the return of the Jews from Babylon. But what connection has this interpretation with the promise or command that every one should acquire his knowledge of religion by reading the Bible?

The fact is, there is no use in examining any of the texts of the Old or New Testaments, by which our separated brethren endeavor to prove their right to interpret the Bible by their own private judgment, unless they prove:

First. That a given text commands the reading of the Bible as the only rule of Faith.

Secondly. That this command applies to all without exception.

This command they seem to have found in the words of Christ to the Jews (John, v. 39): "Search the Scriptures, for in them you think to have life everlasting; and the same are they that give testimony to me." But first of all, it is not settled among the learned, whether the word Ερευνατε should be translated by the second person of the present, or the imperative mode. St. Cyril of Alexandria, and some modern commentators, maintain that Christ stated a mere fact, and that He gave no command. In that case we should read the passage: "Ye search the Scriptures." Secondly, most interpreters consider these words addressed, not to the Jews at large, but to the Pharisees, the doctors, and expounders of the law, whom He wished to convince of the divinity of His mission, by an appeal first to the testimony of St. John the Baptist, next to His miracles, and lastly to the

Scriptures of which they were the expounders. And this seems to be the real purport of His words, for he adds: "If ye did believe Moses, ye would perhaps believe Me also. For he wrote of Me." (Ibid. 46.) This is the more probable, when we consider that the Jews did not, as a general thing, read the Bible; but had it read to them, as is plain from Deut. xxxi. 11, 12. They were forbidden to read the whole of it till a certain age. Moreover, they got their Bible only successively, and certain portions of it were penned only towards the end of their existence as a nation. They were never taught that it alone was every man's rule of faith; for our Saviour spoke in perfect accordance with their established rule and practice, when he said: "The Scribes and Pharisees sit upon the chair of Moses. *All things*, therefore, *whatsoever they shall say* to you, observe ye and do." (Matt. xxiii. 2.) They had to learn, to hear, not to judge for themselves. Again, our Saviour does not seem to approve their reading of the Scriptures, for he adds, with a kind of sarcasm: "for ye *think* ye have in them everlasting life." He does not say, Ye *know*, ye are *convinced*, that in them ye have everlasting life; but—ye *think:* in the same manner as He said of the heathens and their much speaking in prayer. Observe, moreover, that Christ refers to the testimony of the Scriptures for one point of doctrine only, a point which was clearly and distinctly established in all, to wit: the divinity of His mission, and He by no means asserts that they are capable of finding the whole truth by reading the whole Scriptures. Suppose that the Executive should refer the people to the laws for a certain decision, in a given case, it would not follow thence that the people are competent to sit in judgment upon the law itself, and infallibly decide its meaning in every case.

"Now these [the Bereans] were more noble than those in Thessalonica, who received the word with all eagerness, daily searching the Scriptures, whether these things were so." (Acts, xvii. 11.)

You see, thence, exclaim our separated friends, that even in the days of St. Paul, the Scriptures were read by the people.

We grant the fact, that the still unconverted Bereans, did, on that occasion, search the Scriptures; but we deny that they received a command to do so, or that they were even commended for so doing. For, the epithet "*more noble*" does not necessarily qualify the Bereans as searching the Scriptures, but may qualify them as receiving more eagerly than did the Thessalonians, the Word of God, when it was preached to them by St. Paul; and this is obviously the meaning of the passage: for, just before, the author of the Acts tells us that the Jews of Thessalonica, moved with envy at Paul's preaching, took unto them "some wicked men of the *vulgar sort*, and, raising a mob, set the city in an uproar." (Ibid. 5.) The writer, evidently, praises the noble behavior of the Bereans towards the Apostles while preaching, and contrasts it with the ill conduct of the Jews in Thessalonica. Finally, who dare say that they read the Scriptures with the view of finding fault, if they could, with St. Paul's preaching? In that, the Evangelist could not possibly have commended such a course of conduct, nor could our separated friends themselves, approve of it. How, then, did the Bereans search the Scriptures? With no other view than to verify the genuineness of St. Paul's citations, and thus convince themselves that the texts were really to be found in the places indicated by the preacher. Nor do we object to this process. We, too, refer our hearers to the Scriptures, and give them all the liberty to verify the passages which we quote; yea, more, to convince themselves that the doctrine which is taught from the text, is the very doctrine which the Scripture teaches. We do, in these lectures. We allege proof upon proof, from Holy Writ, to show our separated brethren, that our own doctrine has its foundation in the written Word of God, while theirs can find no sanction in the inspired volume. But this does by no means imply, that the faithful, who have believed already, should test the Word of God which has been preached to them, by the written Word, as if they were allowed to doubt the veracity of the Word which was preached to them. This would be a contradiction. For, on the one hand, they would believe, and on the other, they would doubt, the Word of God. They would first receive it from the lips of the preacher, and believe it as the Word of God; and, at the same time they would doubt it, until they should convince themselves, by reading, that it was the Word of God. Precisely the inconsistency into which our separated brethren fall, when their ministers tell the people that the Bible is their only rule of faith, and in the same breath assert that the ministry was appointed by Christ to spread and propagate the Gospel. These good people go every Sabbath to hear the Word of God delivered by one of their ministers, and when they have heard it, they can not yet believe, until, by their own reading, and private judgment, they have proved to themselves, that their minister taught them the truth. Of what use are Gospel preachers among them? The same may be said of confessions of faith, catechisms, and the like; all of which are drawn up by fallible men, who may have been mistaken, and the correctness of whose doctrines must be tested by the Bible. We oftentimes wondered at this inconsistency of our brethren, the more so, that it is accompanied with heavy expenses, levied upon the members of the various churches. To support a minister and his household, who can, at most, preach only his personal views of the Bible—who can not, in the name of an infallible Church, declare the truth, as it is in Jesus—seems to us an absurdity.

Their next proof is drawn from the words of St. Paul to Timothy (2 Tim. iii. 16): "Every Scripture divinely inspired, is profitable for teaching, for reproof, for correction, for instruction in justice." Who ever denied this truth? But, does it follow thence, that the Scripture is intended to be every man's only rule of faith? By no means. The words are addressed to a bishop, who is, of right, a doctor of the law—a teacher and preacher of the Gospel—who must necessarily study the Scriptures, in order that he may instruct the ignorant, reprove the wicked, correct abuses, and guide his flock in the ways of righteousness. But, if every one were to read the Scriptures, as all-sufficient for these purposes, where would be the teachers, correctors, and instructors? Then, it would be true, that we should have no need of any man teaching his neighbor, or his brethren; for then, all would know the truth, by reading the Scriptures only, "from the least of them, even to the greatest. (Jer. xxxi. 34.)

Observe, that the foregoing texts plainly contradict those Scriptures in which preaching the Gospel to every creature, and teaching all nations, are laid down as the means by which we are to come to the knowledge of faith; they contradict the texts which teach that whoever does not hear those whom Christ sends, does not hear Him; that we must hear the Church; that Christ appointed some to be apostles, others evangelists, others doctors; that the spirit of error is known by the fact, that there are those who refuse to hear the ministers of Jesus Christ.

But, we are asked, was not my reason given

me as a guide in all things, that concern my own interests? And what concerns me more intimately than the knowledge of the truths which Christ has deigned to reveal to me for my happiness in time, and in eternity?

No doubt, our reason was given us to attain the end for which we were created; and since the knowledge of the truths of revelation is necessary to reach that end, our reason must be the medium by which to come to that knowledge. But God may have willed that reason should be assisted in the attainment of that necessary knowledge. It does not follow, that each individual reason is, therefore, of itself, sufficient to grasp that knowledge. Providence, no doubt, intended that the various nations of the world should be linked together by the bonds of social intercourse; therefore, that they should exchange thoughts and feelings with each other; but it does not follow thence, that every individual should have physical power to swim the seas or lakes which intervene between them. He may have willed, that there should be vessels to transport them across the waters, and that there should be captains to guide those vessels. So, He may have willed that, to reach the haven of salvation by the chart and compass of His Word, there should be those who, with infallible knowledge, should steer us across the ocean of this world, lest, if left to ourselves, we might be tossed to and fro by every wind of doctrine; lest, being our own teachers in things which are hard to understand, we might wrest them unto our own destruction. (2 Peter, iii. 16.) We do not exercise our freedom less, by asking the advice of others, and following it, than by guiding ourselves. If, by our own reason, we have discovered motives sufficiently strong to rely on the judgment of others, skilled, and, in our present case, appointed by Heaven, to direct, and guide us unto good, we exercise our freedom by following them, as thoroughly, and more so, than if we were to proceed in our ignorance.

Were the Apostles slaves because they were bound to hear their Master, and to understand Him in the sense in which He spoke to them? If the same authority should continue to exist now, as we shall prove hereafter, that it does exist, where is the slavery in following its voice, or obeying its injunctions? Would not such a voice be the voice of truth, and are we not truly free where the truth makes us free? Man's slavery, is in error and in doubt, not in the truth. The Pagan might as well conclude that he needs no revelation from Heaven, because his reason is given him to know all truth that is necessary for his temporal and eternal happiness. Yet this erroneous principle underlies the Protestant rule of private interpretation. It denies the right of guidance and instruction not only to men, but to God Himself. For, while it proclaims the divine Word as our sole guide in matters of religion, it is our own proud reason which it is intended shall direct us. This truth is evident to every one who reflects upon the facts in the case. First, it is reason which must decide what is, and what is not, the Word of God; so that, whatever books or chapters of Scripture reason rejects, even should they chance to be the Word of God, they cease to be such, merely because reason has so decided. Secondly, the objective truth of the books which reason approves as divinely revealed, must obey the subjective understanding of every individual, so that man's sense is God's sense, and man's mind the mind of the Revealer. Who does not see, that this principle is, at bottom, the same which the enemy of our race held up to our common mother, Eve, when he said, in order to dissuade her from obeying the command of God: "No; ye surely shall not die; for

God doth know, that on whatever day ye shall eat thereof, your eyes shall be opened: and you shall be as God, knowing good and evil." (Gen. iii. 4, 5.)

In fine, the principle of our separated brethren can never effect the designs of the Founder of Christianity. If our Saviour intended the Bible to be the world's only rule of faith, then, the world should have been converted by the reading of the Sacred Volume. And yet, what is the historic fact? Can our separated brethren point out a single nation, or tribe, which has been converted to Christianity by the reading of the Bible alone? All history is there to prove, that the nations, which at any time previous to the so-called Reformation, renounced the worship of their idols, and embraced the Christian religion, were converted by the authoritative preaching of the zealous Apostles who went among them. The same success has attended the Catholic rule of faith since the dawn of the Reformation, as we shall have occasion to prove in our next lecture. How comes it that the Protestant rule has proved so barren, and that of the Catholic Church so fruitful in converting the world to Christ and the Gospel? Does not the failure of the one prove its want of Divine sanction, and the success of the other, the approbation of Heaven?

Oh, that our friends would open their eyes to so important, so vital a subject! Their eternity depends upon it. "He that believeth not," says the Saviour, "shall be damned.' (Mark, xvi. 16.) "Without faith," says the inspired Apostle, "it is impossible to please God." (Heb. xi. 6.) And yet, as we have proved, faith, on the principle of our separated brethren, is impossible. Hence their salvation is impossible, so long as they wilfully and obstinately refuse to embrace that only saving rule of faith, with the nature of which we are to acquaint you in the following lecture.

III.

THE CHURCH OF CHRIST.

"All power is given to me in Heaven and on earth. Going, therefore, teach ye all nations; baptizing them in the name of the Father, and of the Son, and of the Holy Ghost; teaching them to observe all things whatsoever I have commanded you; and behold I am with you all days, even to the consummation of the world." MATT. xxviii. 18, 19, 20.

In the preceding lecture we have proved that the Bible alone, interpreted by private judgment, could not be and is not the rule of faith. What then is the rule established by the Founder of Christianity, through which all are to come, and can easily, securely, and certainly come, to the knowledge of the faith, without which it is impossible to please God, without which, all that are capable of faith shall be damned. We answer, the infallible Church of Christ, which is at once the commissioned guardian, interpreter and judge of all the doctrines, that Christ ever taught, and that are to be believed unto salvation. This assertion supposes or assumes that Christ established a Church, but one Church, and that Church still exists. These assumptions need to be proved, and as they are matters of fact, we shall appeal to history. But before we do so, it may be well to define what we mean by the word church, especially as many wrong notions are current on this subject among our adversaries, both Protestants and Rationalists. We scarcely need stop to declare the nominal definition. The word Church, taken literally from the Greek, means, a calling out, or convocation, assembly, or meeting, of some or many individuals. Figuratively, it signifies, at times, a place of meeting, as in Judith (vi. 21): "And afterwards all the people were called together, and they prayed all the night long, within the Church." At other times it means a society or assembly of the faithful, living or meeting in the same town or province; thus St. Paul (Rom. xvi. 3, 5) writes: "Salute Prisca and Aquila . . . and the Church which is in their house." And again (ibid. 16): "All the Churches of Christ salute you." So we read of the Church of the Corinthians, Thessalonians, etc. It is also taken for the faithful all over the earth. St. Paul uses it in this sense when he writes to the Ephesians (i. 17, 22): "That the God of our Lord Jesus Christ ... hath made Him head over all the Church." And Acts, xx. 28: "Take heed to yourselves, and to all the flock, over which the Holy Ghost hath placed you Bishops, to rule the Church of God." Not unfrequently it refers to the teaching or governing portion only, or the Pastors of the Church. In this sense, Christ says (Matth. xviii. 17): "And if he will not hear the Church, let him be to thee as the heathen and the publican."

The real definition, with which we have to do in this lecture, is given by Bellarmine in these words: "The Church is a society of men on earth, united together by the profession of one and the self-same Christian faith, and the communion of the same sacraments, under the government of lawful Pastors, and especially of the Roman Pontiff." (Bell., De Eccl., lib. iii., c. 11.)

That there exists such an institution upon earth, is evident to every one who has eyes to see and ears to hear. There is a society of men spread all over the world, called the Roman Catholic Church, whose members, to the number of at least one hundred and fifty millions, assert and maintain that Christ is their Founder. They profess the same faith, participate in the same sacraments, obey their respective bishops, and, with the latter, are subject to the Roman pontiff, otherwise called the Pope.

You find, besides this Universal or Catholic Church, smaller societies that call themselves Christian, though separated from the society of Roman Catholics, in doctrine, sacraments, and government; and yet agreeing with us in the belief, that Christ established a society of followers, called His or Christ's Church. The proof of this fact can be traced back to the very first ages of the Christian era. Add to this, as incontestable proofs, the histories which have been written, the temples which have been erected, the altars and other monuments of Christian art, extant for ages among nearly all nations and peoples. Witness in the first centuries the "Apologies" of the Christian religion, in which we always read of a society founded by Christ, and in which that society is defended as the true Church of Christ against the innovations of heresies and schisms. Witness the Fathers of the Church, whose historical testimony has, to say the least, as much weight as that of professed historians themselves. Witness the very writings of the heathen philosophers of the primitive ages, all of whom assume the fact that Christ was the Founder of the Church which they assailed in their works. The persecutions from Nero down to the present time prove the same fact, inasmuch as they assail not individuals merely, but the sect of the Galileans, which called itself Christian, and they not unfrequently upbraided them for being the followers of a malefactor who was crucified. The martyrs, in their turn, bore the same testimony by shedding the last drop of their blood. From these authorities, so various, so constant, so universal, given by men of different nationalities, education, prejudices, interests, in all ages, among all people, we conclude that it is proved beyond the shadow of a doubt, that Christ was the Founder of an institution which He called His Church, and which the world has continued to call the Christian Church, or the Church of Christ.

If now we open the Bible, not as the inspired word of God, but merely as an historical record of facts which happened in the days of its authors, we shall find the same distinct and evident testimony. In the first place, we read that the Founder Himself calls the society of His followers, His Church. "Upon this rock," says He to Peter, "I will build my Church." (Matt. xvi. 18.) The same fact may be gathered from the figures or comparisons by which

He expresses the idea of His Church. Sometimes He compares it to a fold of which He Himself is the shepherd (John, x. 1); sometimes to a marriage feast (Matt. xxii. 2); again, to a family (Matt. xxiv. 45); to a city set on a mountain (Matt. v. 14); to a kingdom. (John xviii. 36.) All these comparisons convey the idea of a society, of a visible association, a union of several into one. His acts proclaim the same truth. He chooses twelve men to be His Apostles (Matt. x. 1); He begs His Father that they and all those who through them shall believe in Him, may be one, as He and the Father are one (John, xvii. 20, etc.); selects Peter as the visible foundation stone, or head of the building (Matt. xvi. 18); subjects to him and the other Apostles, according to their rank, the rest of the faithful (ibid. and Luke, x. 16); gives them power to bind and to loose, and constitutes them a tribunal, from which there is no appeal. (Matt. xviii. 17.) To these He associates seventy-two disciples to aid them in the preaching of the Gospel. (Luke, x. 1.)

Then He commands the believers to receive and obey these teachers, to be baptized, and to receive the rest of the sacraments which He instituted for their sanctification.

The Apostles, faithful to their duty, execute every command of their Master, with regard to the society He had established. They nominate and appoint Bishops and Deacons, and colaborers in the vineyard of their Lord. They do it in His name, with His power, or rather Christ continues to do it through them. "He who descended, is the same, also, who ascended above all the heavens, that He might fulfil all things. And some, indeed, He gave to be apostles, and some prophets, and others evangelists, and others pastors and teachers, for the perfection of the saints, for the work of the ministry, unto the edification of the body of Christ." (Eph. iv. 10, etc.) In the same sense the Apostle says: "Take heed to yourselves, and to all the flock, over which the Holy Ghost hath placed you Bishops, to rule the Church of God, which He hath purchased with His own blood" (Acts, xx. 28); and: "Christ loved the Church, and delivered Himself up for it; that He might sanctify it by the laver of water in the word of life. (Eph. v. 25, 26.) He speaks of marriage as a great sacrament, but only in the Church and Christ. (Ibid. v. 32.) Do not all these sayings and acts of Christ and His Apostles prove beyond any cavil that He founded a Church, or society of believers, perfect in all its parts, having all the conditions, all the essential constituents of a real, external, visible association, corporation or living organic body, with which moreover He promises to abide until the consummation of the world (Matt. xxviii. 20); and of which He was to be the head and vital principle for evermore?

The end of that society, besides the greater glory of His Father, was the salvation of mankind. For the end of the society He founded was the same as the end or object of His own mission. He came to save that which was lost (Luke, xix. 10); He came that men might have life, and that they might have it more abundantly. (John, x. 10.)

He intended to perpetuate His own mission through His institution or church; consequently He wished the Church to be the representative person of that mission. Now, one of the means by which He effected His mission was the preaching of all the truth necessary to salvation; hence, to perpetuate this means, He must appoint teachers accredited by Him, as He Himself was by the Father, so that like Him they could say: "My doctrine is not Mine, but of Him who sent me" (John, vii. 16); that is to say, it is not of man, human; but of God, divine. He does so appoint them, saying: "As the Father hath sent Me, I also send you." (John, xx. 21.) "All power is given to Me in Heaven and on earth, going therefore, teach all nations," etc. (Matt. xxviii. 18, 19.) Hence the Apostle had a right to say: "Let a man so look upon us as the ministers of Christ, and the dispensers of the mysteries of God." (1 Cor. iv. 1.) To Peter the command is given: "Feed My lambs;" "feed My sheep" (John, xxi. 15, 17); that is to say, Peter is to supply all the means necessary to salvation. "To thee I will give the keys of the kingdom of Heaven," etc. (Matt. xvi. 19.) He is the janitor who must open the gate to this spiritual city, this kingdom of Christ on earth.

If Christ intended to perpetuate His ministry of teaching in and through the Church, it follows that He must invest that ministry with all the marks of authority which characterized His own teaching. If the Church, as teacher, had less authority, or her teaching were not as fully accredited as His own, the Church could not possibly represent the person of Christ, and it would not be true that Christ is with that Church, that He uses it as His organ, through which to preach and teach whatsoever He had commanded.

What then were the characteristics of Christ as a teacher?

The first characteristic of a teacher is his visibility. The nature of teaching requires pupils to be taught; teacher and disciple must be brought to a communion of mind and action; both must meet face to face. This law God observed from the beginning. He Himself taught Adam face to face, appeared to the Patriarch, either directly Himself or through the ministry of His angels, revealed Himself and His law to Moses and the prophets, and finally, as the Apostle says, "God having spoken on divers occasions and many ways, in time past, to the Fathers by the Prophets, last of all in these days hath spoken to us by his Son." (Heb. i. 1.) Jesus was to fulfill the Scriptures that were written of Him; He was to die, to rise again, and afterwards ascend into Heaven, where now "He sitteth at the right hand of the Majesty on high." (Heb. i. 3.) Yet according to the reasoning of the same Apostle, He was not to cease remaining among us in that capacity in which He was introduced into the world. Hence the Apostle applies to Him the texts of the Psalms: "Thy throne, O God, is for ever and ever, a sceptre of justice is the sceptre of Thy kingdom." (Heb. i. 8.)

"Thou, in the beginning, O Lord, hast founded the earth: and the heavens are the works of thy hands. They shall perish, but Thou shalt continue: and they shall all grow old as a garment. And as a vesture shalt Thou change them, and they shall be changed: but Thou art the self-same; and Thy years shall not fail." (Ibid. 10-12.) The throne, then, of Christ's kingdom, is for ever and ever, and not only the throne but the incumbent of the throne is to continue the self-same. "Jesus Christ yesterday, and to-day, and the same forever." (Heb. xiii. 8.) This is precisely what Christ Himself said: "Heaven and earth shall pass away, but My words shall not pass away" (Luke, xxi. 33); "I will not leave you orphans" (John, xiv. 18); "I am with you all days, even to the consummation of the world." (Matt. xxviii. 20.) But Christ is now no longer personally on earth; He dwelleth in the Heavens. How then reconcile His presence in Heaven with His presence in the Church? Listen to the Apostle again: "Therefore ought we more diligently to observe the things which we have heard; lest perhaps we should let them slip. For if the word, spoken by angels, became steadfast, and every transgression and disobedience received a just recompense of reward:

how shall we escape, if we neglect so great salvation? Which having begun to be declared by the Lord, was confirmed to us, by them that heard him. God also bearing them witness by signs and wonders, and divers miracles and distributions of the Holy Ghost, according to His own will." (Heb. ii. 1-4.) And, further on, the Apostle exalting Christ above Moses, says: "Moses indeed was faithful in all his house, as a servant, for a testimony of those things which were to be spoken. But Christ as a Son, in His own house, which house are we, if we retain a firm confidence and the glory of hope unto the end." (Ibid. iii. 5, 6.)

The Gospel truths, then, which were *begun* to be declared by Christ, were confirmed, that is, made certain, by the Apostles; to whom He communicated at the same time, the identical, visible means of propagating them, which He Himself had employed, such as signs, wonders, miracles, and the outpouring of the Holy Spirit. Thus Christ continues to live in the Church, which He established, as in His own house, through the Apostles, His visible representatives.

The idea of an invisible church, to which ancient and modern heretics have had recourse, is evidently a contradiction in terms. The word church, as we have seen, means a congregation, a meeting, an assembly. Who ever heard of an invisible meeting or assembly of men and women?

It is repugnant to the object of the Church, which is to spread the true faith, to dispense the mysteries or the sacraments, to effect the reconciliation of the sinner with God, all of which require a visible agency. How could an invisible church effect or realize these objects? If the teacher be invisible and therefore inaudible, how will the world be taught? If the dispenser of the sacraments be not known, how shall the people receive them? How then shall the commission of Christ to His Apostles be verified?—" Go ye into the whole world, and preach the Gospel to every creature. He that believeth and is baptized shall be saved; he that believeth not shall be condemned." (Matt. xvi. 16.) How these other words?—" Go ye, therefore, and teach all nations; baptizing them in the name of the Father, and of the Son, and of the Holy Ghost, teaching them to observe all things whatsoever I have commanded you." (Matt. xxviii. 19-20.) How are they "the light of the world," if that light is hidden under a bushel? How is the Church to be the mountain of the Lord's house established on the top of the mountains and exalted above the hills, and how are the nations to flow into it, and to be taught in that house, if it is hid from their eyes, and the teachers thereof are unknown to them? (Isaiah, ii. 2.) The Church is a kingdom, a fold, a city, the house, yea, the body of Christ: by what figure of speech can these be made ideas of invisible things?

How are we to distinguish between orthodoxy and heterodoxy, between the wheat and the chaff, between the good and the bad fishes? How are we to discern those that walk circumspectly and those that walk disorderly in the house of God? (Eph. v. 15.) How are the bishops to reprove, to rebuke, to preach, in season and out of season? (2 Tim. iv. 2.)

Every society must have laws by which it is regulated; these laws must be administered. For that purpose, there must be a government and officers; there must be a Constitution, an Executive, and a Judiciary. How can all these be found in an invisible church? How are inferiors to obey their superiors and be subject to them? How shall the superiors watch over them for the good of their souls, as having one day to give an account of their stewardship (Heb. xiii. 17); how shall the shepherds feed the sheep, if none of these can be known or seen?

If the true Church of Christ was at any time invisible, by what logical premises did you come to such a conclusion? Doubtless the invisible church must have been visible to you who assert the fact of her invisibility, for otherwise, you assert a fact of which you have no knowledge. If you could get the knowledge of the fact, why not others? If others could obtain that knowledge, it was because the invisible church was really visible as invisible, could be seen as unseen, which is a contradiction in terms. Yea, all should be able to see the invisible church: for, on the hypothesis that she was the true Church of Christ, all were bound to be united with her, as the only means of salvation. All, then, should have been able to see the invisible Church, and yet because invisible, none could see it.

Again: Where was the invisible Church before the so-called Reformation? Was she in one or in all the several churches that existed before that time? What were her conditions of membership? Where were the true members? Give us their names, the place or places where they lived and died.

Moreover, did Christ institute a visible or an

invisible Church? If the former, your theory falls to the ground. If the latter, then you do wrong to remain Protestant; for as a Protestant you are a member of a visible institution, which you at least contend is the Church of Christ. In either case, therefore, you are, by your own confession, out of the pale of the true Church, therefore, without the true faith, therefore, under the displeasure of God, and on the road to damnation.

Christ, who appeared a visible teacher of God, and who made His Church His representative upon earth, left us, in the first place, a *visible* Church, whose doctrines and sacraments, whose government, whose whole nature, are open to the eyes of the whole world;—who continues, as she ever did, to preach on the house-tops what she had heard from the beginning. Christ, as a teacher, was necessarily consistent in His doctrines. Consistency, objectively considered, is unity. He that never contradicts Himself in speaking, or teaching, speaks and teaches one and the same thing on the same subject. Christ, therefore, as a true teacher, never contradicted Himself. If the Church is His organ, if He, as the head, continues to speak by her lips, if she is but a permanent incarnation of Himself, she must, like

Him, be thoroughly consistent in her teaching; she must be one in her doctrines, so that both the teachers and the taught, the shepherds and the flock, "be of one mind" (Philip. ii. 2), speaking the self-same thing. One of the essential characteristics of Christ's Church, as we have seen in the definition, is that the society of believers be united by the profession of the same faith. He who founded her is one, for ever the self-same, the God-man Christ Jesus. Such then must His body be, such must His house be, in which He dwelleth, such the fold of which He is the shepherd, the kingdom over which He sways the sceptre. Christ is the *truth;*—"I am the truth." (John, xiv. 6.) The truth, of its nature, is one; it cannot *be*, and *not be*, at the same time. The Church, therefore, in which that truth resides, which is the pillar and the ground of truth, must needs be one. The truth and Christ being identified, and Christ being identified with His Church, the Church is the truth, and is as incapable of contradicting herself as Christ Himself. Hence it follows that the Church can never teach one doctrine in one way, to-day, and in another way, to-morrow. Hence it follows that we, at the present time, are as certain that when the Church speaks as Church, she speaks the truth as if we listened to Christ Himself. And this He has openly declared. "He that heareth you, heareth Me, he that despiseth you, despiseth Me, and he that despiseth Me, despiseth Him that sent Me." (Luke, x. 16. The Church, therefore, brings us into immediate contact with God who is the truth. It follows further that our act of faith in what the Church teaches, is of all other acts the most certain, and imparts the most unshaken and unshakable conviction.

Did Christ really impart this unity to His Church? If not, why did He pray to His Father that the Apostles and disciples might be one as He and the Father are one? And why did He pray that not they alone, but they also who should believe in Him through their word might all be one (John, xvii. 21, 22), if He did not intend that this unity should remain a characteristic mark of the true Church? Yea, He Himself declares that this was the reason of His prayer: "That the world may know that Thou hast sent Me." (Ibid. 23.) We are aware that the prayer of Jesus was always heard for His reverence. (Heb. v. 7.) Hence His true Church is even now really one in doctrine, one in sacraments, one in government.

Our Saviour said (John, x. 16): "And other sheep I have, that are not of this fold; them, also, I must bring, and they shall hear My voice; and there shall be made one fold, and one shepherd." Sheep of one fold are fed together, sheltered together, and led together; go in and out together, under the care and vigilance of the shepherd who is set over them. If Christ has other sheep that must be brought to the one same fold, then, the theory that Christ's sheep are spread and scattered through many folds, led and fed by many shepherds, is a false one, and must be rejected; then, it is not true, that the Church is made up of believers in all the various and contradictory churches which have sprung up in the world, since the beginning of Christianity, and especially since the days of the so-called Reformation.

Again, the Apostle writes, that the Church of Christ is his body (Coloss. i. 24), and that that body is one,—there is " one body and one Spirit, as you are called in one hope of your vocation, one Lord, one faith, one baptism" (Eph. iv. 45); "We being many, are one body in Christ, and each one members one of an other." (Rom. xii. 15). How can members of different bodies compose one symmetrical frame? Would not such a body resemble that described by Horace in the opening lines of his "Art of Poetry"? Would it not be even more monstrous still? In one body all the members obey the same head; the same will governs and commands them all. They are subordinate—not co-ordinate—to each other. On the Protestant theory of the right of private judgment, every member is independent of the other. There is neither subordination nor co-ordination possible. Every one strikes out a course of thought, and of action, for himself. Every one forms a creed of his own; every one determines the nature and the number of the sacraments; every one rules, and no one is ruled. There can be no unity in such a body.

That such unity was one of the characteristic marks of the Christian Church is a fact of history. "All they that believed were together, and had all things common; they sold their possessions and goods, and divided them to all, according as every man had need. And, continuing daily, with one accord, in the temple, and breaking bread from house to house. . . . And the Lord added daily to their society such as should be saved." (Acts, ii. 44–47.) Unity was considered so necessary, that salvation depended upon it as one of the signs of the true faith. "And the multitude of believers had but one heart and one soul." (Ibid. iv. 32.) There was no such thing as setting up independent churches, or societies of believers. It mattered not whether they were Romans, Corinthians, Colossians, Ephesians, Cretans or Cappadocians, Jews or Samaritans, all those who were converted from their various religions to the Christian Church, were members of one and the same mystical body of Christ, in which all national distinctions ceased; in which there was neither Jew nor Greek, bond nor free, male nor female, for they were all one in Christ Jesus. (Gal. iii. 28.) Heresies, divisions, schisms, were not tolerated nor permitted. Those who "cause dissensions" were marked and avoided (Rom. xvi. 17); were regarded as antichrists (1 John, ii. 18), and were not looked upon as belonging to the Church. "They went out from us, but they were not of us; for, if they had been of us, they would, no doubt, have continued with us. (Ibid. 19.)

The idea of Christ in founding His Church, excludes, therefore, all independent organizations, all self-constituted churches, all congregationalism, such as we find in our day. His idea is concentrative. All the members of His Church are one among themselves, all are one with the Church, and the Church with Him.

Individualization was still further from His mind. Every individual is, indeed, to believe, and to practise the obligations laid upon Him; but the faith of one individual is the faith of a second, and of a third, and so on, so that the faith of every individual member of the Church equals the faith of the Church itself; and the faith of both equals the principles of faith, as they exist in the mind of Christ, the Author of the faith. And there is not only a numerical unity as to the precise articles to be believed, and the duties to be practised, but a substantial and formal unity, which comprises the sense—the meaning of these things as they lie in the mind of Jesus. Every believer and doer of His Word may say, with truth, that it is now no longer he that lives, but Christ that lives in him (Gal. ii. 20); that he is one with Christ; that he is a Christian—another Christ—by living the life of Christ, in spirit and in truth.

Thus, the ideas of Christ become the ideas of the Church, and of every member of the Church, and the truth of these ideas as it lies in the mind of Christ, lies in the mind of the Church, and in the minds of its members. The same may be said of the life of the heart. By conforming the individual will to the will of the Church, which, in her turn, always conforms hers to the will of Christ, there is a oneness of vitality, of spiritual life, which makes us partakers, through grace, of the Divine nature, which causes us to live in Christ, and Christ in us, so that we become, after our own measure, one in Him, as He is one in the Father (John, xvii. 21.)

To produce this wonderful, this more than natural unity, more than a natural authority was absolutely necessary. No human power was ever able thus to unite the individual members of society among themselves or with the head of the social body. A material union of an outward nature, binding the members of the same society together by bonds of natural and material interests, may be effected and maintained for a time. But to cause all to be of one mind and one will, to make all think and desire the same thing, is a rare spectacle, and, so far as we know, never seen on earth, except in the Church or Christian society. The authority of the State can never reach the mind and heart of all its members, so as to subject *them* to its rule. To unite individuals after this manner, the head of the social body should not only have authority to command, but should be able to infuse his own vitality into the members. This Christ alone could do and has done in His Church. The authority of society, although, like all real power, it comes from God, is not so intimately identified with Him as not to admit a distinction. Human authority can act independently of the source of its power. It is not infallible. It can abuse the trust which it has received of God; and may err concerning the nature and extent of its power as well as in the manner of exercising it. God grants to the heads of nations the power to rule their subjects, but He has not promised them that divine assistance by which they shall be able to avoid all mistake or abuse in applying it. Not so with His Church. He has lodged His own divine authority in her rulers, and He governs in them and by them. He communicates it to them by a continual presence, by a perpetual influx of His own mind into their minds, and of His own will into their wills, thus securing them against all possible error, not only as to the nature and extent of their power, but as to the manner of exercising it. He does more. He influences the ruled, in turn, by His divine grace and spirit, so as to make them at once know the nature and extent of the rulers' power, and help them in subjecting themselves heart and soul to it.

The infallibility of the Church is a privilege

received by her from Christ, in virtue of which she cannot be deceived, nor deceive others, in proposing to the world doctrines of faith and morals. Hence, whatever she proposes to be believed or practised, is infallibly true, whether she proposes these truths from the Bible. or from Tradition.

Christ was witness of the truth as He learned it from the Father. He was the Judge of that truth, and its Teacher. Such is also the threefold office of the Church, and in each she is, like Him, infallible. "Behold," exclaimed the prophet Isaiah, "I have given Him for a witness to the people, for a leader and a master to the Gentiles." (Isaiah, lv. 4.)

And St. John: "Grace be unto you . . . and from Jesus Christ who is the faithful witness . . . who hath made us a kingdom and priests to God and His Father." (Apoc. i. 4–6.)

"Amen, amen I say to thee," so spoke Jesus to Nicodemus, "we speak what we know, and we testify what we have seen, and you receive not our testimony." (John, iii. 11.)

"I am one that give testimony of Myself; and the Father that sent Me giveth testimony of Me." (Ibid. viii. 18.)

Christ asserts that His judgment is true, "because I am not alone, but I and He that sent me, the Father." (John, viii. 16.) He judged between falsehood and truth in the doctrines of the Pharisees and condemned their innovations. He settled disputes that arose between His own Apostles before they were imbued with virtue from on High. He came unto the world to teach all truth. Both the Jews and the Apostles called Him Master and Teacher. They bore testimony to His teaching "the way of God in truth." (Matt. xii. 38; xxii. 16.)

These same offices were by Christ transmitted to His Apostles and their successors. "But you shall receive the power of the Holy Ghost coming upon you, and you shall be witnesses unto Me in Jerusalem, and in all Judea and Samaria, and even to the uttermost part of the earth." (Acts i. 8.) "We are witnesses," said St. Peter, "of all things that He did in the land of the Jews and in Jerusalem." (Ibid. x. 39.) "And He commanded us to preach to the people, and to testify that it is He who had been appointed by God to be judge of the living and of the dead." (Ibid. 42.)

You have but to read the acts of the Apostles and their epistles to be convinced that they claimed and exercised the right, in the name of Christ and in the power of the Holy Ghost, to approve and condemn in matters of doctrine and morals and worship, according as circumstances required.

That they were appointed teachers is evident from St. Matt. xxviii. 18, 20. "All power is given to Me in Heaven and in earth, go ye, therefore, and teach all nations; baptizing them in the name of the Father, and of the Son, and of the Holy Ghost—teaching them to observe all things whatever I have commanded you."

As a witness, the Church will never misunderstand nor pervert the truths, concerning which she is to testify; as a judge she will never draw from God's word, whether written or unwritten, any false meaning or conclusions; and as a teacher, she will always propose those truths and practices so as safely to provide for the salvation of all. Thus the doctrines of Christ and of the Apostles, by the infallible presence and assistance of Christ and His Holy Spirit, shall go down, from age to age, without any mixture of error, pure and spotless as they came from them.

This infallibility is absolutely necessary, to realize the end for which Christ founded His Church. His mission was not a transitory one. He came to save, not only those who lived in

His own day and time, but all mankind, of all times and ages. He sincerely wished that we, and those that are to come after us, should have the same means of salvation as the Jews had in His own age and country. For this purpose He entrusted His doctrines and His sacraments, and the power to govern His Church, to His Apostles; for this purpose He promised them His infallible aid and presence; for this purpose He communicated to them the fulness of the power which He Himself had received from His Father; for this purpose He commanded that all should hear and obey them, as if He Himself were personally and actually present on earth. But the Apostles were mortal men. If He wished all to be saved by the same means and in the same way, He must have provided for all even until the end of time. Now, the means which He employed were the infallible preaching of His word, the infallible administration of His sacraments, and His government. He must, therefore, continue till now to propose His doctrines, to communicate His sacraments, and to govern His Church in the same manner. This He does; for He promised the Apostles and their successors His ever-abiding presence: "I am with you all days till the consummation of the world." (Matt. xxviii. 20.) That consummation is not yet come; Christ, therefore, is still with His Church as He was with His Apostles. With them and through them He Himself teaches; with them and through them He Himself baptizes and administers the other sacraments as means of salvation; with them and through them He governs His Church, He identifies their authority with his own: "He that heareth you heareth Me, and he that despiseth you despiseth Me." (Luke, x. 16.) He places those who are rebellious to His Church on the same footing with the heathen and the publican, who, as such, have no share in the kingdom of God. He that " will not hear the Church, let him be to thee as the heathen and the publican." (Matt. xviii. 17.) He makes faith in their preaching, and in the baptism administered by them, conditions without which none can be saved; "Go ye into the whole world, and preach the Gospel to every creature. He that believeth and is baptized, shall be saved, but he that believeth not, shall be condemned." (Mark, xvi. 16.) The Apostles act on these principles. St. John tells the world: " He that knoweth God, heareth us, he that is not of God, heareth us not;" and he gives it as a characteristic sign of truth and error: " By this we know the Spirit of truth, and the spirit of error." (1 John, iv. 6.).

Now, how can you reconcile all this with a fallible Church? If the Church could err, then the error would redound on Jesus Christ Himself. For, on the one hand, He makes the Apostles and their successors, or in other words, the teaching Church, His organ; He identifies Himself with her;—and, on the other, He binds all creatures to subject themselves to that Church, as a condition without which they remain in error, without which they are sure to be condemned; and yet, He would not have made that Church infallible, in proposing to them the doctrinal and practical means of salvation. Would not, in that case, the errors into which men might and would naturally fall, redound on Him, who had given such a power and such a commandment? He would, on the hypothesis that she can deceive and mislead men, command them to obey her under pain of damnation, whether she teaches error or truth, which is an absurdity.

He promises to work signs and wonders through His Church, that the people may believe the doctrines which she proposes, and she has enjoyed, till this day, the privilege of confirming the doctrines which she proposes, by unmistakable and undoubted miracles. How could He allow this unless He really approved the doctrines of the Church, in behalf of which these miracles are wrought?

Finally, if there is no infallible Church, then there is no rule of faith at all; therefore, no faith in Christ; therefore, no salvation. For, according to our separated brethren, the only rules of faith apart from the infallible authority of the Church, are the private spirit, and private reason of each individual. But, as we have proved in our preceding lecture, neither of these can impart to any one the infallible certainty that he has the faith, as it is in Christ Jesus; therefore, no one can be infallibly certain that he has the true faith. It is not enough to imagine, to think, to hope, that what anyone believes, is the doctrine of Christ; for, "faith is the substance of things hoped for, the conviction of things that appear not." (Heb. xi. 1.) Whoever has not such evidence must necessarily doubt; and he that doubts cannot believe. Faith and doubt exclude each other. Nor, will it do to say, that every one becomes infallible by the aid of the Spirit, or by reading the Bible. For, this assumption no Protestant Church has ever set up as a claim to its own infallible orthodoxy. And rightly so; for then, since the assistance of the Divine Spirit is promised to all, all must needs be infallible. Then, we are as infallible as our separated brethren. Then, the Socinian, reading the Bible, is as infallible as the Episcopalian, the Jew as infallible as the Presbyterian, and so on.

Neither will it do to say, "But the Bible which I read, and the Spirit, who testifies to my inmost conscience, what is the inmost faith in Jesus, are infallible." We do not deny the infallibility of either; but we maintain, that you and the Bible are two different things; that you and the Spirit are two different persons. To prove your infallibility by the fact that the Bible and the Spirit are infallible, you must first prove that your understanding becomes infallible by the mere fact, that you read the Bible and that the Spirit assists you in reading it. The objective truths of the Bible become subjective in the mind of the reader. It is your subjective understanding of the truth which is the recipient of the objective truth, as proposed in the Bible, or by the Spirit. How do you prove that your subjective understanding seizes with infallible certainty, the objective truth proposed by the Spirit or the Bible? Until you prove this, you prove nothing. A fallible recipient faculty cannot exceed its own powers, which are essentially fallible, till it receive an assistance which is infallible, and endows it with infallible power. If you answer, the fault is with the reader, not with the Bible nor the Spirit, the same question returns: But, how do you infallibly determine which of the two is in fault, you or we? If you say, this is to be settled by the Scriptures, you beg the question. For, suppose we do not understand texts which tell us how to avoid misunderstanding the Bible and the Spirit, as you do, who, or what, in the last resort, is to decide between us? No longer the Bible; for the difficulty is precisely about the meaning of the Bible on that score. Nor the Spirit; for the Spirit witnesseth two contradictory things on the same subject. Nor, in fine, private reason, for your private reason contradicts ours, and *vice versa*, ours contradicts yours. The only reasonable theory, therefore, is, that Christ has established a supreme tribunal apart from the Bible, composed of living men, to whom He promised the Spirit of Truth, so that it would never, yea, could never misunderstand the doctrines of faith and morals propounded for the belief and practice of the faithful. When He began to preach His Gospel, He Himself, was at once the infallible witness of all the truths He taught, the infallible Judge of the meaning of His own Word, and its infallible Teacher and Expounder. The same method He continued, by appointing His Apostles and their successors, the infallible witnesses, judges, and expounders of all things whatsoever He had taught them; obliging the hearers to hear them, as if He Himself were judging and teaching; obliging them, under the threatened penalty of eternal damnation if they refuse, to believe their word, or His own, and making their obedience or disobedience the distinctive marks of the spirit of truth and the spirit of error. For that purpose, He promised His Apostles and their successors, His own presence and assistance, and that of the Holy Spirit. "Behold! I am with you all days, even to the consummation of the world." (Matt. xxviii. 20.) "And I will ask the Father, and He shall give you another Paraclete, that He may abide with you for ever, the Spirit of truth, whom the world cannot receive, because it seeth Him not, nor knoweth Him; but you shall know Him, because He shall abide with you, and shall be in you. He will teach you all things, and bring all things to your mind, whatsoever He shall have said to you." (John, xiv. 16,

17, 26.) And that Spirit is the Spirit of Jesus. "He shall not speak of Himself, but what things soever He shall hear, He shall speak." (Ibid. xvi. 13.)

That spirit was to accompany them always and everywhere, so that, when interrogated at the bar of human justice, for the faith that was in them, "it is not you that speak," says Christ, "but the spirit of your Father speaketh in you." (Matt. x. 20.) It is thus that Christ loves His Church; it is thus that He sanctifies it, in order "that He might present it to Himself a glorious Church, not having spot or wrinkle or any such thing, but that it should be holy and without blemish." (Eph. v. 26, 27.)

Whatever we have hitherto said concerning the necessity and the fact of the existence of an infallible Church, may be confirmed by a comparison. The Church is the society of believers in the doctrine of Christ. As a society, it is made up of many individuals. It is a corporation, a body composed of many members. Every society must necessarily have a head, that head must have authority. A society in which all are sovereign, is no society at all. To meet as a collective individual, there must be a point of contact somewhere. Individual sovereignty is individual independence, and excludes the possibility of contact with the rest of individuals. There must be laws. No society can exist without laws; these laws must be observed; to have them observed, there must be an authority which can interpret the meaning of the laws, and enforce their observance. A law whose meaning cannot be settled, is no law at all; for law binds as something defined, something positive. If the meaning cannot be agreed upon, the positiveness of the law disappears, consequently its binding obligation. There must, therefore, be a tribunal, a court of final appeal in every society, to determine the real meaning of the law. To this court must be referred all doubts, all disputes concerning the law, and it must be able to settle them. Otherwise, the meaning of the law remaining in doubt, the law itself will be doubtful, and doubtful laws can never impose positive obligations. Hence the maxim: *lex dubia non obligat,* a doubtful law is not binding. To meet this difficulty, every well-constituted society has established a judiciary, or court, whose decisions, in disputed cases of the law, are, by the common consent of the individual members, and from the very necessity of the case, considered final; and it is, therefore, called the Supreme Court. To this court the members of society implicitly ascribe an infallible authority of its own; namely, a judicial infallibility; that is to say, though the Supreme Court may and does sometimes actually err in its decisions, yet as the last and highest authority in such cases, its decisions cannot be repealed by the authority of the individual nor by another court. If this is deemed essential to the well-being of human societies, how much more so to the well-being and existence of a divine society among men? And just in proportion as the one is more important than the other, must the divine society have a means more secure than the other. The divine society should, therefore, have a divine means to secure her own well-being and existence. If so, then, instead of a mere *judicially* infallible, she must have an *actually* infallible authority, to decide questions of the divine law. That is to say, her final decision must not only be ultimate to the litigant, because there is no higher court of appeal for him, but because her decision is indeed, in reality, the *only possible* decision in the case, so that the voice of that tribunal is always, and in every instance, the voice of truth itself. Without such a tribunal the litigant would always retain the right, and, indeed, would be under the obligation of doubting the truth of the decision. As this decision would, on our hypothesis, be a decision in matters of faith or morals, the faith of the litigant would remain a doubtful one, and hence no faith at all. Christ, therefore, would not have sufficiently provided for His society, if He had not established an actually infallible authority, an actually infallible Church.

A church constituted as we have hitherto proved her to be, must needs be indefectible and perpetual. She must, in this respect, too, resemble her founder and her keeper. Christ founded His Church on the day of Pentecost, when He sent down His Spirit upon His Apostles in the form of fiery tongues. He had Himself risen from the grave, and having died once, dieth now no more. His kingdom and His throne are for ever and ever. All other things were to perish, but He was to continue the self-same, and His word was not to pass away. If His Church was destined to be the representative of His own mission, then she, like Him, must continue to exist forever. She must be indestructible in her essence, and perpetual in her duration. That is to say, the Church of Christ must continue to possess the same internal and external constitution, properties, and marks, with which she was founded in the beginning. In one sense, the Indefectibility characteristic of the Church is the same as her Unity, but, considered in connection with duration, a thing may be one, without being indefectible or perpetual. Hence when that oneness is considered as indefectible and perpetual, it constitutes a new property, a new characteristic of that thing. Christ came to save all men; for that purpose He instituted His Church as His representative, His organ, by which all should be able to come to the knowledge of the truth.

Now, if the Church could ever fail, it would follow that the end of His mission could fail. The moment you suppose the means to fail, that very moment the end fails. If you suppose the Church could fail at any period of time, it would be because her constitution, her essential properties, her characteristic marks would fail: if they or any one of them fail, she is no longer cognizable; for it is by these that she is cognizable as the Church of Christ. It she ceases to be cognizable, she ceases to be a means of salvation; and since she is the representative of Christ's mission, the mission of Christ fails with her. The fact is, her essential constituents or properties are so inseparably interwoven with each other, that if you take out a single one, you destroy the whole Church. For instance, suppose her defectible; the moment she fails, she ceases to be Apostolical, for that moment she breaks away from the chain that binds her to the Apostles. You destroy her Unity, because she teaches no longer the same doctrine. You take away her Catholicity, which makes her existence universal as to the sum total of the doctrines taught, and as to the time in which, and the people among whom they are taught. You take away her Sanctity; for she ceases to be the medium by which sanctification is to be effected. You destroy her Infallibility, because she fails in teaching and believing the doctrines as they were laid down by her Founder. Finally, you make her invisible; for she would no longer be cognizable as the true Church of Christ. The Church, therefore, as the representative of Christ's mission to men, must be indefectible and perpetual.

To suppose her defectible, is not only to open the way to all heresy and schism, but to sanction them. If she can cease to exist in her primary and essential constituents, she can fail at any time, at any period. All that heretics will require to justify their separation from her, is to proclaim the fact that she has actually failed.

Moreover, if the Church ceases to be the medium through which Christ effects the sanctification and salvation of mankind, He must have provided another means in her stead. He must have pointed out that means as distinctly as he pointed out His Church. Has He done so? Has He foretold that when His mission failed, He would raise up another man to make a new covenant with His people? Where is that promise? Who was that man to be? Did He point out any of the heretics of the first ages of Christianity? Did He accredit Luther or Calvin as His successors in the fulfilment of His Divine yet defectible mission? Did He help them to establish it as He did His own? Did He assist Luther, Calvin, or any others, as He did the Apostles, as He promised all those would be assisted who truly believe in Him? Did Luther, Calvin, or any heresiarchs prove the Divinity of their mission by miracles, by signs and wonders, by prophecies made in confirmation of their doctrines? Yet this would be necessary; for, otherwise, the world would have no sufficient evidence to conclude that the old form of things had passed away, and that a new one was to succeed in its place.

It will not do to answer, that the purity of

their doctrine, in opposition to the corruption which had crept into the Church, was sufficient evidence of the Divinity of their mission. For that is precisely the thing in question. The question among so many different and contradictory creeds, is, precisely, which constitutes the only true, the only divine creed. Doctrines cannot be assumed as the first and only evidence of the truth and divinity of the Church which proclaims them.

The proofs of the indefectibility of the Church, both in the Old and New Testaments, are plain and numerous. We read in Daniel: "And in the days of those kingdoms the God of Heaven will set up a kingdom that shall never be destroyed: and his kingdom shall not be left delivered up to another people, and it shall break in pieces, and shall consume all these kingdoms; and itself shall stand for ever." (Dan. ii. 44.) This kingdom is, according to the interpreters of the passage, no other than the spiritual kingdom of Christ, the same of which it is said, "Of His kingdom there shall be no end;" the same of which the Archangel Gabriel said to Mary, "The Lord shall give unto Him the throne of David His Father, and He shall reign in the house of Jacob for ever." (Luke, i. 32, 33. See also Dan. vii.

14; Isaiah, ix. 7; lix. 20, 21; Ezekiel, xxxvii 24, etc.) In the text already often quoted from Matthew (xxviii. 20), our Divine Saviour promises His Apostles that He will be with them even till the consummation of the world. It is evident, from the text, that He promises them His divine assistance, His divine though invisible presence in those things which are necessarily infallible to carry out the object of His mission, till the end of time. Hence He promises to be with them in teaching, in baptizing, that is to say, in administering the sacraments, until the consummation of the world. He thus consoles them for the loss which they should sustain by His bodily absence, and strengthens their conviction, that, though far away in body, His invisible Spirit will always be with them, teaching and ministering with them always, or as the Greek expresses it, all *the* days, even till the end of time. But the Apostles could not live for ever. They were mortal, and, like their Master, they were to disappear from earth. Yet, like Him, in another sense, they were to remain until the consummation of the world. How could this be, save by a moral presence with their successors, so that they, in their turn, appointing representatives of the mission of Christ on earth, should morally continue to live with them, in the oneness of faith, sacraments, and government, and thus preserve the interior and exterior properties and essential marks of the Church. In other words, Christ promises to remain with His Church, so that He will provide for her always, as He would do if He were still visibly present on earth; that, as invisible Head, He would continue to do for her what He would have done had He remained her visible Head during all the stages of her existence. Were He Himself to remain Her visible Head on earth, He would certainly never allow her to fail; therefore, she is yet what she always was, and she shall be the selfsame for ever.

He made a similar promise to Peter, when He appointed him the head of His Church. "Thou art Peter" (a rock), "and upon this rock I will build My Church, and the gates of hell shall not prevail against it." (Matt. xvi. 18.) The gates of hell would prevail against the Church the very moment that she would become other than she was when founded. An institution, a particular form of government, ceases to be, as soon as its first institution—its essential characteristics—cease to exist. So it is with the Church. The moment her constitution—her essential properties—as originally given her, cease to exist, that very moment she ceases to be the Church of Christ. Hence it follows, that a radical reformation is impossible in such an institution. Abuses which are external to the primitive constitution—to the formal nature of the institution—may be, and should be, corrected; but you cannot change the formal constitution, without changing the institution itself. This change the God-man designed to be beyond the power of man, yea, even of hell.

If the true Church of Christ is indefectible and perpetual, she is necessarily Apostolical. For then she remained formally the selfsame throughout the ages. That the Church of Christ is Apostolical in her origin is a fact of history, which no one, in his sound senses, dare deny. To His Apostles He gave the commission to preach the Gospel to every creature. To them He intrusted the ministry of Sacraments. To them He left the governing power. Hence St. Paul tells the Ephesians: "Now, therefore, you are no more strangers and foreigners, but you are fellow-citizens with the Saints, and the domestics of God, built upon the foundation of the Apostles and prophets, Jesus Christ Himself being the chief corner stone; in whom all the building framed together groweth into a holy temple in the Lord: in whom you also are built together into a habitation of God in the spirit." (Eph. iv. 19–22.) No Church, therefore, can claim to be the Church of Christ, which does not proceed either immediately or mediately from the Apostles, and therefore from Christ. All those Churches which have another than an Apostle for founder, are by that very fact strangers and foreigners to Christ and His Church. They lack what Tertullian calls the "consanguinity of faith;" they are not of the "household of the faith;" they enter not like living stones into the "spiritual house." (1 Peter, ii. 5.) A church is *immediately* Apostolical, when it is founded by one of the Apostles. Such were the Churches of Corinth, Ephesus, Rome, and others. It is *mediately* Apostolical, when founded by any one appointed by one of the Apostles. Thus the Church of Alexandria was founded by St. Mark, appointed and empowered for that purpose by the Apostles. Or when a church founded by an Apostle produces through her Apostolic missionaries another church, as the Apostolic Church of Rome founded the churches in Africa and most of the Western churches.

But it is, moreover, necessary that all these Churches remain united with the centre. This centre was Peter, whom Christ made the Head of the Apostles. Hence there can be no Apostolic Church which is not in union with the Church of Peter. This was the doctrine of all ages. Thus St. Irenæus writes: "They who would behold truth, may see in every Church the Apostolic Faith manifested to the whole world; and we can enumerate those bishops who were appointed by the Apostles and their successors down to ourselves; none of whom taught, or even knew, the wild opinions of these [heretics]. Had the Apostles really professed any doctrines which the perfect only were to hear, surely they would have communicated them to those to whom they intrusted their churches. However, as it would be tedious to enumerate the whole list of successions, I shall confine myself to that of Rome, the greatest, most ancient, and most illustrious Church founded by the glorious Peter and Paul; receiving from them her doctrine, which was announced to all men, and which, through the succession of her bishops, is come down to us. Thus we confound all those who, through evil designs, or vain-glory, or perverseness, teach what they ought not. For to this Church, *on account of its superior headship,* every other must have recourse, that is, the faithful of all countries; in which Church has been preserved the doctrine delivered by the Apostles." He then enumerates the Popes who had succeeded Peter till his day, in the See of Rome: "Linus Anacletus, Clement, Evaristus, Alexander, Sixtus, Telesphorus, Hyginus, Pius, Anicetus, Soter, and Eleutherius, the twelfth from the Apostles, who now governs the Church." He then continues: "Things being thus made plain, it is not from others that truth is to be sought, which may be readily learned from the Church. For to this Church, as into a rich depository, the Apostles committed whatever is of divine truth; that each one, if so inclined, might thence draw the drink of life. This is the way to life; all other teachers must be shunned as thieves and robbers. If there be any dispute on a point of minor importance, must we not have recourse to the most ancient churches, where the Apostles resided, and from them collect the truth? And had these Apostles left us nothing in writing, must not we then have followed that rule of doctrine which they delivered to those to whom they intrusted their churches? To this rule many barbarous nations submit, who, deprived of the aid of letters, have the words of salvation written on their hearts, and carefully guard the doctrine which has been delivered." (Adv. Hær. 1. c. 3, 4.)

Tertullian holds the same language concerning the Apostolic Churches. "We are not allowed," says he, "to indulge our own humor, nor to choose what another has invented. We have the Apostles of our Lord for founders, who were not themselves the inventors nor authors of what they have left us; but they have faithfully taught the world the doctrine which they received from Christ. Therefore, if an angel from Heaven should preach another Gospel, we would say anathema to him." (De Præscript. c. vi., vii., viii.)

The Apostolicity of faith follows, therefore, from the fact of the Apostolical origin of the Church. And justly so; for the faith of the Church cannot at any given period be other than the faith of Christ; but the faith of Christ was the faith of the Apostles; therefore, the faith of the Church must always be Apostolical. Christ, surely, wished His faith to be for ever the self-same. Since, then, He gave His faith in all its fulness to the Apostles, the Apostolical faith alone can be identified with the faith of Christ. On the supposition that there could be a Church not founded by the Apostles, and not receiving the faith of Christ as delivered to the Apostles, there would be a Church of Christ which does not profess the same faith as that of the Apostles and of Christ. To know what that Apostolic faith really is, it is not necessary to compare doctrine with doctrine; it suffices to ascertain what Church is in uninterrupted communion with the Apostles till this day. The Fathers and Doctors of the Church insist upon this fact, as conclusive evidence of the falsehood of the doctrines of all other Churches not in uninterrupted communion with the Church of the Apostles.

Thus, besides the passages already quoted, Tertullian says: "What will you gain by recurring to Scripture, when one denies what the other asserts? Learn rather who it is that possesses the faith of Christ; to whom the Scriptures belong; from whom, by whom, and when that faith was delivered by which we are made Christians. For, where shall be found the true faith, there will be the genuine Scriptures; there the true interpretations of them; and there all Christian traditions. Christ chose His Apostles, whom He sent to preach to all nations. They delivered His doctrine, and founded Churches, from which Churches, others drew the seeds of the same doctrines, as new ones continue daily to do. Thus these, as the offspring of the Apostolic Churches, are themselves deemed Apostolical. Now, to know what the Apostles taught, that is, what Christ revealed to them, recourse must be had to the Churches which they founded, and which they instructed by word of mouth, and by their epistles. For it is plain that all doctrine which is conformable to the faith of these Mother-Churches, is true; being that which they received from the Apostles, the Apostles from Christ, Christ from God; and all other opinions must be novel and false." (Ibid., c. xvii., xix., xx., xxi.)

From all we have hitherto said, it follows that the first Church is still the true Church, and that all the Churches posterior to the Church of the Apostles are proved false by the mere fact that they were not founded by them. This truth Tertullian presses with his usual clearness and strength of argument: "It is a maxim not to be controverted, that what was first delivered is evangelical and true, and *what was afterwards imported is extraneous and false.* By this rule all future heresies may be tried. But should they dare to arrogate to themselves the name of Apostolic, because at that time they may have been in existence, let them produce the origins of their churches, the regular succession of their bishops; and so show that the first in that order was an Apostle, or, at least, constantly united with the Apostles. For, in this manner the Apostolic Churches deduce the order of their successions. Smyrna has her Polycarp, appointed by St. John; Rome, her Clement, ordained by St. Peter; and so the other churches. Let the heretics show this. And should they invent something like it, they have gained nothing; since their doctrine, compared with that of the Apostles, by its diversity and contrariety, will show that it came not from any Apostle, or Apostolic man. For as the Apostles would not have taught discordant doctrines, so neither would their immediate followers have taught differently from them." (Ibid., c. xxxi., xxxii.)

Besides the faith, the sacraments, and the legitimate government of the Church can come only from the Apostles. Here the same reasoning applies. To the Apostles Christ intrusted the ministry of the sacraments, and the government of His Church. These were to be continued through their successors. No churches, therefore, can claim these as their own, unless they can prove that they have received them in regular succession from one of the Apostles; and that they received them as they were delivered to them, namely, united to the central authority of St. Peter. To do this, they must prove that every bishop, or head of their Churches, can trace up his appointment to an Apostle or his successor, and that the appointment was approved of by the central power.

From the Apostolicity of the Church we pass to her Catholicity, which is another of her essential marks. The Catholicity of the Church has a twofold aspect. One regards her identity of faith, sacraments, and government, throughout all ages, and among all peoples, or her internal and external organization, with regard to all times and places; and the other, her diffusion throughout all times, places, and among all nations. On this subject Vincent of Lerins remarks: "But, in this Catholic Church we must be particularly careful to hold fast that doctrine which has been believed *in all places, at all times, and by all.* For, as the word itself plainly denotes, there is nothing truly and properly Catholic but that which comprehends all in general. Now, it will be so, if we follow universality, antiquity, and unanimous consent. We shall follow *universality*, if we believe that doctrine alone to be true, which the Church everywhere admits. We shall follow *antiquity*, if we depart not from the opinions which our ancestors and fathers openly maintained. We shall follow *unanimous consent*, if we adhere to the sentiments of all, or of almost all, the priests and teachers." (Common. i., n. 2.)

The general diffusion of the Church must be understood in a moral, or relative, not in an absolute sense. For it is evident, that the Church could not be strictly Catholic at the very commencement of her existence. She had within her the seeds of growth, which were to be scattered, and to germinate gradually and successively all over the world. It does not mean, that the whole world should be actually Catholic, nor that her faith should be practically embraced by every individual of the nations of the earth. But her doctrines were to reach successively every empire and kingdom in the world; so that all might, at least, hear of them, and that it would be easy, if they wished, to become acquainted with them. Nor is Catholicity destroyed by the defection of any kingdom or nation from the doctrines of the Church. First, because in their case, the command of the Saviour has been fulfilled: "Go and preach the Gospel to every creature; go teach all nations." (Matt. xxviii. 19.) Secondly, because these defections have been foretold, and therefore enter into the plan of the divine economy of Christ with regard to His Church. Thus we read: "For it must needs be that scandals come" (Matt. xviii. 7); and, "there must be also heresies, that they, also, who are approved, may be made manifest among you" (1 Cor. xi. 19); and again: "For there shall be a time when they will not bear sound doctrine; but according to their own desires, they will heap to themselves teachers, having itching ears, and will turn away indeed their hearing from the truth, but will be turned unto fables." (2 Tim. iv. 3, 4.) Our Divine Saviour Himself foretold, that, at the end of time, the faith of a large number will have failed; for, He says: "There shall arise false Christs, and false prophets, and they shall show great signs and wonders, in so much as to deceive (if it were possible) even the elect" (Matt. xxiv. 24), and "they shall seduce many;" so many, that He adds: "But yet, when the Son of man cometh, shall He find, think you, faith on earth?" (Luke, xviii. 8.) So, in like manner, we are told, that the Apostles and their successors in the ministry, will be rejected by many, banished, or otherwise persecuted by others. Yet, this much must be asserted, that the Church of Christ shall always be more widely diffused, and better known by a larger majority of mankind than any heretical or schismatical Church in the world, or she will be, at least, distinguishable from all other Churches by the mutual agreement of all her members in the same doctrines, and their union with the whole Church, so that she will evidently be the religion of all times and peoples. This much was promised her by the voice of God's prophets in the old, and by Christ's own lips in the new dispensation. The Church is Christ's inheritance, and it is to comprise all the nations: "Ask of Me, and I will give thee the Gentiles for thy inheritance, and the utmost parts of the earth for Thy possessions." (Ps. ii. 8.)

It is His kingdom, which is universal. "He shall rule from sea to sea, and from the river unto the ends of the earth. Before Him the Ethiopians shall fall down and His enemies shall lick the ground. The kings of Tharsis and the islands shall offer presents; the kings of the Arabians and of Saba shall bring gifts. And all kings of the earth shall adore him: all nations shall serve Him." (Ps. lxxi. 8–11.) "All the ends of the earth shall remember, and shall be converted to the Lord. And all the kindreds of the Gentiles shall adore in His sight." (Ps. xxi. 28.)

When Christ sent His Apostles and their successors "to preach the Gospel to every creature,—to teach all nations," He certainly designed that their preaching should be efficacious; but it could not be efficacious, unless there were some in all nations who should obey the Gospel, at least for a time. And if they did obey, the Church of Christ was really Catholic, since it had believers in every clime and nation. This was fulfilled in the days of the Apostles, who, according to St. Mark, "going forth, preached everywhere." (xvi. 20.) This made the Apostle St. Paul write to the Romans, that although all did "not obey the Gospel," yet the voice of the preachers "went over all the earth, and their words unto the ends of the whole world" (Rom. x. 16, 18); and in the eighth verse of the first chapter, he tells them that their "faith is spoken of in the whole world." To the Colossians he writes, that the Gospel had come not only unto them, but it is also "in the whole world, and bringeth forth fruit and groweth, even as it doth in you." (i. 6.) The fact is, this Catholicity was, to a great extent, established on the very day of the foundation of the Church. For we are told that the Apostles, being filled with the Holy Ghost, began to speak with divers tongues to Jews, devout men out of every nation under Heaven. "Parthians and Medes," were there, "and Elamites and the inhabitants of Mesopatamia, Judea, and Cappadocia, Pontus and Asia, Phrygia and Pamphilia, Egypt and the parts of Lybia about Cyrene, and strangers of Rome, Jews also, and Proselytes, Cretes, and Arabians." (Acts, ii. 4–11.)

Catholicity, then, is one of the distinctive marks of the Church of Christ. This made St. Augustine say: "We must hold fast to the Christian religion, and to the communion of that church which is Catholic, and is called Catholic not only by her own children, but even by all her enemies. The heretics and followers of schisms, whenever they talk not with their own, but with strangers, despite themselves, call nothing else Catholic Church, but *the* Catholic. For they cannot be understood unless they call her by the name which she bears throughout the world." (Lib. de Unit. Eccl., cap. vii., n. 12.

Finally, the true Church of Christ must be holy; holy in her Founder, holy in her doctrine, and that holiness must be manifested in the lives of her members. The Church is the body of Christ. She receives continually the influence of holiness: He owed it to Himself to sanctify that body.

The object of the Church is to bring all nations to the way of truth and salvation; yea, "this is the will of God," says the Apostle, "your sanctification" (1. Thess. iv. 3). But she cannot make others holy unless she herself be intrinsically holy. The true Church must always be identified with the Church of the Apostles and of Christ, but she would not be thus identified, unless she were holy; for the Church founded by Christ and the Apostles, was a holy Church. Moreover, Christ loved the Church, and delivered himself up to her, that He might sanctify her, and "present her to Himself a glorious Church, having neither spot nor wrinkle, nor any such thing, but that it should be holy, and without blemish." (Eph. v. 26, 27.) Are His designs to be frustrated? Did He pay the price of her ransom in vain?" "He chose us," continues the same Apostle, "that we should be holy and unspotted in His sight." (Eph. 1. 4.) He gave Himself for us, "that He might redeem us from all iniquity, and purify unto Himself a people acceptable, pursuing good works."

(Titus, ii. 14.) The object of Christ, in transferring His mission to the Apostles and their successors, was that they should go and should bring forth fruit, and that their fruit should remain. This fruit was the sanctification of believers, by the preaching of the word, the ministration of the Sacraments, the practice of every Christian virtue. The mission being perpetual, the same fruit must attend the labors of the ministry now as in the days of the Apostles, and, as the means of sanctification were accompanied with signs and wonders, so now, there must exist in the true Church, miracles, which shall testify to the truth and the sanctity of the doctrines, and the means of salvation proposed to the believer. Hence the true Church must continue to work miracles, especially among unbelievers.

Moreover, it is necessary that in a holy Church, there should always be saintly children. Otherwise, the means of holiness would be useless. In every age and in every country, therefore, there must be found men and women in the true Church of Christ, whose exterior sanctity is a visible proof of the interior holiness of the Church of which they are members. This does not mean that every individual member of the Church must actually be a saint.

For although the Church continues to possess intrinsically all the means necessary to sanctify each one of her members, although her ministers never cease to exhort them to pursue the way of justice, yet it will always remain true, that in the Church there will be chaff as well as wheat, and that her net will contain bad as well as good fishes. For her Founder has permitted that the tares should grow together with the wheat until the great harvest-day, when He will say to the reapers: "Gather up first the cockle, and bind it into bundles to burn; but gather the wheat into My barn ... The Son of man shall send His angels, and they shall gather out of His kingdom all scandals, and them that work iniquity; and shall cast them into the furnace of fire; there shall be weeping and gnashing of teeth. Then shall the just shine as the sun in the kingdom of their Father." (Matt. xiii. 30, 41, 42, 43.)

Having seen which are the essential properties and characteristic marks of the true Church, we are to prove, in our next lecture, that they belong to one only existing Church, and that that Church is the Roman Catholic.

IV.

THE ROMAN CATHOLIC CHURCH THE CHURCH OF CHRIST.

"Thou art Peter; and upon this rock I will build my Church, and the gates of hell shall not prevail against it." MATT. xvi. 18.

To prove that Christ established a church, we had recourse to history. The same facts which prove that Christ established a church, prove that that church is no other than the Church of Rome. The Apologists who defended Christianity against the calumnies of the infidels; the Fathers who vindicated its doctrines against heretics and schismatics; the Confessors who were banished from home and country; the Martyrs who sealed their faith with the last drop of their blood during the first three centuries of the Christian era, were members of the Roman Catholic Church, defended, vindicated her doctrines, her sacraments, her government, suffered and died for her. The bishops, the priests, the missionaries, who preached the Gospel to every creature, who went forth to teach and baptize all nations, went forth from her, as from the only house in which Christ dwelled, as from the only fold of the one true shepherd. Her temples and her altars, her sculptures and her images, everywhere testified to her doctrines, her rites, her worship. Her pontiffs have succeeded each other in uninterrupted succession from St. Peter down to Pius IX. She, in all ages, as in our own, was pointed out even by her enemies, as the *only* Catholic Church in the world. She alone can trace back her existence to the days of the Apostles, whence her enemies are agreed in calling her the Old Church. She alone has preserved her doctrines, her sacraments, her government, unchanged throughout the course of nineteen centuries; she alone has withstood the violence of earth, and proved herself built upon a rock, against which the gates of hell could never prevail. She alone has been a mother ever fruitful in saintly children, whose sanctity was approved by Heaven in many wonders. Now, whatever church unites in herself the above enumerated properties and marks, is the Church of Christ. The Roman Catholic Church, therefore, is the Church of Christ.

The true Church of Christ is a society of believers, who are united by the profession of one and the same faith, by participation of the same sacraments, under the government of lawful Pastors, and especially of the Pope of Rome.

This definition contains the idea which the Scriptures and Tradition give us of the true Church of Christ.

As we have seen in our preceding lecture, the Church of Christ is a real society, organized by her Founder according to the essential principles of all societies. This society has rulers and subjects, superiors and inferiors; and since the object of the society is the attainment of the ultimate end of the members, the salvation of their immortal souls, there are teachers and disciples, ministers and those to whom they minister. Furthermore, the ruled, the taught, and those who are ministered unto, are all linked to one supreme head, who has received power and jurisdiction over all, who is the source of unity in the faith, communion and government, of the Pastors and the flock.

This body of teachers, pastors, ministers of the sacraments, was to exist in uninterrupted succession, till the end of the world. To this body of pastors and teachers Christ promised His moral presence, His divine assistance in teaching, in administering the sacraments, and in governing His Church, among all nations, till the consummation of the world. And He obliged the taught and the ruled to obey those pastors, to hear them as if they heard Himself, under pain of eternal reprobation.

Now, this ideal of the Church of Christ is realized in the Roman Catholic Church alone. For all other churches lack these essential properties of the Church of Christ. They have not Christ for their Founder, because every one of them sprang up since the foundation of the Church by the Saviour. They are not Apostolical for the same reason. The Apostles had already organized the Church of their divine Master, before these laid the foundation-stones of their separate societies. By the very fact, then, that every sectarian church comes necessarily later than the Church of Christ and the Apostles, it is proved not to be the Church of Christ; therefore not the true Church; therefore not the Church without which none can be saved. To the Roman Catholic Church alone belongs the title Apostolical, because she alone descends from the Apostles in uninterrupted succession till the present time. Dare any one deny this fact? Show us the sect in the world which can prove it was founded by an Apostle. Doubtless it is none of the so called Protestant sects of the last three and a half centuries. We know the names of their founders, and the date of their origin. We know that Campbell, who is still living, is the author of the sect that bears his name; we know that John Wesley founded the Methodist, George Fox the Quaker Church. Swedenborgians, Mennonites, Calvinists, Lutherans, all bear the names of the respective authors of these heresies. Anglicanism was not known in England before Henry VIII., nor Presbyterianism in Scotland before Knox.

So it is with all other sects that sprang up at various periods of the Christian era. Before Peter Waldo there were no Waldenses; before Peter Bruys, no Petro-Bruysians; before Berengarius, no Berengarians. Pelagians, Eutychians, Nestorians, Collyridians, Donatists, Helvidians, Tationists, Novatians, Nicolaites, Cerdonians, Valentinians, Carpocratians, Basilideans, Marcionites, Ebionites, Menandrians, Simon-Magians, all derived their origin, as well as their doctrines, from the men whose names they bore, or still bear, in the annals of history.

It is not sufficient for any of these Churches to say: "Oh, we are the true Church of Christ: we teach His doctrines; we observe His ordinances; we govern ourselves according to His plan." They should prove these assertions. And they cannot prove them satisfactorily, save by proving that they were founded by one of the Apostles; that they remained faithful and obedient to the central authority of St. Peter and his legitimate successors in the see of Rome.

The moment that you cut off any Church from the Apostles—sever it from the rock upon which Christ built His Church—that moment it ceases to be the Church of Christ.

The Church of Christ was to be indefectible—indestructible. The gates of hell should never prevail against her. Hence, there is no possibility of her becoming corrupted in her faith, her sacraments, or her government. If so, there can be no reason for any reformation in her faith, her sacraments, or her government. Every attempt at such a reformation is an explicit denial of the indefectibility of the Church of Christ, and consequently, a denial of the truth of Christ's promises to His Church. For, to assert, that the Church failed, is to assert, that Christ did not keep His promise when He said " The gates of hell shall not prevail against her" (Matt. xvi. 18); " I am with you all the days, even to the consummation of the world."

(Ibid. xxviii. 20.) But if He did not keep His promises, it must have been either because He could not do so, or would not; to assert either of which, is to blaspheme Christ. Christ is God; hence nothing is impossible to Him; hence He does not change; for, Christ is to-day, and yesterday, and the same for ever. (Heb. xiii. 8.) If His Church was to remain, like Himself, for ever the self-same, then we reason as follows: whenever, since the days of Christ and His Apostles, any man or woman established a so-called Christian Church, different from any other till then existing, the Church of Christ either existed or did not. If she existed, there could not be any need of another; yea, it was impossible to establish another Church of Christ; for the Church of Christ is essentially one, and therefore, necessarily excludes a second or a rival Christian Church. If the Church of Christ did no longer exist at that time, then Christ belied His solemn promises to be with His Church until the end of the world. Furthermore, the only Christian Church existing always, at any given period, since the beginning of Christianity, was the Roman Catholic Church; therefore, she is the only true Church of Christ. This conclusion is strictly logical. If you find the Roman Catholic Church at every period of the Christian era, you find her existing from the days of the Apostles. Let us apply the same reasoning to the Churches that sprang up since the days of Luther. When Luther left the Roman Catholic Church, she was either the Church of Christ or not. If she was the Church of Christ, Luther did wrong to separate himself and others from her; if she was not the Church of Christ, then the Church of Christ had failed,—to assert which, as we have seen, is to blaspheme Christ. For, if the Church of Rome was not at that period the Church of Christ, where, then, pray, was that Church? Will you say it was the Church of Wickliffe or Huss, or the Waldensian or the Albigensian? The same reasoning always returns with the same force. When Wickliffe, Huss, Peter Waldo, or Simon Magus, separated from the Church of Rome, she was then either the true Church of Christ, or she was not; if she was, then all the separatists did wrong, and were real heretics, who, according to St. Paul, should be avoided as men who are perverted, and whom St. John forbids us even to salute. If she was no longer the Church of Christ, then the Church of Christ had failed; then Christ's promises had failed, and He was an impostor.

The true Church of Christ must have a body of teachers, and a visible central head, who have authority to preach, administer the sacraments, govern the Church, and appoint their successors, with the same powers which were originally given to them. Every pastor and head of the true Church must, therefore be able to show the series of pastors and heads of the Church, from whom he derives the three-fold power of preaching, administering the sacraments, and governing the Church of Christ. How will any pastor, minister, or head of a separate Church, be able to do this? Let Luther, Calvin, Wesley, Cranmer, Knox, Campbell, point out to us the line of bishops, and sovereign pontiffs from whom they derived the power of preaching, ministering in, and governing the Church. They certainly did not receive them from the Roman Catholic Church. From what Church, then? From the Greek schismatical Church, perhaps. But the Greek schismatical Church is in the same predicament as they. She, too, came too late into the world, to be the Church of Christ. From whom did she receive these powers, in the ninth century? Not from the Church of Rome; for she separated herself from Rome, and incurred her excommunication.

as far as you can, and say, from Simon Magus. But, from whom did Simon Magus get his power? Not from the Apostles, although he lived in their day, for he was condemned by the Apostle St. Peter. Therefore, from no one; therefore, these reformers are of the class of prophets who run without being sent—to whom Christ hath not spoken—of those of whom St. John writes: "Verily, verily I say unto you, he that entereth not by the door into the sheepfold, but climbeth up some other way, the same is a thief, and a robber." (John, x. 1.) But those who are not sent by Christ nor the Apostles cannot preach, according to the saying of St. Paul: "How can they preach unless they be sent?" (Rom. x. 15.) "Neither doth any man take the honor to himself, but he that is called by God." (Heb. v. 4.) And if they have no authority to preach, the nations have no obligation to listen to them; if they have no right to dispense the sacraments, the people are not bound to receive them at their hands; if they have no delegated power to govern, the people cannot be forced to obey them. But no sectarian Church can have such an authority or power; therefore, the Roman Catholic Church alone has this power; therefore, she alone is to be heard and obeyed as the Church of Christ.

As this subject is of vital importance to every individual, inasmuch as our eternal salvation depends upon our belonging to the true Church, let us place this question in another light. If the Church of Rome is not the Church of Christ, then, we suppose, you will say it is the Protestant? Which of the many Protestant Churches? We have seen in the preceding lecture that the Church of Christ is essentially one in her faith, sacraments and government; we have also seen, in the second lecture, that the Protestant Church is divided into a hundred and more fragments, each of which pretends to be the Church of Christ. Well, then, which of the many Protestant Churches, think you, is the Church of Christ? Suppose you answer: The Lutheran. Very well. You mean to say, then, that Christ and the Apostles taught the same doctrines, the same ordinances, established the same Church-government, as Luther professed and taught in his turn. The question naturally arises, where was that Lutheran Church throughout the length of sixteen centuries? Point out to the world the Pastors, Teachers, Bishops, Pontiffs, Fathers, Doctors, who taught like Luther. If you cannot do that, you own that the Church of Luther, which was the

Church of Christ, failed during sixteen centuries. Then, during sixteen centuries, men could not be saved; for, according to Luther, all must be saved by true faith.

It will not do to have recourse to an invisible church; for we have proved that an invisible church cannot be the Church of Christ yea, cannot be a church at all. Nor do you meet the difficulty by answering that the true Church existed there, where the fundamental doctrines of Christianity were taught and believed by its teachers and its members. For the question returns: Where were those fundamental doctrines taught? In what particular Church or Churches? If you answer, in no particular Church, but in all of them together; we urge the question: What are those fundamental doctrines, and who is to decide upon their number as well as their nature? If an authority is necessary to tell us what Christ taught; that same authority is much more necessary to determine, with unerring certainty, which of these doctrines are fundamental, and which are only accessory. For, if we understand the meaning of our brethren's distinction between the fundamental and non-fundamental doctrines of Christianity, they hold that the former are those which it is absolutely necessary to believe in order to have faith, and therefore, to be saved; whereas the latter may be admitted or rejected, at will, without thereby forfeiting the purity of faith or the hope of salvation. Is every individual to determine this knotty yet all-important question by himself? Then there will likely be as many faiths as there are individuals, and yet faith is essentially one. Is it left to the judgment of the several Churches? Then there is the same danger as in the case of the individual; for every Church will use its own judgment and authority to determine the nature and the number of her fundamental doctrines; and as long as there is no unity among them, there can be no unity in the faith. Now, take the facts as they stand: Do all the Churches, actually existing, outside of the Roman Catholic Church, believe in the same fundamental doctrines and in the same way, as to their meaning and number? Among these Churches you have the Eastern heretical and schismatical Communions called the Greek Church, and the Nestorian, Eutychian, Arabian, Armenian Churches. Do they hold the same fundamental doctrines, as the Lutheran, Calvinistic, Anglican, Baptist, Quaker, Methodist, Swedenborgian or Campbellite Churches? You know they do not. Most of them hold the same doctrines as does the Roman Catholic, on the necessity of the episcopate, the power of the priesthood to forgive sins, to consecrate the body and blood of Christ. They hold the seven Sacraments, purgatory, invocation of saints, etc., and all of these they consider to be fundamental doctrines, without faith in which no one can be saved.

But do the modern sects agree among themselves? Does the Presbyterian hold the doctrine of episcopacy and priesthood as a fundamental doctrine of Christ's Church? Does the Baptist believe in Infant Baptism as do, or at least used to do, the Episcopalians, Presbyterians, Methodists, etc.? Do these latter believe it an essential doctrine of Christ, that people should be immersed when they receive Baptism, as do the Baptists? Do any of these believe, as Luther did, in the Real Presence of the body and blood of Christ in the Lord's Supper? Do the Universalists consider the eternity of hell a fundamental dogma of Christianity, as do, till this day, most of the other Churches? Is the Socinian right, is the Unitarian orthodox, when he discards the Divinity of Jesus Christ, and considers it fundamental to believe only in a divine adoption of the Son by the Father? Which of the doctrines is fundamental: that man shall be saved by faith alone, as Luther, Calvin, and others maintained, or that good works are moreover necessary to salvation, as Wesley and Swedenborg taught?

Who is to settle these differences, even as to fundamentals and non-fundamentals? The Church? But which Church? Doubtless no other than the one which Christ has appointed with full authority to decide upon these matters. That Church is no other—as our adversaries themselves concede, when they deny it to their own Churches—than the Church of Rome, which has always claimed and exercised the right, from the beginning of her existence in the days of the Apostles, to decide what must be believed and done in order to salvation.

Moreover, on what ground do our separated brethren distinguish between fundamental and non-fundamental articles of belief? Do they not maintain that the Bible is the Word of God; the whole Bible, and every thing that is written in the Bible? If so, is not the whole Word of God to be believed? Is there any reason for accepting one portion of the Word as non-fundamental, any more than another? Is not the Word of God as worthy of our belief in one case as in another? If you have a right to distinguish between article and article you have a right to reject any you please. For it will depend on your private judgment to determine whether such an article is fundamental or non-fundamental; whether you can, or cannot, be saved without believing it.

The formal motive of faith is the veracity of God, who reveals, and that veracity is as worthy of belief in one article of faith as in another. He can no more be deceived Himself nor deceive us, in one than in another; consequently we are bound to believe Him whenever we know that He has spoken, and to refuse our assent is to refuse to believe, and to expose ourselves to the dreadful anathema, "He that believeth not shall be damned." (Mark. xvi. 16.)

The Church of Christ, is, in the next place, essentially one. None but the Roman Catholic Church ever possessed or does now possess unity of faith, communion, and government. This unity is evident from her constant and uninterrupted union with the central head, St. Peter, and his successors in the see of Rome. "Though," as St. Cyprian reasons most beautifully, "though extended by her fecundity, the Church is one. There are many local, many provincial churches, as there were in the days of St. Paul. These are as so many branches of the same tree, so many rays of the same sun; so many rivulets of the same stream. The Church sends forth her rays over the whole earth; yet is the light one, and her unity is undivided. He that does not hold this unity of the Church, can he think that he holds the faith? He that opposes and withstands the Church, can he trust that he is in the Church? Whoever, separated from the Church, is united to an adulteress, is cut off from the promises of the Church. Whoso deserts the Church of Christ, obtains not the rewards of Christ. He is an alien, he is an enemy. He cannot have God for his father who has not the Church for his mother." (St. Cyp., De Unitate Eccl.) And the same St. Cyprian calls the chair of Peter and the Church of Rome "the principal Church, whence the sacerdotal unity took its rise." (Ep. lix.)

St. Athanasius says that whoever falls away from her Communion, neither is nor can be called a Christian. (Ep. i., ad Serap.) Lactantius writes: "The Catholic Church alone retains the true worship. This is the source of truth, this is the dwelling of faith, into which he that enters not, and from which he that goes out, forfeits the hope of life and of eternal salvation." (Inst., lib. iv., c. 30.)

She is ever one in her faith. Travel whither you will, from pole to pole, from rising to setting sun, among barbarians or enlightened nations, the Church of Rome holds the same articles of faith, administers the same sacraments, obeys the same government. When or where did she contradict herself on the score of her doctrines? Everywhere her bishops and her priests preach the same articles of belief; everywhere do they threaten the same punishment to the unbeliever. She knows no national boundaries, no national prejudices, no national predilections. She proposes the same faith to emperor and king as she does to subject and slave. And she did so throughout the nineteen centuries of her existence. She is the same, when Pius IX. and the bishops define the doctrine of the Immaculate Conception, as when Peter and the Apostles, in council assembled, wrote: "For it hath seemed good to the Holy Ghost, and to us, to lay no other burden upon you than these necessary things," etc. (Acts, xv. 28.) Still the same, when hundreds of Apostolic missionaries go to announce the Gospel to China, Japan, or the savages of our land, as when St. Paul stood before the Areopagus arguing on the resurrection,—a unity which was never affected by distance of time or space. Still the same where perpetual snows cover the dreary wastes of the North, and where eternal spring clothes the earth with fragrant flowers. Still the same where the Arabian pitches his tent amidst the driving sands of the desert, as where the red man roams the boundless prairie in search of the bison and the elk. How beautiful, how sublime, how God-like this unity of faith and union of heart which binds our ancestors of nineteen hundred years ago to their posterity, in one unbroken link of thought and action, without so much as the whisper of a dissenting voice! How beautiful the spectacle which exhibits king and subject, master and slave, husband and wife, brother and sister, rich and poor, lettered and unlettered, genius and semi-idiot, kneeling around the same altars, professing the same creed, practising the same ordinances, of one mind and one heart, as were the primitive Christians mentioned in the Acts of the Apostles!

The Church is the home of concord and of peace. Bishop meets bishop, priest embraces priest, with the same brotherly feeling and love, whether he comes from Asia, or from Europe, from America, or from Africa, because they are all of them grafted on the same vine; because the same spirit is diffused through their hearts, and bringeth forth the same fruit in their souls. How different this scene from that not unfrequently witnessed in sectarian families and Churches. Here the father goes to one, the mother to another meeting-house, while the children, when grown up, often differ from both father and mother, and among themselves, in their religious convictions.

The Church of Rome is the only one which is truly Catholic. Her constitution, her doctrines, her sacraments, the form of her government go whithersoever she extends, and she extends all over the world. It is she who has wrought all the conversions to Christianity, that were ever wrought among pagan and barbarous nations. By her pastors and teachers were fulfilled the words of Christ: "Go ye into the whole world, and preach the Gospel to every creature" (Mark, xvi. 15); and those others: "Go ye, therefore, and teach all nations, baptizing them in the name of the Father, and of the Son, and of the Holy Ghost; teaching them to observe all things whatsoever I have commanded you." (Matt. xxviii. 19, 20.) Of the Church in communion with Rome, it was always true to say with St. Paul: "Your faith is spoken of in the whole world." (Rom. i. 8.) Not to mention the labors of the Apostles, who were her founders, study the work accomplished by their followers in the ministry. The success with which they met was so great that Tertullian could defiantly write to the authorities of Rome, in the second century "We are but of yesterday, and we have over spread your empire. Your cities, your islands your forts, your towns, and your assemblies—your very armies, wards, companies, tribes, palaces, Senate, and Forum, swarm with Christians. We have left you nothing but your temples." (Apol., c. 37.) Remember that the Christians were of that class who believed, like Tertullian, that there was but one Church, and that whoever were not united with that Church, were not Christians, and that "the Lord left the keys of that Church to Peter, and through him to the Church." (Scorp. x.)

The seed was sown; it multiplied from thirty to sixty, and, finally, to a hundred fold. "Every Christian," says Dœllinger, "became an Apostle. The father announced the Gospel to his family, the slave to his master, the soldier to his companions in arms, and the friend to his friend. Many of the new converts devoted their whole life to this Apostolic duty."

St. Gregory, the Enlightener, subjects the Armenians to the Cross of Christ, and fulfils the prophecy of Isaiah. (Is. lx. 3, etc.) Tiridates, their king, believes, as did the Romans, the Corinthians, and Colossians before him.

As early as the year 326, the faith of the Church flourished in the valleys of the Caucasus. About the same time the Albanians and the adjacent tribes embraced the only saving doctrines of the Church. The Iberians owned her gentle sway, the Lazi, Tzanni, and Albasgi received the Gospel from missionary priests of the Eastern part of the Roman Empire.

In the fourth century the fire-worshipping Persians bowed down before the divine sun of justice, which had risen upon the world from Bethlehem.

The Ethiopians next fulfill the prophecy of David, and fall down before the Lord. "The kings of Arabia and Saba bring Him gifts." (Ps. lxxi. 9, 10.)

The Goths, Burgundians and Suevi were Catholics long before they became Arians, and many years did not elapse before they returned to the faith of the "mother and mistress of all the Churches."

Hermenegild had overcome the violence of his heretical father, and in dying a martyr's death, dropped the mantle of his apostolic zeal upon his brother Riccared, who, on ascending the throne, professed the Catholic faith, and induced the greater part of his subjects, and many heretical bishops, to renounce the errors of the Arians.

During the same century, Theodolinda, aided by pious missionaries, became the instrument of propagating the Catholic faith among the Lombards.

Meanwhile, the Franks had received the faith of Rome from St. Remigius, and with Clovis, three thousand declared themselves Catholics.

The empire of the Cæsars falls to pieces, the empire of the Popes builds its throne upon the ruins. The standard of the Cross is unfurled, where the Roman eagle had never flapped his wings. The voice of the Fisherman was obeyed, where decrees of the Senate were contemptuously sneered at, and rejected.

The great St. Patrick next conquered Ireland to the faith, and made her the sanctuary of learning and virtue whence issued forth, at sundry times, a host of holy missionaries, who, in their turn, became the Apostles of foreign countries.

From Ireland the faith spread among the Picts by the zeal of St. Columba. The Hebrides were likewise christianized by this great Apostle.

St. Austin is sent to Britain, and establishes the faith there.

Melitus baptizes the king of Essex; Paulinus converts the chief priest of idolatrous Northumberland and its king.

The sovereign of East Anglia receives baptism from Felix, who, in seventeen years, completes the conversion of the entire nation.

Finian converts the middle Angles, and Birinus receives the Southwestern Britons into the one fold of the one shepherd.

St. Wilfred completes the conversion of the Heptarchy, in 678, by subjecting the inhabitants of Sussex to the empire of the Cross.

The Frieslanders, Hollanders, and Zealanders, obey the voice of St. Willibrord; and the Danes receive him and his eleven companions, as they would angels from Heaven.

Meanwhile, the nations on the Rhine and Helvetia, Rhœtia and Vindelicia, had embraced the religion of Christ.

As early as 511, St. Fridolin, after many and long labors in France, founded the nunnery of Seckingen, and preached the Gospel on both banks of the Rhine.

There was a bishopric in Steiermark at the close of the third century; while Trent in the Tyrol had its Catholic prelate in the fourth.

Strasburg sent its first Catholic bishop to the Council of Sardica in the same century, and the name of the Bishop of Spire still figures on the records of that illustrious assembly. The Bishopric of Treves was founded about the same period. Belgium had its several bishoprics and representatives in the Councils of Sardica and Rimini. Some years later, St. Victricius of Rouen preached the Catholic faith in the land of the Nervii and Morini, now called Flanders. St. Severinus had catholicized the greatest part of Noricum, the modern Bavaria, and Austria.

In the seventh century, St. Kilian converts Franconia. St. Amandus overthrows the last idols in Belgium, and pursues his Apostolic labors through Carinthia, and Sclavonia to the banks of the Danube.

In the eight century, St. Boniface converts the Germans.

In the ninth century, St. Siffroy is sent to Sweden, and Anschar builds a Church at Schleswig, where he baptized many pagans.

Rombert continues the successful labors of Anschar in Hamburg and Bremen, and Denmark and Norway fulfill the prophecy that ' the ends of the world shall be converted to the Lord." (Ps. xxi, 28.)

Iceland was catholicized in the year one thousand, and the Faroe islands soon followed its example.

The celebrated Norman chief Rollo became an humble follower of the faith of Rome shortly after the treaty of Epte, in 912, and his warlike subjects followed the example of their leader.

As early as the year 650, Porga, prince of the Croatians, received, with open arms, missionary priests sent by Rome, at the request of the emperor Constantine Pogonatus; and the Servians, yielding to the inducements held out by Heraclius, became docile children of the common Father of the faithful.

The Carontani were converted in the eighth century.

Arno and Virgilius, Bishops of Salzburg, were instruments in the hands of God to convert the Moravians.

From Moravia, the Gospel spread through Bohemia, and thence it made its way to Poland; bishoprics were founded at Breslau, Cracow, Colburg, and Gnesen.

Benno, Bishop of Misnia, became the Apostle of the Sorbi, while Methodius and his brother Cyril made known the name of Jesus to Russia. Passau wrote in 974 to the Roman Pontiff that the priests whom he had sent into

Hungary had already baptized more than five thousand of the inhabitants, and St. Stephen left at his death eleven bishoprics and many monasteries, and seminaries for the education of young priests.

We might continue this sketch of Catholicity by instancing the conversion of Pomerania, in the eleventh, and of the island of Rugen, in the twelfth century. The conquests of Rome in Livonia, and Cumania, in the thirteenth, and in Tartary and Lithuania, in the fourteenth century, might furnish as brilliant a page for a lecture as they present for history.

But we must stop here, and give a synoptical view of the victories which Catholic Rome has achieved over infidel and pagan nations since the so-called Reformation.

The great Apostacy from Rome took place in 1517. Shortly after began the conversion of the aborigines of Cumana, under the leadership of Las Casas. In 1521, the kings of Zebu, and Messana, the prince and nephew of the latter, and five hundred more, were regenerated by the waters of baptism. About the same time the religion of Rome gained ground in Yucatan and Mexico. Over twenty-nine millions, says Torribio, were baptized within the space of twenty years.

In Honduras the conquest of the Church kept pace with those of Cortez; but while the harvest was great, the reapers were proportionately few.

Meanwhile, the schismatics and heretics of the East were not forgotten. Towards the middle of the sixteenth century, the Franciscan friar, John Franco de Potenza dispelled the errors of the Maronites, who, through three ambassadors, abjured them in the Council of Lateran.

No one needs to be reminded of the more than human success of St. Francis Xavier and his companions among the Asiatic Indians. This one man repaired in great part the losses which the Church sustained in Germany, Switzerland, France, England, and the northern kingdoms.

It was Catholic missionaries who planted the Cross upon the heights of the Citade Alta, and the prostrate temples of the sun in Brazil and Florida. Anchieta, Peter Correa, and Brother John Souza triumphed where the Calvinist Peter Richer, and William Cartier had failed.

What shall we say of the Catholic conquests in the kingdom of Congo, during the reign of king Diego; and in Hindostan, where, according to Fontana, the Dominicans built eighteen churches and converted sixty thousand idolaters to the Church of Rome.

Gaspar of the Cross destroyed numerous idols in China; Monomotapa admitted the services of Father Silveira, and about the year 1577, its emperor, his mother Maria, together with three hundred Caffirs, bowed their neck under the sweet yoke of Jesus Christ.

The inhabitants of the Archipelago of the Moluccas hailed Nuñez and Alfonso de Castro with open arms, and in one single village these holy men baptized five hundred children. In 1581, the Dominicans carried the saving word to the kingdom of Siam, and baptized many converts.

But, not to become tedious, we must refer you for beautiful and interesting details on the success of the Catholic Church in converting barbarous, and pagan nations, to Dœllinger's History of the Church, and Henrion's and Marshall's works on Catholic missions.

In our own country, too, the Roman Catholic Church is the only one which has really succeeded in reclaiming a portion, at least, of the superstitious savages, from their idolatrous worship and vicious habits. Wherever the "black-robe chief" comes with his guides and companions, there yet takes place the scene so graphically described by Henry Wadsworth Longfellow:

"The noble Hiawatha
With his hands aloft extended,
Held aloft in sign of welcome,
Waited, full of exultation,
Till the birch canoe, with paddles,
Stranded on the sandy margin,
Till the black-robe chief, the pale face,
With the Cross upon his bosom,
Landed on the sandy margin.
Then the joys of Hiawatha
Cried aloud, and spoke in this wise:

Beautiful is the sun, O strangers,
When you come so far to see us!
All our town in peace awaits you;
All our doors stand open for you;
You shall enter all our wigwams,
For the heart's right hand we give you.
Never bloomed the earth so gaily,
Never shone the sun so brightly,
As to-day they shine and blossom
When you come so far to see us.
Never was our lake so tranquil
Nor so free from rocks and sand-bars,
For your birch canoe, in passing,
Has removed both rock and sand-bar.
Never before had our tobacco
Such a sweet and pleasant flavor;

> Never the broad leaves of our corn-fields
> Were so beautiful to look on,
> As they seem to us this morning,
> When you come so far to see us."

Add to these victories among the heathen the daily conquests she makes among the ranks of Protestantism in Germany, England, and the United States. Who has not heard of the return to the Church of such men as Henry Edward, prince of Schœnburg; F. A. Charles, of Hesse Darmstadt; the Duke of Saxe Gotha; of Ingenheim; Frederick of Mecklenburg; the Duke and Duchess of Anhalt-Cœthen; Princess Charlotte Frederic; the Countess Solm-Bareuth; Count Stolberg; men of letters and science, and statesmen such as Werner, Frederic Von Schlegel, Clement Brentano, Baron Eckstein, Goerres, Adam Müller, Haller, Esslinger, Hurter; the minister of state, Laval; Petit Pierre, Bermay, and others in Switzerland and France; the saintly Spencer, the learned Newman, the eloquent Manning, the ascetic Faber, Canon Oakley, Capes, Northcote, Wilberforce, the ministers of Leeds, a dozen or more Fellows of Oxford and Cambridge, and scores of distinguished members of the bar, the pulpit and other honorable professions in life.

You have not forgotten the former Episcopal Bishop of North-Carolina, the now zealous and devoted Catholic, Dr. Ives; you remember the Brownsons, Walworths, Heckers, Prestons; the judges, Bayne, Burnett, Wilkins, Wilkinson; the Huntingtons, Bakewells, and others, many of whom sacrificed all earthly hopes, in abandoning their sectarian Churches. Contrast these names with the Achillis, De Sanctis, Hogans, Gavins, Leaheys, Gavazzis, and a few others of the same class, and you will be able to form an idea of the respective merits of those who leave the ranks of Protestantism, to join the Church of Rome, and those who leave us rather than repent of their insubordination and scandalous example.

On this subject we dare assert, without fear of being contradicted, that as far as experience goes, no intelligent, well instructed Catholic ever left the Church, whose pride had not been stung, or whose immoral conduct had not brought him under the censure of his ecclesiastical superiors. If there are exceptions to these prevailing causes, they must be sought in temporal, political, social, or domestic interests; but never can they be imputed to a well-grounded conviction that Catholicity was wrong, and Protestantism right.

The infallibility of the Church is the next of her heavenly prerogatives. We have proved that there exists a Church of Christ; that the Church of Christ is one, and that she must be infallible. If you have been convinced by our arguments, you are bound to conclude that the infallible Church is the Roman Catholic alone. The conclusion is logical. For since there must be an infallible Church, and there are no claimants to that infallibility, except the Roman Catholic Church, it follows that she is really the lawful claimant.

That none of the many Protestant Churches claim any infallibility in deciding questions of faith, sacraments, or church-government is a fact of history. So far from claiming it, they deny its existence and possibility altogether.

Some of the earlier heresies and schisms, such as Nestorianism, Eutychianism, or the Greek Church, might be thought to assert this prerogative, but certainly it is without any reasonable grounds. First, because the infallible Church of Christ must exist from the days of Christ and the Apostles, and the Greek schism dates back to the ninth, the Eutychian heresy to the fifth, and Nestorianism to the fourth century. Secondly, because, according to their own confession, they separated from the Church of Rome because she had ceased to be the Church of Christ; therefore, ceased to be infallible; but they, being united with the Church of Rome, must have ceased to be infallible with her, for they erred with her, while they were united with her; that is, if the Church of Rome did err at all. But a church that errs, even once, in matters of faith or morals, is no longer infallible; therefore, the Eastern churches have forfeited their title to infallibility. If the Church of Rome had not erred till the day of their separation, then they erred in separating from her, and consequently ceased to be lawful claimants for infallibility.

The Church in communion with Rome has never ceased to claim and to exercise her claim as the infallible Church of Christ. From the day on which she held her first œcumenical council in Jerusalem, till she held the last in Trent: from the time that Pope Victor threatened to excommunicate, or, as Eusebius has it, did excommunicate Polycrates, Bishop of Ephesus, for keeping Easter at an undue time, till the excommunication fulminated against the enemies of the Church in our own days, by his successor Pius IX., the Church of Rome has always asserted unerring authority as her special and exclusive right, intrusted by Christ to His Apostles in union with St. Peter, and to their successors till the end of time. This fact should have its weight with every reflecting mind. Constantly to claim and to exercise a right in virtue of which she sat in judgment upon every doctrine and practice that did not agree with her own; to cut off from her communion, without mercy, all those who knowingly and obstinately refused to submit to her authority; to doom to misery here, and eternal destruction hereafter, all unrepenting sinners, or criminals on these scores, could not have been done without serious opposition, not only on the part of those who smarted under her ban, but on the part of her own children, who must needs have known and seen that she had no divine right to proceed to such lengths, if she were not really the only infallible tribunal instituted by Christ. It would be next to impossible to conceive any institution so universally corrupt, as to have no members who would have the moral courage to remonstrate against it for overstepping its own powers, when it exercises them publicly and severely as did the Church of Rome. Strange, indeed, it was, that none of her children should have reasoned as follows: One who does not know with certainty, cannot decide with certainty;

but you do not know what you decide upon with certainty, therefore, you cannot decide with certainty what is and what is not to be believed and done unto salvation. Stranger still, that none should continue the argument, and say: Whoever condemns without sufficient knowledge, condemns unjustly; but you condemn other doctrines and practices without sufficient knowledge, therefore, you condemn them unjustly. This would be the more readily objected, because she would act unjustly towards her own children, as we said, in making it obligatory on them, under pain of eternal damnation, to believe her decisions to be the decisions of Christ and the Holy Ghost. Such tyranny could not but meet with stern and constant opposition. And yet the Church has always pursued this course of conduct towards heretics and schismatics whose errors were to be condemned in her councils; towards pagans and infidels, whom she was to convert by her missionaries; towards catechumens, whom she instructed by her priests and bishops; towards her own children whom she warned against seduction. A testimony so universal, exposed to so many evident absurdities if false, or probably false, given by those whose every interest for time and eternity were at stake;

borne to her by every nation in every clime, against the natural inclination of the heart, against the dictates of natural reason, which, in cases of doubt, generally asserts its own liberty rather than submit to a doubtful authority, such testimony as this of her own infallibility must stand as infallibly true;—for a testimony which is based upon such grounds as these, is, according to all sound philosophy, an infallible criterion of the truth which is asserted.

But, even on mere Protestant principles, she has, to say the least, as much right to assert her own infallibility as they have to deny it, and with greater certainty than Protestantism can possibly have for its denial. Protestantism asserts the right of private interpretation for every individual. The members of the Church, therefore, have as much right to interpret the meaning of the Scripture as they themselves. If, then, all the members of the Church assert with one voice that the texts which we have often quoted in our last lecture prove the infallibility of the Church, on what ground can our dissenting brethren justly condemn the assertion? This argument gains in strength when we reflect that the Protestants themselves are not agreed among themselves upon the real and precise meaning of these texts, whereas the interpretation given by the members of the Roman Catholic Church is invariably the same throughout the ages of her existence.

Add to this that the Church was in possession of the Scriptures, and of their meaning, before they were entirely written, and upward of two hundred years before they were declared authentic and inspired by her rulers. She had taught all the doctrines which they contain, all the practices which they enjoin; she had acted with the fulness of her authority upon the promises of her infallibility, so that she practically asserted the meaning of those texts, before they were written. She had taught the nations, she had preached the Gospel to well nigh every creature, she had held a solemn œcumencial council, and she had exercised the power of excommunication, before her doctrines were either written or pronounced upon as containing the Word of God. This she could not have done (as we saw before) without great injustice to the people whom she taught, and the rebellious subjects whom she placed under her ban, and delivered over, as St. Paul did, to the power of Satan, unless she was infallibly certain of the meaning of those texts. The Roman Catholic Church, therefore, is the infallible Church promised by the Scriptures; therefore, she is the Church of Christ. If infallible, then, all her decisions on matters of faith and morals, are essentially true, are the decisions of the Apostles and of Christ—the decisions of the spirit of truth, who was promised to the Church, and who would teach her all truth, who would abide with her *forever*, and bring back to her mind whatsoever Christ had taught her.

Once convinced of this fundamental principle, there can be no longer a difficulty in the way of any one, young or old, learned or unlearned, civilized or barbarian, to find out, with a corresponding infallible certainty, what he is to believe and to do in order to be saved. All that is required of him is to go to Mother Church, and ask her: "What do you teach on this and that subject? What do you teach on the Trinity, on the Incarnation, on the procession of the Holy Ghost, on baptism, on confession, on the Eucharist, on the saints, purgatory, prayers for the dead, indulgences, and so on?" Whatever answer she gives you on any of these subjects, you know is the answer which Jesus Christ Himself, which the Holy Ghost would give you, if they were visibly present, in reply to your interrogations. Admit her infallible authority to teach, to administer the sacraments, to govern herself, and your mind is secure·you have found the easy, the certain, the infallible rule of faith. We insist upon this question, because it is for ourselves, as well as for our brethren, the question of questions. Without infallibility there is no certainty, without certainty there is no faith, without faith it is impossible to be saved. Again, according to our separated brethren, there is no infallibility in their churches; according to our former proofs, there can be none in the elder churches, such as the Greek, Nestorian, etc.; therefore, since there must needs be an infallible Church, and there can be no other than the Church in communion with Rome, the Roman Catholic Church is infallible, and therefore the Church of Christ. But the Church of Christ alone possesses the saving faith, therefore without the faith of the Church of Rome none can be saved. Hence, if you desire to be saved, you must abandon your errors, clear up your doubts, shake off your apathy, and knock at her door, that you may enter her house, which is the dwelling of Christ. Besides its infallible certainty, this rule of faith has all other necessary conditions. It is easy. What more easy than to find a teacher, who by his office is bound to devote his life to the instruction and the guidance of his people. The more so, that the Church of Rome is, as we said before, truly Catholic, and her pastors can be found in every country under the sun? It is universal. It is within the reach of all. All cannot read,—all that can read, cannot read intelligently,—all have not the time to read,—all cannot get a copy of the Bible to read,—but all can go to a teacher, listen to him; and when they doubt, question him, till their doubt is removed. When they are dull of understanding, they can return, and return again to the task. The teacher can accommodate himself to the capacities of all. He can question his pupils and ascertain whether they have seized his meaning,—whether they desire any further explanation. In one word, the Catholic rule of faith is all that it must and can be to satisfy the wants of all in all times, and among all nations.

It is the natural rule, or in other words, a rule dictated by sound reason and common sense. Natural reason and experience dictate that all things necessary to the preservation of human life should be taught us by those whom God has placed over us as the secondary causes of our existence. The same law holds good in an order of things which it is much more difficult to learn than the laws of self-preservation. If we have need of a guide to teach us the expression and the meaning of the expressions of our natural wants, how much more have we need of learning the expressions and the meaning of the expressions which convey our supernatural wants? If, without guidance, without instruction in the manner of securing our earthly prosperity, we need the voice of authority and experience, how much more do we need an authority which can, with infallible certainty, direct us in the way of securing the eternal interests of our immortal souls? This the Roman Catholic Church does for her children. She does not give them a dead letter, however holy and divine, and say to them: "Take this book, study it, read it, interpret it for yourself; make your eternal fortune or misfortune; as you understand it, so you will fare;" but she takes her children on her knees, presses them to her bosom, and says: "Come hither and hear the word of the Lord your God." (Jos. iii. 9.) "Come, children, hearken to me. I will teach you the fear of the Lord." (Ps. xxxiii. 12.) Her children come, they hearken, and they learn the word of the Lord their God, and they walk in his holy fear. Self-education in religion is as impossible as in human science, and even more so. We learn every thing from others, the most we can do of ourselves, is to improve upon the principles we have been taught, in a practical manner, or by way of practical application. We draw conclusions, we do not generate principles. The principles are given us; they are transmitted to us in one way or in another, but always by way of instruction, by way of communication. Language itself, the medium of our thoughts, is not originated, it is communicated. How much more so the language of Heaven? If the word of man needs an interpreter, how much more so the word of God? Observe, beside, that the world proceeds on an implicit conviction of the human infallibility of the teachers in matters that concern the preservation of human life. The child never doubts the accuracy of the alphabet it has been taught by its mother. It never, even in maturer years, calls A, B, C, by any other name than those given by its first instructors. The value of arithmetical numbers and algebraical quantities remain the same to a Laplace at the age of sixty, as at the age of six. God has willed it so, and it is well it should be so. Why, then, should we refuse to accept a teacher of truths, that lie without the range of our natural reason? Surely we cannot object to such an order of things on the score of its intrinsic impossibility. Is there any thing impossible to God? Is there no natural infallibility among men? Are there no intuitions of reason, of which she is infallibly certain? Can reason mistake when she asserts that two and two are four, that a part is less than the whole? Are not our senses under certain circumstances applied to their proper objects, an infallible criterion of truth? What prevents God from establishing an infallible criterion of truth in things which regard His divine revelation? What prevents Him from assisting a body of men, by His divine grace, so as to place their intuitions of, or reasonings on His Heavenly Truths, above the danger of illusion or deception?

The true Church of Christ must be holy, as well as infallible. Hence, if the Church of Rome is the Church of God, she must be holy in her Founder, holy in her doctrines, holy in her sacraments, holy by the lives of her children. And such she undoubtedly has been, and is till this very day. Her founders, as we have seen, are Jesus Christ and the Apostles; and who dares doubt the holiness either of the doctrines which they taught, the sacraments which they administered, or their personal sanctity? But the doctrines taught by Christ and the Apostles, the sacraments administered by them, were to remain, and are still the doctrines, the sacraments of the Roman Catholic Church; therefore, she is holy in her doctrines and in her sacraments.

To be convinced of the personal holiness of millions of her children, you need but open the annals of history. There you read of men and women, in every age, and in every country through which the Catholic religion spread, who gave every possible evidence of fulfilling, in their daily conduct, the saying of the Apostle: "This is the will of God, your sanctification." (1 Thess. iv. 3.) Scrupulous observers of the commandments of God, they fulfilled the whole law and the prophets. Many of them went further, and practised the evangelical counsels, so highly recommended by Christ and the Apostles. How many millions of the children of the Church followed that saying of the Lord, "Be ye perfect, as also your Heavenly Father is perfect" (Matt. v. 48); and, "If thou wilt be perfect, go, sell what thou hast, and give to the poor, and come, follow me." (Ib xix. 21.) How many, wishing to be true disciples of Christ, left their father, mother, brothers, sisters, lands, estates, and all that they had dear and near in this world, that they might the more closely imitate their Master, who, being rich, became poor for our sakes. Witness the hermits and anchorets of the first ages; witness all the religious orders of men and women that have sprung up under the fostering influence of the Church of Rome. Witness the chastity of her countless virgins; the spirit of prayer in her contemplatives; the spirit of mortification in her penitential orders; the spirit of charity in her various institutions of mercy and benevolence; the spirit of elevated love in her million martyrs.

Cast a retrospective glance over the catalogue of her saints, holy missionaries, and religious, during the nineteen hundred years of her existence, and then show us something—we do not say equal—but similar, to the array. Show us, in our own day, a clergy, who, like ours, follow the advice of Christ concerning continency, and fulfill the wish of St. Paul, who desired that all might be like him in this regard. Show us an order like the sisterhood of the "Good Shepherd," who, without any earthly recompense, without even the hope of ordinary gratitude, on the part of those unfortunate creatures to whose moral reformation they devote their every care, live only to do good to such as the world rejects as hopeless castaways. Show us a "Sisterhood of Mercy," where the poor servant girl finds a shelter, whom a cruel master, or a whimsical mistress, after depriving her of her just wages, and loading her with reproaches, abandons, upon the street, homeless and friendless. Every Church has its needs. There are orphans to be cared for; deaf and dumb to be taught; the maimed, the blind, the decrepit, to be fed and clothed; there are sick to be nursed; poor children to be instructed,—show us another Church, besides the Roman Catholic, in which you find devoted "Little Sisters," heroic "Sisters of charity, "Sisters of Providence," "of the Cross," "of St. Joseph," who, all, according to their own spirit, provide for these wants, ministering to them with an angel's care, and an angel's love. Observe, moreover, that most of the virtues practised in the Church by her saintly children, are above the power of fallen nature, and can be practised, constantly and perseveringly, only with the assistance of Divine grace. It is not a dictate of human nature which makes a man renounce father, mother, wealth, hope of inheritance, and lead a life of voluntary poverty. It is not the voice of nature which bids a man refrain from the enjoyment of lawful pleasures, that he may the better devote himself to the Lord. Nor is t an impulse of the fallen heart of man, to give up his own will, and seek his true freedom in dependence on, and entire obedience to his superiors. Yet these virtues have always flourished, and still continue to flourish, in our Church, and in ours only. So far are other churches from practising them, that they ridicule the observance of the evangelical counsels as something absurd, and deserving only contempt or pity.

That God approved the sanctity of His servants by many signs and wonders, is a fact of history which it would be too tedious to develop in these pages. Any one who desires to be convinced of the facts in the case, may read the "Lives of the Saints," by Alban Butler, or any of the numerous ecclesiastical histories.

We know* that it is customary among a class in other churches to denounce the immorality of the clergy, detail the corruption which reigns in monasteries, and write tirades against the vices of Catholic countries. We are aware that some scruple not to identify the Church of Rome with every thing that is wicked, criminal, abominable in iniquity; that they apply to her names borrowed from the Apocalypse and the Prophets which modesty forbids us to set down on paper; but we know, too, that such has been the conduct of all the enemies of Christ and the Church throughout the ages. The Scribes and Pharisees, who were outwardly great sticklers for the law; who made a show of fasting and almsgiving; who talked constantly of the Scriptures and the Covenant, found fault with Christ and His Apostles; slandered them; invented all manner of lies against them; yet the Saviour, whose judgments were always true, said of them: that they did "all these works to be seen of men;" that they were full of pride, because they made their phylacteries broad, and enlarged their fringes; that they loved the first places at feasts, and the first chairs in the synagogues, and salutations in the market-places, and to be called by men, Rabbi; and addressing them, He said: "Wo to you, Scribes and Pharisees, hypocrites; because you make clean the outside of the cup and of the dish but within you are full of extortion and un cleanness. Wo to you Scribes and Pharisees, hypocrites, because you are like to whited sepulchres, which outwardly appear to men beautiful, but within are full of dead men's bones, and of all filthiness. So you, also, outwardly, indeed, appear to men just, but within you are full of hypocrisy and iniquity." (Matt. xxiii, 25, 27, 28.) We know that there are those who are called the leaders of others, who never weary of describing the ungodliness of Catholics; their breaking of the Sabbaths of the Lord, and the like; but we remember that all these things happened to our Master, and yet He said to His censors: "Blind guides, who strain out a gnat, and swallow a camel." (Ibid 24.) History repeats itself. The impure and filthy Gnostics, who gave themselves up to every abomination, called the Catholics Psychici, that is to say, mere animals, while they styled themselves spiritual, or perfect. (St. Irenæus, ch. vi.) So did the Montanists. The Donatists arrogated to themselves the title of *just*, and derided Catholics as *sinners* and *traitors*. All of us know the morality of the Latter Days" Saints, and every reader of history knows the lives of the so-called first reformers: Luther, Calvin, Henry VIII., Edward VI., Queen Elizabeth, and others. We do not deny that there have been, and still are, bad Catholics. But we do deny, that they are such in virtue of their religious principles. Our lessons in morality never were, that we have no free will of our own: that we are to be saved or damned without any regard to our good or evil works; that good works are bad works; that the best of them are venial sins, as Luther taught, and many after him. All we contend for is, that our separated brethren should contrast the lives of their progenitors in the faith, with those of ours; the conduct, in general, of our ministers with theirs; of our people with their people. It is easy to find exceptions to general rules. It is not difficult to find a Judas among twelve Apostles; but let them find as many holy men and women, and as many confessors and martyrs of the faith, as many virgins, as we can point to in history, all of whom derived their sanctity from the principles of our faith, and we shall be willing to own, that where the greatest sanctity is, there, also, is the best religion.

Here we leave the argument that the Roman Catholic Church is *the* Church of Christ, and we beg our readers to give it a serious, an attentive perusal.

We are aware that there are objections to the argument, and we are ready to meet them in the same spirit in which we are writing these pages.

The first of these objections is this: From

the course of reasoning which you have pursued, it would follow that out of the Church of Rome there is no salvation. Logically, this conclusion follows from our premises, and we do not shrink from it. Nor is this doctrine our own. It is taught most clearly by the Scriptures. Our Divine Saviour positively asserts: "He that believeth not shall be condemned," or damned, as the authorized version of our separated brethren has it: again, our Saviour says, in St. John: "He that doth not believe, is condemned already, because he believeth not in the name of the only begotten Son of God." (John, iii. 18.) St. Paul tells us that "without faith it is impossible to please God." (Heb. xi. 6.) The same Apostle wrote two epistles to prove the same truth. One of these is to the Romans, in which he informs them, that both Jews and Gentiles, before they receive the faith, are all under sin: "That the justice of God is by faith of Jesus Christ unto all, and upon all them that believe, for there is no distinction (Rom. iii. 22), all have sinned ... being justified gratis by his grace through the redemption that is in Jesus Christ. (Rom, iii. 24.) But we have proved that there is and can be but one faith, and that faith is to be found in the Roman Catholic Church only; therefore, out of the Roman Catholic Church there is no salvation.

In order to have the true faith, we must be subject to the Church; for Christ says: "He that will not hear the Church let him be to you as the heathen and the publican" (Matt xviii. 17); but heathens and publicans are out of the path of salvation; therefore, since the Church of Rome is the Church of Christ, there is no salvation out of the Church of Rome.

St. Paul reckons heresies or sects among the works of the flesh of which he says: "They who do such things shall not obtain the kingdom of God." (Gal. v. 21.) But it has been proved that all churches, except the Church of Rome, are heretical or schismatical; therefore, those who are not in the Church of Rome cannot inherit the kingdom of God.

In the Acts we read that "the Lord added daily to their society (the Church) such as should be saved" (ii. 47); therefore, to be saved it is necessary to belong to the Church; but that Church is the Church of Rome; therefore, out of her communion there is no hope of salvation.

The Apostle St. Paul writes: "Now, I beseech you, brethren, to mark them who caused dissensions, and offences, contrary to the doctrine which you have learned, and avoid them.

For they that are such, serve not Christ our Lord" (Rom. xvi. 17, 18); but they that do not serve Christ our Lord, cannot be saved; and sects and heresies cause dissensions, and offences, contrary to the doctrine of the Apostles; therefore, all such cannot be saved. But the Church of Rome alone has always avoided such; therefore, out of her bosom there is no salvation.

Again: "But though we, or an angel from heaven, preach a Gospel to you besides that which we have preached to you, let him be anathema." (Gal. i. 8.) The Gospel, therefore, is essentially one; but the sects do not hold the unity of the Gospel; therefore, none can be saved, save in union with Rome.

"A man that is a heretic, after the first and second admonition, avoid: knowing that he, that is such a one, is subverted, and sinneth, being condemned by his own judgment." (Titus, iii. 10, 11.)

If a heretic is to be avoided, when he does not renounce his heresy; if he is subverted, if he sinneth, if he is condemned by his own judgment, and dies impenitent, he cannot be saved; but all those who wilfully and knowingly reject any of the doctrines of the Church of Christ are heretics, and the Church of Rome is the Church of Christ; therefore, any one, dying wilfully and deliberately, out of the Church of Rome, cannot be saved.

St. Jude tells us that all such men as deny the faith are "clouds without water, which are carried about by winds, trees of the autumn unfruitful, twice dead, plucked up by the roots, raging waves of the sea, foaming out their own confusion, wandering stars to whom the storm of darkness is reserved for ever." (Jude, i. 12, 13.)

The doctrine of exclusive salvation appeared so reasonable to the reformers themselves, that they all adopted it as an article of their creed.

Luther reproached Zwingle for having fallen into the modern error of admitting all promiscuously to the kingdom of Heaven.

The Anglican Church declared in the eighteenth of the Thirty-Nine Articles, to which all the clergy were obliged to subscribe, that "those are to be accursed who presume to say, that every man shall be saved by the law or sect which he professeth, so that he be diligent to frame his life according to that law and the light of nature."

The Protestants of Scotland in their profession of faith, in the year 1561, say: "As we believe in one God, the Father, the Son, and the Holy Spirit, so we firmly believe, that there was from the beginning, that there now is, and that to the end of the world there will always be, one Church, which is the Catholic, that is, the universal Church, out of which there is neither life nor everlasting happiness." (Conf. Scot., cap. 16.)

The Protestants of Switzerland, in their profession of faith, in the year 1566, say: "We set so great a value on being in communion with the true Church of Christ, that we affirm, those cannot have life in the sight of God who are not in communion with the true Church of God, but separate themselves from it." (Conf. Helv., cap. 16.)

The Dutch, in their profession of faith of the year 1561, approved by the Synod of Dort, in the year 1619, say in the Twenty-seventh Article: "We believe and confess one only Catholic or universal Church." And in the Twenty-eighth: "Since this holy society and congregation is the society of those who are to be saved, and since there is no salvation out of it, we believe that no one of what place or dignity soever he be, ought to separate himself from it, to live apart by himself; but that all are equally bound to join themselves to it, and to be united with it, to preserve the Church's unity, to submit to its doctrine and discipline, and to subject their necks to the yoke of Christ." (Conf. Belg., Art. 27, 28.)

The French Protestants ask the following question in their catechism: "Why is this article of forgiveness of sins put after that of the Church?" "*Answer.* Because no one obtains pardon of his sins, unless he be first incorporated with the people of God, and continue in unity and communion with the body of Christ, and so be a member of the Church." "*Q.* Out of the Church, then, there is nothing but death and damnation?" "*A.* It is certain; for none of those who withdraw from the communion of the faithful to make a sect apart, ought to hope for salvation, as long as they continue separated."

It is not necessary to prove that the same doctrine was taught in all ages since the commencement of Christianity. It was the doctrine of St. Ignatius, martyr, who, in his epistle to the Philippians, declares that whosoever follows those that make a separate communion, shall not inherit the kingdom of God. St. Irenæus describes the Church as having but one soul, one heart and mouth, dwelling in one house, and adds: "She is the gate of life, but all the rest are thieves and robbers, and therefore to be avoided." (Adv. Hær., iii.) St. Clement of Alexandria says: "The ancient and Catholic Church is but one in her substance, origin, and excellence." (Lib. Strom., vii.)

St. Cyprian wrote a whole work to prove the necessity of being a member of the one only true Church, out of which, he says, there is no salvation.

"But is it not uncharitable to say that there is no salvation out of the Church of Rome?"

We answer, is it uncharitable to tell a man the truth, when his very life is in peril? Is it uncharitable in a physician, for instance, to warn his patient that there is great danger of his dying, if he refuses to comply with certain prescriptions and regulations regarding his diet and the like? Is it uncharitable for a mother to caution her child against such and such company, because she has reason to know that the child will be ruined by it? Would it be uncharitable in you to inform your friend of a plot which his enemies are making against his life, and which he can avoid by seeking shelter in your house? If the Church believed that men may and can be saved by any religion, or even without any, it would be uncharitable in her to tell the world that out of her bosom there is, ordinarily speaking, no salvation. But, as we have proved, she maintains that there can be but one faith, as there is but one Lord of all, and that she is in possession of that one faith. She knows from the Bible that without faith it is impossible to please God or to be saved, hence it is very charitable in her to announce to the world that all must seek salvation through her.

It is true, therefore, that no one shall be saved out of the Church,—most undoubtedly true.

"Then, my parents before me, are all in hell, because they died out of the Church of Rome?"

To answer this question, you must distinguish certain truths, and carry out the distinction in applying them to individual cases. When we say that out of the Church of Rome there is no salvation, we do not assert that all must needs be externally united to that Church, and externally profess her faith and practices. For there are persons who, through invincible necessity or invincible ignorance, cannot be outwardly united to the Church of Rome, and yet die in her bosom. Let us suppose the case of a man who is suddenly stricken by apoplexy. He has consciousness enough left him to look into himself, repent of his sins, and desire baptism; he receives the grace to believe all that our Lord may have revealed, though he actually knows very few if any of the doctrines of Christ in detail. There is no minister, no priest, no person present to instruct him or baptize him, yet he is so disposed in his heart, that he would do any thing that might be required of him, if he had the opportunity. That man dies. Does he die a Protestant or an infidel? Apparently, to those who knew him before his death, he died as he lived, either a Protestant or an infidel. Is it so in the eye of God? By no means; in the eyes of God and of the Church, he dies a very good Catholic, because he had every disposition that was necessary to be outwardly joined to the Catholic communion. He belonged to the soul, as theologians say, though he was not outwardly united to the body of the Church. Hence we are taught to suspend our judgment as to the salvation or reprobation of those who die apparently out of our communion; it is a question which we leave to God, who searcheth the earts and reins of man.

True, the Church does not perform any external rites for those who die out of her bosom, and with good reason. For, since they were outwardly joined to other religions, or made public profession of infidelity, she cannot possibly treat them, in her external service, otherwise than they treated her during their lifetime. But her children may, if there be no certainty of their reprobation, pray for them privately, and remember them in their works of penance or devotion. No Catholic need be more Catholic than his mother the Church. She teaches that heresy and unbelief are sins, and deadly sins, which exclude those who die in them from the kingdom of Heaven. But she also teaches that two things are necessary to commit a mortal sin: sufficient knowledge of the evil, and malice of the will. And as there may be persons who, for want of these conditions, commit an action which is materially wrong, but formally not criminal, so there may be, and doubtless are, persons who live in material infidelity or heresy, without being formally guilty of that crime in the sight of God. Should such persons be invincibly ignorant of their obligation to leave sectarian churches or any other association, and to join themselves to the Roman Catholic Church, should they have been baptized or desire to be baptized and repent for their sins, believing all that God wishes them to believe, they die Roman Catholics. By this we do not mean to convey the idea that it is all the same to which religion a man belongs. We merely say, that a person who is invincibly ignorant of the Church, and puts no other obstacles in the way to heaven, may be saved, though outwardly he is not joined to the Church. We believe this to be the case with a great many good, simple country people, who never heard of the Church of Rome, never read any of her doctrines; who conscientiously believe themselves right in their own religion, and who, if they but knew that the Church of Rome is *the* Church of Christ, would immediately renounce their error, and enter the one fold of the one Shepherd.

We believe this to be the case with a great many children born of sectarian or infidel parents, whose religion is neglected, and who are never spoken to on the subject; these, living in ignorance of their duty, and dying in that invincible ignorance, will be saved if they have wilfully put no other obstacle to their salvation.

But the same exception does not apply to those who have the opportunity of becoming acquainted with the true Church of Christ, and wilfully reject or neglect availing themselves of it. Much less to those who know that the

Catholic Church is the only saving Church, but dare not enter her communion, for fear of the world, or through motives of interest. These persons act in opposition to their own conscience, and evidently live in sin; consequently, can never hope to be saved, so long as they remain in that disposition of mind. Alas, how many such are there among our Protestant and infidel countrymen! How many who depend upon their relatives or their friends for whatever religious opinions they form for themselves. How many who dread the prospect of being called a Papist; of being looked upon with contempt, abandoned by their friends, insulted by their foes, disinherited by their relations, and who sell their soul as Esau sold his birthright, for a mess of pottage, or, like Judas, barter their eternal salvation for a handful of silver. Of such the Holy Spirit says: "I called, and you refused: I stretched out My hand, and there was none that regarded; you have despised all My counsels, and have neglected My reprehensions: I will also laugh in your destruction, and will mock when that shall come to you which you feared. When sudden calamity shall fall on you, and destruction, as a tempest, shall be at hand; when tribulation and distress shall come upon you;

then shall they call upon Me, and I will not hear; they shall rise in the morning, and shall not find Me : because they have hated instruction, and received not the fear of the Lord." Proverbs, i. 24, etc.)

"But does not the Church of Rome make new articles of faith, and thus prove that she fluctuates in her doctrines, that she is neither one, nor Catholic, nor indefectible?"

The Church *defines* articles of faith, but she does not make new ones. She holds in her depository all and every truth revealed by Almighty God, but she does not always propose every article of faith, in particular, to the express belief of her children under the penalty of eternal damnation. She obliges her children to believe all that was revealed, whether through Scripture or tradition, but she does not always define under anathema every particular article of that revelation. This she does when heresies or schisms make it necessary to show her subjects what must be believed, on the score of the doctrines or practices which are impugned by error. Thus the Council of Nice defined the consubstantiality of the Son with the Father, against Arius, though the Church had always believed this doctrine from the days of the Apostles. In a similar manner did she define many of her doctrines against Luther in the Council of Trent, although she had taught and believed them before the uprising errors made it necessary to define them in so many precise and accurate terms. In the same way she defined, some years ago, the doctrine of the Immaculate Conception of the Ever blessed Virgin Mary. Previously to her solemn decisions on these matters she, at times, allows her children that freedom of discussion which, while it is disposed to abide by her decision, calls in question the fact of the revelation of the still undefined doctrines. Nor does she thereby forfeit her title to unity. For, there is this difference between the denial by a heretic of any of the doctrines of the Church, and a denial by her own subjects, that the latter remain always willing to abide by her authority, no matter what decision she may come to, when she will deem it necessary, or useful, to define her doctrine, or any given subject of revelation; while the heretic obstinately refuses to recognize and to abide by that authority. When Catholic doctors, or divines, dispute concerning certain dogmas still undefined by the Church in her solemn councils, or by the Pope, with the consent of the bishops, they continue to profess an implicit faith in the truth upon which she may decide in the future.

The same happens in every organized society. The Constitution of a State is, for various reasons, open to many disputes, which circumstances evolve. When there are two contradictory views presented, one or the other must necessarily be false, yet so long as no real danger is threatened to the State from the misinterpretation, the supreme tribunal may suspend its decision in the case. Meanwhile both parties remain loyal, and faithful citizens, so long as they are willing to abide by the decision which future circumstances may make it obligatory on the court to pronounce. But the parties would forfeit their claim to loyalty, should they positively make up their minds not to submit to the decision, if given against them.

This shows, that the Church, so far from enslaving the intellect of her children, leaves them every possible freedom; and it is only when liberty degenerates into license, that it becomes her duty, as teacher and judge of the truth, to speak out, and to define her position.

"But there are many sects in her own bosom: for instance, there are Gallicans, who do not believe in the infallibility of the Pope; and there are Ultramontanists, who vigorously contend for that infallibility. The Thomists are at war with the Molinists, and the Augustinians with both, on the subject of grace and free will in connection with grace. Then there are Franciscans who wear shoes, and others that do not. Some shave their heads, and others wear beards. Some dress in one way, and others in another."

Although, as we have just said, there are different opinions among our divines concerning matters that relate to faith and morals, yet they all agree on the faith itself. Neither the Thomist, Jesuit, nor Augustinian, denies the defined faith of the Church concerning grace or free will. All they do is to discuss the *manner* in which grace, and free will, under the action of grace, operate in man. The manner of a thing differs from the substance of the thing. Whether the blood operates in one way or another on the heart, the lungs, the various parts of the human system, may be matter of antagonistic views among doctors of medicine; but, so long as they do not deny the existence of the blood, nor its action and influence on the human system, they cannot be said to err substantially on that subject. So it is with many questions of theology. The *modus operandi*, the manner in which any mystery or article of faith is to be conceived, may cause differences of opinion among the learned, but they cannot be said to differ about the faith. As to the various religious orders which exist in the Church, and their different customs and costumes, every one, not wilfully blind easily perceives, that they have nothing to do with faith or morals. No one will deny, that a man who shaves his head or his beard—who dresses in gray or in white—may be as sound and as good a Christian as one who wears a beard, or dresses in blue or black. You might as well argue, that our citizens are divided in their loyalty to the Constitution, because some of them wear felt hats, others beavers, and others panamas; or, because some take their dinner at noon, and others at five or six o'clock in the evening.

In conclusion, let us sum up the reasons which should make every one seriously determine on embracing the doctrines and practices of the Roman Catholic Church, in preference to any other.

First, Because without faith it is impossible to please God, or to be saved, and that saving faith can be found in the Roman Catholic Church alone.

Secondly, Because she alone has those essential properties, which, according to the Scriptures and common sense, should characterize the Church of Christ. She alone has existed from the days of the Apostles. She alone is one in her faith, her sacraments, and her government; she alone is Catholic, or universal; she alone is holy and infallible; she alone is indestructible. All other Churches have had their day; the Church of Rome has survived all the persecutions of earth, and of the powers of hell. She alone offers security in life, and at the hour of death.

At the worst, our Protestant brethren admit, with Luther, that a good Catholic has as fair a chance of going to Heaven as a Protestant, or any honest man, consequently he loses nothing worth speaking of, by remaining a Catholic. That he gains much, those testify who have left the ranks of infidelity, indifferentism, scepticism, and Protestantism in its various forms, to join the one fold of the One Shepherd.

Let all those who read these pages pray that God may enlighten them, and pour out His Spirit upon them, that they may find the old path, and securely and faithfully walk therein, until they reach the happy goal where all are one, in the same undivided Godhead, for evermore. Let all strive to enter that brave and long-tried bark, whose eventful history is thus summed up by the poet:

"Two thousand years—two thousand years,
    Our bark o'er billowy seas
Has onward kept her steady course,
    Through hurricane and breeze;
Her Captain was the Risen One—
    She braved the stormy foe,
And still He guides, who guided her—
    Two thousand years ago.

"Sound Scripture and tradition were
    The charts, her course to steer;
Her Helmsman was the Holy One,
    A helper ever near.
Though many a beauteous boat has sunk
    The treacherous waves below,
Yet, ours is sound as she was built,
    Two thousand years ago.

"The wind that filled her swelling sheet,
    From Rome's great centre blown,
Still urging her unchanging course
    Through shoals and breakers on;
Her fluttering pennant still the Cross,
    Whatever breeze might blow,
It pointed, as it does, to Heaven,
    Two thousand years ago.

"When first our gallant ship was launched.
    Although our hands were few,
Yet, dauntless was each bosom found,
    And every heart was true;
And still, though in their mighty hull
    Unnumbered bosoms glow,
Her crew is faithful as it was
    Two thousand years ago.

"True, some had left their noble craft,
    To sail the seas alone,
And made them, in their hour of pride,
    A vessel of their own;
But they, when clouds portentous rise,
    And storms tempestuous blow,
Re-entered that old vessel, built
    Two thousand years ago.

"For, onward rides our gallant bark,
    With all her canvas set,
In some few nations still unknown
    To plant her standard yet.
Her flag shall float where'er a breath
    From human life shall glow,
And millions bless the boat that sailed
    Two thousand years ago.

"On Britain's coast three centuries since,
    She lay almost a wreck,
Her mainmast gone, her rigging torn,
    The boarders on her deck;
There Becket, Fisher, More, did fall,
    Queen Mary's blood did flow,

Defending our good vessel, built
  Two thousand years ago.

"Ah! many a martyr's blood was shed,
  We may not name them all;
They tore the peasant from his hut,
  The noble from his hall;
When, Erin brave, thy children's blood
  For faith did freely flow,
As pure the stream as was the fount,
  Two thousand years ago.

"Yet onward still our vessel pressed
  And weathered out the gale,
She cleared the wreck and spliced the mast,
  And mended every sail:
And swifter, stauncher, mightier far,
  Upon her cruise did go,
Strong hands and gallant hearts had she
  Two thousand years ago.

"True to that guiding star which led
  To Israel's cradled hope,
Her steady needle pointeth yet
  To Calvary's bloody top!
Yes! there she floats, that good old ship,
  From mast to keel below,
Seaworthy still as erst she was
  Two thousand years ago.

"Not unto us, not unto us,
  Be praise or glory given,
But unto Him, who watch and ward
  Has kept for her in Heaven,

Who quelled the whirlwind in his wrath,
    Bade tempest cease to blow,
That Lord who launched our vessel forth
    Two thousand years ago.

"Then onward speed thee, brave old bark,
    Speed onward in thy pride,
O'er sunny seas and billows dark,
    The Holy One thy guide!
And sacred be each plank and spar,
    Unchanged by friend or foe,
Just as she left Jerusalem
    Two thousand years ago."

V.

CONFESSION.

"And he said to them again: Peace be to you. As the Father hath sent me, I also send you. When he had said this, he breathed on them; and he said to them: Receive ye the Holy Ghost. Whose sins ye shall forgive, they are forgiven them, and whose sins ye shall retain, they are retained." JOHN, xx. 21, 22, 23.

MAN is a sinful creature. Ever since the fall, the wickedness of men has been great on earth, and all the thought of their heart has been bent on evil, at all times (Gen. vi. 5); "for the imagination and thought of man's heart are prone to evil from his youth." (Gen. viii. 21.) And St. John, the Evangelist, tells us that "all that is in the world is the concupiscence of the flesh, and the concupiscence of the eyes, and the pride of life, which is not of the Father, but is of the world." (1 John, ii. 16.)

This inclination to sin, this concupiscence, is universal. It exists in the just man, after his regeneration through baptism, as well as in the unregenerated pagan; and through passion and temptation it leads the greater portion of mankind to rebel against their Maker, and transgress His Law.

Now, the question is: Did Christ, the Founder of Christianity, leave us any visible, palpable remedy against sin,—against all sin? Not only the sin of unbelief and transgressions of the moral law, committed before baptism, but also against all kinds of sin, which we may have the misfortune of committing after baptism? Or, in other words: Did Christ leave to His ministering Church the power of pardoning sin committed after baptism? And, if He left such power, is it a logical sequence, that those whose sins are to be forgiven should confess them to the ministers of His Church?

The questions are plain, and we hope to make the answers equally so.

The better to understand the questions and the answers, allow us to premise certain truths, which most Christians admit, with the Roman Catholic Church.

The object of Christ's mission to the world was chiefly twofold. He came, first, to destroy error and to teach all truth. Secondly, to do away with sin, and to establish the empire of virtue in its stead. These may be called the fundamental objects of Christ's coming, and therefore, of Christianity, of the Church, as a divine institution.

Both these objects He came to realize in a visible, palpable manner. These objects were to be the objects of Christianity as long as t would exist on earth. But, according to Christ's promises, Christianity was to exist till the end of time; therefore these primary objects remain to be realized by Christianity till this day, and till the end of time. And, if there is no evidence of a change in the original plan of their realization, they continue to be realized in a sensible, visible form—the very same as He established it from the beginning of Christianity.

The first object, the destruction of error, and the teaching of all truth, together with the plan which Christ established for that purpose, we have fully discussed, in a previous lecture. We there proved, that He did not leave the knowledge of truth to the arbitration of the individual intellect, but established a living, an authoritative, an infallible tribunal, which should guide men into all truth, and free them from all error opposed to the doctrines of salvation.

Is it not natural to suppose, even before entering upon a Scriptural examination of the fact, that He adopted, with regard to the destruction of sin, and the establishment of the empire of virtue in the heart, a method similar to that which He adopted to establish the reign of truth in the minds of men? Did He leave the manner of atoning for sin- the manner of getting rid of it—to the arbitrary will of every individual sinner? Did He leave the judgment of the validity or invalidity of the conditions and dispositions for efficacious repentance, to the same arbitrary will of each sinner? Or, did He not appoint a ministry with power at once to take cognizance of the sins committed, of the conditions and dispositions of true repentance, and invest them with the power to apply, or to retain the pardon, for for those sins?

Our separated brethren contend for the former, we for the latter, as the true method established by the Founder of Christianity.

We proceed to prove the truth of our doctrine: that Christ gave to His Apostles the full and exclusive power of forgiving and retaining whatsoever sins might be committed by men after baptism. This He did, when, having laid down, as a last resource, to convert an offending brother, that they should tell the Church, He enjoined, that if he would not hear the Church, they should let him be to them as the heathen and publican. (Matt. xviii. 17.) And He added: "Amen, I say to you, whatsoever you shall bind upon earth, shall be bound also in Heaven: and whatsoever you shall loose upon earth, shall be loosed also in Heaven." (Ibid. 18.) The power of binding and loosing supposes bonds—what bonds? Surely not physical, but spiritual bonds. What are spiritual bonds, if not sins and the effects of sins? Christ, then, conferred upon His Apostles, upon the first ministers of His Church, the twofold power of binding and loosing whatsoever sins might be brought under the action of their judicial power, and, promised, in a most solemn manner, that the power thus exercised by them, on earth, would be ratified in Heaven.

After He has made the general atonement for sin, by his bloody death upon the ignominious cross; after He has triumphed over death —which is the wages of sin—our Divine Redeemer, by His glorious resurrection, before returning to His Heavenly Father, speaks to them again, and, if possible, in still clearer terms, upon this subject. Observe, that the ransom for all sin had now been paid to an offended Deity; the reconciliation, through the

Mediator's death, of sinful man with his God, had been effected; the price was paid and accepted, but the conditions of the acceptance remained to be fulfilled according to the plan of Divine Providence. The merits of the redeeming blood were to be applied to the souls of those for whom it had been shed. This must be done according to the method intended by the Mediator and His Heavenly Father.

What is that method? Is it, that every sinner shall, by faith and hope, by repentance and sorrow, apply this blood himself, and be the judge of the conditions and personal dispositions required in the application? We answer: By no means. The Redeemer willed that these merits of His redeeming blood should come to sinful man through the visible, external channel, the sacrament of penance, which He instituted for that purpose, and that His Apostles and their successors should be the dispensers of this wholesome remedy, the judges of the dispositions with which it was to be received by the applicants.

"Now when it was late that same day, being the first day of the week, and the doors were shut, where the disciples were gathered together for fear of the Jews, Jesus came, and stood in the midst, and said to them: Peace be to you... As the Father hath sent Me, I also send you.

"When He had said this, He breathed on them and He said to them: Receive ye the Holy Ghost

" Whose sins ye shall forgive, they are forgiven them: and whose sins you shall retain they are retained." (John, xx. 19, 21, 22, 23.)

The Protestant version here reads: "Whosesoever sins ye remit, they are remitted unto them; and whosoever sins ye retain, they are retained."

To remit and to forgive sins, mean the same thing; the only difference is that the word "remit" is derived from the Latin, whereas to "forgive" is a native word of our multiform language.

Let us analyze the meaning of the passage:

"Peace be to you." How fitting a salutation to those disciples of His whom He was about to make His ministers of peace and reconciliation!

"As the Father hath sent Me, I also send you." Recall the nature and object of Christ's mission to a fallen world,—to do away with all error and sin, and to establish the Kingdom o truth and virtue in the minds and hearts of all men. With what power? With all power; for "all power was given to Him in Heaven and on earth." With divine power; for Christ came to us with the fulness of the power of God.

Next: "He breathed upon them." Why this peculiar ceremony? When our separated brethren assist at the Catholic baptism, and see among other rites, the priest breathing upon the person to be baptized, they not unfrequently smile, and whisper into each other's ears: "Look at the old priest blowing in his face." I wonder whether these same brethren would have smiled at Jesus, breathing upon His Apostles. But to the point:

"Receive the Holy Ghost." Who is the Holy Ghost? The third person of the ever blessed and adorable Trinity, consubstantial with the Father and the Son, one in nature, distinct in person, to whom, in an especial manner, belongs the work of sanctifying the souls of men by the infusion of divine grace, purchased for us by the blood of the Redeemer.

Why all these imposing and significant preludes? Why say to them, "Peace be to you... As the Father hath sent Me, I also send you?" Why this solemn breathing upon the disciples? Why this imparting of the Holy Ghost? Christ neither says nor does a thing uselessly. There must be something grand, to follow such impressive preparations. Listen, and understand the object: "Whose sins you shall forgive, they are forgiven them; whose sins you shall retain, they are retained."

The words are plain, they need no elaborate comment: "Whose sins," or as the Protestant version reads, "whosoever sins, you shall forgive" (remit). The proposition is universal in all its parts. There is question of forgiving *sins*, *all* sins, without restriction, *whosoever* sins; no persons are excepted. The power of pardoning sins is to be exercised by the Apostles, with regard to all persons whatsoever, who are the subjects of that power. The same reasoning applies to the other part of the text. Whose sins you shall retain, they are retained. He confers a double power, therefore, upon His Apostles, and promises to ratify its exercise by them.

Furthermore, these Apostles are *men;* they are not angels; much less, Gods. As men, therefore, having a human nature, they are clothed with this divine power of forgiving and retaining whosoever sins.

Nothing can be plainer, than the fact that the power of binding and loosing, of remitting and retaining sins, was by these words, and on this particular occasion, entrusted by the Founder of Christianity to His disciples.

But not to them only. The mission of Christianity was intended to be perpetual; coextensive with time. Hence the objects of the mission are of their nature coextensive with time Hence, the ministry which is empowered to effect those objects, is destined to be perpetual till the end of time. As there will always be error to be refuted and condemned, so there will always be sin to be forgiven or retained. The ministry, therefore, of reconciliation is not to cease with the death of those who first exercised the power. It is a moral body whose members shall never cease to succeed each other till the objects of its mission cease to exist.

The identity of the mission requires a corresponding identity of the powers devolving successively upon the delegates of those powers. There must be, therefore, at this day, a ministry which claims and exercises, in behalf of sinners, the same powers that Christ conferred upon the first recipients of those powers, His beloved Apostles.

Where is that ministry? Not among our separated brethren, nor in any of the so-called Protestant Churches. For all of them, even those who claim the power of forgiving and retaining sins, in their printed confessions of faith, or liturgical manuals, reject it in their teaching and in their practice; or if any do claim and exercise that power, they do so to the great indignation of the rest of their brethren, and have innovated upon the universal doctrine and practice of Protestantism during the last two centuries.

Where, then, is that ministry! Evidently nowhere, in its perpetuity, in its uninterrupted and uniform manner of belief and practice on this score, except in the Roman Catholic Church. The Roman Catholic Church, then, proves herself the Church of Christ, by the fact that she has always claimed and exercised the power of forgiving and retaining sins, which Christ conferred upon His disciples, and which, according to the very object of that power, was to be claimed and exercised by the successors of those disciples till the end of time, while those so-called Christian Churches, which discard this power, thereby prove themselves no longer in union with the Church of Christ, which has always believed remission of sins an article of the Christian faith. What is the great objection urged by our separated brethern against this doctrine? That it is a presumptuous assumption of power which belongs to God alone. "Who," say they, "who can forgive sins but God only?" This is no new objection to this article of Christian faith. Do you know, dear reader, who were the first to urge this objection, and how, and by whom it was refuted? Open your New Testament, and read the beginning of the second chapter of St. Mark's Gospel. We are told by the Evangelist that when Jesus was again in Capharnaum, they brought to him one who was sick of the palsy; and when with much labor the bearers had succeeded in placing him at the feet of Jesus, "He saith to the sick of the palsy, Son, thy sins are forgiven thee." Then the historian proceeds: "And some of the scribes were sitting there, and thinking in their hearts, Why doth this man speak thus? He blasphemeth. Who can forgive sins but God only." (Mark, ii. 5, 6, 7.) You observe the objection is precisely the same as that of our separated brethren. It is made by the scribes, that is to say, the sworn enemies of our Lord, and of the truth, who never rested till, by calumny and persecution, they succeeded in having Jesus put out of the way and nailed to the cross. They denied the divinity of Jesus, and therefore thought Him a mere man. And yet they heard Him say, "Thy sins are forgiven thee." This they considered blasphemy, because they did not believe it possible that man could have such power given him. How does incarnate wisdom answer, and refute their objection? Read on: "And Jesus presently, knowing in His spirit that they so thought within themselves, saith to them: Why think you so in your hearts? which is easier to say to the sick of the palsy: Thy sins are forgiven thee, or to say, Arise, take up thy bed and walk? But that you may know that the *Son of man* hath power *on earth* to forgive sins (He saith to the sick of the palsy), I say to thee, Arise! take up thy bed and go into thy house. And immediately he arose, and, taking up his bed, went his way." (Ibid. 8–12.) Our Saviour then answers their objection in the very sense in which they made it. He proves to them and confirms his proof by a miracle, that it is possible, yea a fact, that the *Son of man,* not the Son of God as such only, but the *Son of man* hath power, not in heaven, but on *earth;* here among men, to forgive sins; and by that same miracle He proved, once for all, that the same power may be possessed by other men, not indeed through condignity of nature, but by delegation of power. The power of forgiving sins is not so absolutely God's own that He cannot communicate it to His creatures. We delegate certain powers to each other, which as to its legitimate exercise, do not lie in our individual natures as such. We by our suffrages elect a governor of State, who, in his official character, can pardon crimes against the State and reprieve the culprit, though we, as individual citizens, have not the power of life and death. No priest pretends to have the power of forgiving and retaining sins in virtue of his birth, parentage, talents, genius, or education. He claims it in virtue of a commission granted him by the authorized depositaries of this power, namely St. Peter and the Apostles, and their legitimate successors, who received it from Christ, as He in His human nature, received all power from God. The only question to be settled is the question of fact: Did Jesus Christ give such power to men?—to His ministers, to His Apostles? This fact we have settled by an appeal to the Scripture, and it decides the matter beyond all dispute.

This fact, some of the strongest enemies of the Church have candidly acknowledged to be beyond all reasonable controversy.

Chillingworth, commenting on the text from

St. John, ch. xx., writes: "Can any man be so unreasonable, as to imagine, that, when our Saviour, in so solemn a manner, having first breathed upon His disciples, thereby conveying and insinuating the Holy Ghost in their hearts renewed unto them, or rather confirmed that glorious commission, etc., whereby He delegated to them an authority of binding and loosing sins upon earth ... can any one think, I say, so unworthy of our Saviour, as to esteem those words of His for no better than compliment? Therefore, in obedience to His gracious will, and as I am warranted and enjoined by my Holy Mother the Church of England, I beseech you that by your practice and uses you will not suffer that commission, which Christ hath given to His ministers, to be a vain form of words, without any sense under them. When you find yourselves charged and oppressed, ... have recourse to your spiritual physician, and freely disclose the malignancy of your disease ... And come not to him, only with such a mind as you would go to a learned man, as one that can speak comfortable things to you; but as to one *that hath authority, delegated to him from God Himself, to absolve and acquit you of your sins.* (Serm. vii. Religion of Prot., pp. 408, 409, apud Milner, Let. xli.)

But there are authorities that are more venerable and significant than that just cited from the champion of Protestantism.

Luther, in his little catechism, requires his own to believe: "that the forgiveness of the priest is the forgiveness of God;" and the Lutherans, according to Dr. Milner (Letter xli.), in their Confession of Faith and Apology for that confession, expressly teach that *particular absolution* is to be retained in confession, that to reject it is the error of the Novatian heretics; and that by the power of the Keys (Matt. xvi. 19), *sins* are remitted not only in the sight of the Church, but also *in the sight of God* (Augsb. Conf., art. xi., xii., xiii.; Apol.)

In the book of Common Prayer of the Church of England we find this ordinance for the minister who visits any sick person: "The latter should be moved to make especial confession of his sins, if he feels his conscience troubled with any weighty matter; after which confession the priest shall absolve him, if he humbly and heartily desire it, after this sort: Our Lord Jesus Christ, who hath left power to His Church to absolve all sinners who truly repent, and believe in Him, of His great mercy forgive thee thine offences, and *by His authority committed to me, I absolve thee from all thy sins*, in the name of the Father, and of the Son, and of the Holy Ghost. Amen." (Order for the Visitation of the Sick.)

According to these authorities, there is then an absolving power in Christ's Church, which, in certain cases, at least, can and should be exercised by the ministers in whom it is lodged. If in one case, why not in all, since Christ made no distinction? If in sickness, why not in health, should the sinner need and apply for the exercise of that power?

But if Christ did really leave power to His ministering Church to forgive and retain sins, it follows that the confession of sins is a necessary condition of the exercise of that power. The power is of a twofold character; to *forgive*, and to *retain*. There are instances, therefore, in which the minister of this Sacrament is obliged to forgive, and others in which justice and prudence, or both, require him to postpone, or even absolutely refuse the pardon of offences. This power, consequently, is discretionary and judicial. He is obliged to form an equitable judgment concerning the case which is brought before his tribunal. Woe to him if he abuses his power! Woe, if he uses it rashly and without justice! The responsibility rests on his own conscience.

But to form and exercise an equitable judgment, he must needs know the matter on which he is to decide. What would you think of a judge of one of our courts, who, without any examination of the accused, without any self-accusation on the part of the defendant, would take his seat, and pronounce sentence upon him? Suppose he should address the prisoners at the bar, in this way: "A, such a one, guilty, and condemned to ten years of penitentiary. B, not guilty, go home and join your family. C, guilty, and condemned to death." Would not such a judge deserve your condemnation!

Make application of this case to the priest. Suppose he should, without any clear and distinct knowledge of the conscience of each penitent, pronounce sentence of absolution over some, and sentence of condemnation over others; would he not expose himself to commit the grossest injustice to many of the sinners, who stand before his bar? Perhaps the very individual to whom he should refuse forgiveness, is the one whom he absolves, and *vice versa.*

He must, therefore, possess full knowledge of the cause on which he is to exercise his judgment. But this knowledge is possible on one of the two following suppositions only.

Either God, who gives His minister the twofold power, reveals to him in every instance the guilt, and the nature of the guilt, of the penitent; or the penitent himself must become his own accuser. Now, we know that the ordinary providence of God has not established the former of these means, as the usual channel by which the minister of the sacrament of penance can come to the knowledge of the guilt of his penitents; it follows, therefore, that the self-accusation of the guilty parties is the method which He established for that purpose. But what is this self-accusation except confession? The necessity of confession is therefore a logical conclusion, drawn from the divinely revealed proposition: that Christ left to His Church the power of forgiving and retaining "whosoever sins."

Nor, let it be said, that a general knowledge of man's sinfulness, on the part of the minister, or a general accusation of that sinfulness, on the part of the penitent, is sufficient to the discreet and just exercise of that power. For it must be remembered that sin is a violation or transgression of the law, and that these violations are, of their own nature, specifically and numerically different. There are different kinds of sins, and these different kinds may be committed repeatedly. The mere knowledge of the general sinfulness of mankind, or the general self-accusation, on the part of the penitent, would, by no means, lead the spiritual judge into anything like a knowledge of the sinner's real claims to pardon, or his unworthiness therefor. Unbelief, for instance, differs specifically from superstition; blasphemy from cursing. All manslaughter is not murder, nor is all manslaughter criminal to the same degree. Fornication and adultery constitute two distinct and specific crimes.

Furthermore, a judge who has the power to pardon and retain must take cognizance of the moral dispositions of his penitents. Are they really sorry? Are they resolved to amend, to avoid the occasions of sin? Have they made restitution, or are they willing to repair the damage which their sins may have caused to a second or a third party? All these are dispositions, the presence or absence of which, in the heart of the guilty party, will influence and determine the judge in the judgment which he is to pronounce. But all these lie hidden in the heart, and cannot be known unless the penitent himself reveal them to the confessor.

Suppose a penitent should come to me, and say, "Father, I am a great sinner, and I crave the benefit of your pardoning ministry in my behalf," and I should, without more ado, say to him, "Well, my child, I absolve thee of all thy sins, in the name of the Father, and of the Son, and of the Holy Ghost," and suppose you know that said penitent swindled you out of ten thousand dollars, and is well able to restore them, would you deem my absolution such as Christ intended I should impart in the given instance? Why not, if the general knowledge of man's sinfulness, or the general self-accusation of the sinner, is all that Christ required of the penitent?

It is evident, therefore, from these reflections, that as soon as you admit the fact, that there is a judicial power to forgive and retain sins, you must admit the duty of confession by the penitent, as a consequence of that power. Therefore, He who willed the pardoning power, also willed confession, as a condition necessary to execution. Hence the command of St. James (v. 16), "Confess, therefore, your sins one to another." He had previously said: "Is any one sick among you, let him bring in the priests of the Church, and let them pray over him, anointing him with oil in the name of the Lord." Whereupon he concludes: "Confess, *therefore*, your sins one to another." The confession is to be made to those brought in to the sick man; to those who are to anoint him; to those who are to pray for him; but these are the priests. The confession of sins is made with a view to their remission, but, as already proved, none but the lawfully appointed ministers of the Church have the power of remitting sins; therefore, the confession here enjoined must be made to them.

It was thus that the primitive Christians understood the doctrine of Christ and of the Apostles. For we are told (Acts, xix. 18), that "many of them that believed came, confessing and declaring their deeds." Observe, it was not the unbelievers, it was they *who believed* that made the confession and declaration of their deeds. And the fruit of their confession was made manifest by the fact, "that many of them who had followed curious arts, brought together their books and burned them before all." (Ibid., 19.)

This practice we observe throughout the ages.

St. Irenæus mentions some women who accused themselves of secret crimes: "Some," says he, "touched in conscience, publicly confessed their sins, while others, in despair, renounced their faith." (Adv. Her., xiii.)

On this passage Cardinal Wiseman remarks: "Look at this alternative; some confessed, and others renounced the faith. If there had been any other means of forgiveness, why should they have abandoned their faith?" (Moorfield Lect., 2d ser., p. 23.)

Tertullian inculcates the same doctrine, and urges the same alternative: "If you still draw back, let your mind turn to that eternal fire, which confession will extinguish; and that you may not hesitate to adopt the remedy, weigh the greatness of future punishment. And, as you are not ignorant, that, against that fire, after the baptismal institution, the aid of confession has been appointed, why are you an enemy to your own salvation?" (De Pœnit., c. xii.)

St. Cyprian tells us, that those who entertained the mere *inward* thought of sacrificing to idols or of surrendering the Scriptures, "confessed this sin, with grief, and without disguise, *before the priests* of God, unburdening their conscience, and seeking a salutary remedy, however small and pardonable their failing may have been." (De Lapsis, p. 190.)

Here you have confession "*before the priests,*" with the full conviction, that it is from the priests of God they are to expect the salutary remedy, namely, the remission of their sins.

In another place he writes: "I entreat you, my brethren, let all confess their faults, while he that has offended enjoys life; while his confession can be received, and while the satisfaction and pardon imparted by the priests are acceptable before God." (Ibid., p. 190.)

The satisfaction and pardon imparted by the priests of the Church were, therefore, deemed the satisfaction and pardon of God, since they are said to be acceptable before God.

Origen, a Greek Father, says: "They who have sinned, if they hide and retain their sin within their breast, are grievously tormented; but if the sinner become his own accuser, while he does this, he discharges the cause of his malady. Only let him carefully consider to whom he should confess his sin; what is the character of the physician; if he be one who will be weak with the weak; who will weep with the sorrowful, and who understands the discipline of condolence and fellow-feeling, so that when his skill shall be known, and his pity felt, you may follow what he shall advise. Should he think your disease to be such that it should be declared in the assembly of the faithful,—whereby others may be edified, and yourself easily reformed,—this must be done with much deliberation, and the skilful advice of the physician." (Homil. ii., in Psal. xxxvii.)

According to Origen, *private*, or *auricular confession*, always preceded public confession, and it depended on the advice of the physician in private, whether the penitent should make the same confession in public.

Again, this learned Father says: "They who are not holy die in their sins; the holy do penance; they feel their wounds; are sensible of their failings; *look for the priest;* implore health; and *through him, seek to be purified.*" (Homil. x., in Num.) "If we discover our sins, not only to God, but *to those* who may apply a remedy to our wounds and iniquities, our sins will be effaced by Him who said: 'I have blotted out thy iniquities as a cloud, and thy sins as a mist.'" (Is. xliv. 22; Homil. xvii., in Luc.)

Confession to God alone, is, according to Origen, not sufficient; to be purified and to have our sins effaced by Almighty God, we must, moreover, look to the priest for that purpose.

St. Basil teaches that we must not rashly communicate our sins to everybody, but that "the confession of sins must be made to such persons as have power to apply a remedy." (In Regul. brev. Quæst. ccxxix., tom. ii.)

"Necessarily our sins must be confessed to those to whom has been committed the dispensation of the mysteries of God." (In Regul. brev. Quæst. cclxxxviii.)

St. Ephrem of Edessa, in his work on the Priesthood, writes: "The exalted dignity of the priesthood is far above our understanding and the power of speech. *The remission of sins is not granted to mortals*, but through the ministry of the priest."

St. Pacianus, refuting the objections of the Novatians, repeated by our separated brethren in our day, says, "But God alone, you Novatians will say, can grant the pardon of sins. That is true; but what He does by His ministers, is done by His own power. What did He say to His Apostles? *'What you shall bind on earth shall be bound in heaven; and what you shall loose on earth shall be loosed in heaven.'* And why this, if sinners might be bound only and not loosed?" He then continues and refutes another objection, which our separated brethren have borrowed from their Novatian ancestors of the fourth century. "But," says he, "perhaps the Apostles alone had this power? Then they alone, it must be said, had power to baptize, to confer the Holy Spirit, and to purify the Gentiles from their sins; for in the same place where He gives them power to administer the sacrament of baptism, He also gives them the power to loose sinners. Either, then, these two powers were peculiarly reserved to the Apostles, or they are both continued to their successors; and, therefore, since it is certain that the power of baptism and unction is descended to the bishops, to them has likewise come the power of binding and loosing." (Ep. i., ad Sympron.)

The same Father, in another letter, refuting the Novatian error that the Church cannot admit sinners to penance after baptism, because she cannot forgive mortal sins, asks: "Who is it that proposes this doctrine? Is it Moses, or Paul, or Christ? No, it is Novatian! And who is this Novatian? Is he a man pure and blameless who has forsaken the Church; who was lawfully ordained bishop, and, in the ordinary course, succeeded in the place of a bishop deceased? What do you mean, you will tell me? It suffices that he has thus taught. But when did he thus teach? Was it immediately after the Passion of Christ? No, it was nearly three hundred years after that event. But did this man follow the prophets? Was he a prophet? Did he raise the dead? Did he work miracles? Did he speak various tongues? For, to establish a new Gospel, he should have done some of these things; and though he had, yet the Apostle assures us, *that should an angel from heaven preach another Gospel, let him be anathema.* (Gal. i. 8.) Has no one, from the coming of Christ to Novatian, understood the Christian doctrine? And since that time is he alone in the way of salvation? But, you add, we do not acquiesce in authority, we make use of reason. As to me, then, who hitherto have been satisfied with the authority and tradition of the Church, I will not now dissent from it; I will not seek after disputes; and you who have separated from this body, and divided from your mother, search in books for what is most hidden, that you may disturb those who are at rest. It is not we, but you, who have raised this dispute." (Epist. iii.)

Who does not see with what overwhelming effect the same argument tells upon those authors of the so-called Reformation, who adopted this particular error of the Novatians! Whatever may be said of the authority of tradition on matters of doctrine and faith, this much must be conceded by our separated friends: that its history bears stubborn evidence to the fact, that the Church has always believed the doctrine and practice of confession to be the doctrine of Christ, and His Apostles, and that every departure from that doctrine and its practice is, in so much, a departure from the truth of Christianity.

We now come to the leading objections which our adversaries are accustomed to urge against confession. They are differently put by different writers and antagonists, but the substance is throughout the same.

The first among these objections is of a practical nature. When our friends hear the word confession, a thrill comes over their nerves, a panic seizes their hearts. "What! go to confession? Never! It is too hard for any men or women to go and tell all their sins, aye and their very thoughts and most hidden desires, to a fellow-mortal; to a man like themselves."

Grant that it is hard, to poor human nature, to declare its hidden weaknesses and secret miseries to a fellow creature; does it follow thence that there is no divine command to do so? The inference seems very illogical, indeed. Your reasoning, thrown into its proper logical form, would read thus: Whatever is hard to flesh and blood cannot be instituted by Jesus Christ; but to confess one's sins is hard to flesh and blood; therefore, confession was never instituted by Jesus Christ. The fault of your reasoning lies in the principle which you assume. Is it really true that Jesus Christ could not institute anything that would cause some pain or hardship to man's fallen nature? If so, then you will be obliged to reject most of those moral doctrines which you have hitherto believed. Thus, for instance, is it not hard for human nature to deny itself, to take up its cross daily, to be slandered, persecuted even unto death, for justice' sake?—yet all these things were to be done and endured by the disciples of Him, whose life was a perpetual cross and martyrdom.

Is not sin the greatest evil of God and man? What more natural than that, to get rid of it, to have it healed, man should be obliged to undergo some humiliation and hardship? When there is question of recovering the health of our corruptible bodies, we submit ourselves to the judgment and treatment of temporal physicians; we declare, in detail, the symptoms of the most private and shameful diseases; and why should we demur against the obligation of manifesting to our spiritual physicians the maladies of our immortal souls, that they may be saved from everlasting death?

Where is the felon, the criminal of State, who, having deserved death, would not be willing, in order to save his temporal life, to acknowledge in full to the minister of State the crimes of which he has been guilty? And why should we deem it hard to confess our sins to the ministers of God, in order to free our souls from eternal destruction?

But your objection, kind reader, suggests a new and unanswerable proof of the divinity or the institution which it assails.

If it is true, as Calvin says, that confession is a rack, a torture applied by the priests of Rome, to the consciences of men, how comes it that so many millions of men and women have, in all ages and countries, submitted so willingly, so readily to this torture? Why did they not rise up against the tyrants who stretched them out on that moral rack? And not only the ignorant, the vulgar crowd, but the learned, the geniuses of the world, have subjected themselves to this so-called torture. Emperors and empresses, kings and queens, eminent judges and skilful lawyers, magistrates, military chieftains, statesmen, philosophers, orators, poets, artists, have submitted and still submit to this painful ordeal. Our Gastons and Taneys on the bench of the Supreme Court of their country, our Ives, Heckers, Walworths, Bakers, go to confession as well as our poor hod-carriers and navvies. How will you account for this fact, on your principle that Christ could not require confession of sins to a priest, because it is too humiliating to our manhood? You cannot account for this fact, except on the principle that all these millions were and are convinced, in their inmost mind, and on the most irresistible evidence, that it is an obligation, a duty enjoined by the Founder of Christianity on all sinners, who wish to be reconciled with His Heavenly Father. And is it probable that a conviction so universal, so lasting, should be the result of sheer falsehood in principle, or of sophistry in its application!

We can understand, that people will adopt false views, and follow erroneous practices, on subjects which flatter human pride and human passions; which second the evil propensities of our fallen nature; but we cannot conceive it possible that any very considerable number of people, spread over different regions of the world, born with different ideas, educated in different prejudices, should conspire, and continue to conspire, in obliging themselves to the performance of certain painful duties—which, as your objection says, are too hard on poor human nature, too humiliating to their manhood—without a well grounded conviction that it is an obligation imposed upon them by the

Author of their faith. The more you exaggerate the difficulties of confession, the more clearly you prove its divinity; if, notwithstanding those difficulties, it is practised by the greater number of Christians.

"But, I would not kneel and confess to a man, who has no other claim over me than his humanity."

Neither do we, Catholics, kneel and confess to man as man only. We recognize, in the priest, the ambassador of God, the dispenser of the heavenly mysteries, the minister of reconciliation. We look upon our father-confessor as St. Paul desired the Corinthians to look upon himself, when he wrote: "For, what I forgave, if I have forgiven anything, for your sakes have I done it, *in the person of Christ*" (2 Cor. ii. 10): and again, "We are, therefore, ambassadors for Christ; God, as it were, exhorting by us. For Christ, we beseech you, be ye reconciled to God." (2 Cor. v. 20.)

"But is not confession the invention of the Pope, the bishops and the priests of the Roman Catholic Church, who, in order to make money and enrich themselves, laid this burden upon their benighted people?"

A remarkable invention, indeed; perhaps, the most wonderful and astonishing that was ever made by man. And, who, pray, was its author? What was his name? In what century did he live? Over what Church did he preside? How did he manage to introduce this novelty into the Church? Was it by dint of argument, or by the sword? Was there no opposition to his invention? Did all the bishops, and priests, and people, agree with his new view, at once, or gradually? Did they all go to bed, one night, without even the suspicion that confession might be a Christian duty, and wake, on the next morning, convinced that it was? Where are the proofs of all, or any of these necessary suppositions in the case? It is true, our adversaries have asserted the introduction of confession into the Church at a period later than Christ and His Apostles. But, have they proved it? Are they agreed among themselves as to the period, and the author of its introduction? By no means. Let them, first, prove and agree among themselves, on this subject, and, then, we shall hear them again. Suffice it to have proved—from numerous sources in the Primitive Church, that the practice of confession is as old as Christianity itself.

Moreover, if popes, bishops, or priests, had invented confession, how came it that they did not exempt themselves from the humiliating obligation? How is it, that the hierarchy, the clergy of the Church, deem themselves bound to confess their sins, as well as the people? For you must know, that the ministers of this sacrament, from the sovereign pontiff down to the humblest priest, are conscientiously convinced, that they, no more than their spiritual subjects, can, ordinarily speaking, obtain the forgiveness of their sins, except by confession, and the absolution of one of their co-laborers in the ministry.

As to the motive of sordid interest, alleged by our adversaries, we have little to say. It belongs to that class of objections which time and experience have proved to be the result, either of the grossest ignorance, or the most shameless propensity to slander our holy religion. If the result of the former, it deserves to be pitied; if of the latter, it merits sovereign contempt. To the ignorant we would answer, there is no more truth in the assertion, that priests make money by hearing confessions, than there is in the popular notion, which was rife, some years ago, in what are called the backwoods of the West, that Roman Catholic priests, being the imps of the devil, had cloven feet, and that their foreheads were graced with a pair of horns. If this reply is deemed insufficient to convince the ignorant or the prejudiced, allow us to add, that since our missionary career began, a few years ago, we, together with our companions and assistant priests, have heard thousands of confessions, in nearly every city and town of any note in the West and East, and among them, the confessions of at least two thousand converts, from the various sects of Protestantism; and we declare, that, if upon investigation, it shall be proved that any one of us ever asked for money, as a condition of absolution, we will hold ourselves ready to suffer the highest punishment the law can inflict. Why, the priest who would require from his penitent money for his absolution, would commit simony, a crime which would incapacitate him from exercising the functions of his sacred ministry!

So rigorous are the laws of the Church on this subject, that in some dioceses of the United States, the bishops have threatened with suspension those confessors who receive money otherwise due to them, in the confessional, for fear of giving grounds of suspicion to the ignorant or the wicked *among those outside the Church*. On those who assert that confession is an invention of the Roman Catholic priesthood, we would urge a few more common-sense reflections.

Would not those popes, bishops, and priests, have proved themselves madmen by instituting a practice which, while it is painful to the people, is a hundred times more so to themselves? These men would have bound themselves to a labor, which, of all others, is the most wearing on the constitution, and, naturally speaking, the most disagreeable to the mind and heart. They would have doomed themselves, day after day, to the unwholesome task of being cooped up for hours in a narrow and ill-ventilated box, where the variety of noisome breaths and odors is outnumbered only by the variety of the loathsome crimes and vices, which are whispered into their ears. The only ministers of a sacrament so necessary to salvation, they would have obliged themselves to be ever ready to respond to the call of any wretched sinner, who might need the benefit of their services. And as none need the benefit of this sacrament more than the sick and dying, they would be bound to answer the furthest as well as the nearest, the most inconvenient as well as the easiest calls that would be made upon their charity. To sit by the bedside of the dying penitent, in the hospital, the asylum, and the pesthouse, to breathe the fetid and often contagious atmosphere of the bedroom, to walk or ride for miles, in all manner of seasons and weather; surely these were not the motives which could have induced them to invent an institution, the arduous duties of which would naturally impair the health of their body, and perhaps endanger the salvation of their souls. As to the argument of indelicacy in having the priest's ears become the "common sewer" of the sins of his people, we have simply to say, that it proceeds rather from passion than from reason. Those same men who are so nice in their taste in the question of confessing revolting crimes to a priest, are, perhaps, the first to communicate the contagion of their infectious vices to their innocent and virtuous companions in the daily walks of life. Certain it is, that this boasted sense of propriety is not invoked as a reason for discarding the assistance of the physician or the surgeon, when diseases, often the physical consequences of the same moral crimes which constitute the sinner's burden of confession, are to be submitted to the treatment of medicine, or the scalpel of the operator. Nor is the same prudishness manifested, when the witness at the bar of human justice is called upon to detail the minutest circumstances of the most revolting crimes. Our brethren should know that the confession of sins, a duty imposed by the Christian law, is not a forced, but a voluntary act of the accuser; and that no secret is drawn from the human breast, which the penitent is not only willing, but anxious to discover.

Moreover, in the examination of his spiritual patient, the laws of theology require the priest to use all the delicacy of human prudence, that the keenest sensitiveness of a refined moral nature could possibly exact under the circumstances. The penitent is his own accuser, and nothing but the necessity, springing from a well-grounded fear of the possible invalidity of the sacrament, if he should neglect to examine his spiritual child, will induce a discreet father-confessor to inquire any further into the nature and circumstances of the offence committed. These are the real facts in the case; all other statements are the exaggeration of men who are ignorant of the practical workings of the confessional, or declamations gotten up for the purpose of maligning an institution which none abhor more, than those who need it most.

But is it not true that the practice of confession, as existing in the Roman Catholic Church, is an encouragement to sin and to the sinner?

What more easy to a sinner than to convince himself that, all he has to do, to be shrived of his most enormous trespasses, is to go to his priest, confess them and get the absolution? Our brethren represent confession as made after some such manner as the following. A sinner, say a drunkard or blasphemer, goes to his priest; tells him, "Father, I was drunk, I cursed, I swore." And the father-confessor says, "Well, my child, pay me five dollars. I absolve thee: In the name of the Father, and of the Son, and of the Holy Ghost. Amen. Go, my child, and sin for five or six months more!" That we do not misrepresent the views of our brethren, may be learned from almost any of their authors who have written on confession. Take, as a specimen, the following extract from a work entitled "Abominations of the Church of Rome," by the Rev. C. De Coetlogon: "In the Church of Rome, you may purchase, not only pardon for sins already committed, but for those that shall be committed; so that any one may promise himself impunity upon paying the rate that is set upon any sin he hath a mind to commit. And so truly is Popery the mother of abominations, that, if any one hath wherewithal to pay, he may not only be indulged in his present transgressions, but may even be *permitted to transgress for the future.*" (Page 13.)

We have already disposed of the calumny, that Catholics pay for the pardon of their sins; let us examine the question: Does the practice of confession encourage sin and the sinner? To answer this objection, nothing more is necessary, than briefly to state the conditions which, besides confession proper, are required of every penitent for the pardon of his sins. Those conditions are, to say the least, as strict as any of our separated brethren do, or can require in their own system for the same purpose. These conditions are, contrition and satisfaction for our sins. "What is contrition?" asks our catechism. Answer: "A hearty-sorrow and detestation of the sins committed, with a firm purpose of amendment." "How many conditions must that sorrow have?" "It must be sincere, universal, supernatural, and supreme or sovereign."

The first condition, then, absolutely necessary to obtain the pardon of sin, is a true, a sincere, hearty sorrow for sins committed, with a firm purpose of amendment. What more do our adversaries require for the pardon of their sins? Do they not call conversion from sin to righteousness, a change of the heart? In what does that change of the heart consist, if not in the act of sorrow, just defined, by which the sinner hates, abominates, and detests all the evil he has done, and firmly, efficaciously resolves never, never to sin again? But, moreover, the motives of that sincere and universal sorrow must be supernatural, that is to say, they must be sought in the order of grace, and not in the order of nature merely. What more natural, than, that a drunkard, for instance, after spending a competency, or a fortune, in saloons or grogshops, after reducing his family to poverty and destitution, should, when his eyes are opened, regret the evil consequences of his passion,—that the thief, when caught in the commission of the crime, should feel sorry for the consequences of his theft? But the motives of their sorrow are by no means sufficient, to obtain the pardon of their sins before God, or the priest. Our Catholic sorrow must, from the heart of men, reach the heart of God. Sin is an insult to divine majesty, a violation of divine law; our sorrow must tend thither whither tended our sin. Hence we must sorrow either because of the deformity, the heinousness of sin in the sight of infinite justice and infinite holiness; or because by sin, we have separated ourselves from God, lost Heaven, and deserved hell, or because by it, we have crucified anew in our hearts the Redeemer of the World. Or, better still, we should grieve through motives of pure, disinterested love, as when an otherwise dutiful daughter has offended a loving mother, she exclaims in the excess of her remorse: "Not because, O dearest mother, by my disobedience to thy will, I have deserved to live forever under thy displeasure, and the frown of thy anger; not because, by my affront, I have merited to be banished from my dear loved home, and to be deprived of my inheritance, does my heart break with grief and sorrow for having offended thee! No, dearest of mothers; but because, by my crime, I have ruffled the loveliest of natures, marred the happiness of the best of mothers, insulted the goodness of the most amiable of earthly characters, therefore do I grieve and sorrow. To live under thy frown forever; to wander, an exile, the wide world over; to be deprived of the richest inheritance, which it is in thy power to leave to thy child, were nothing, if I could but restore that sweet calm, that happiness, which I have troubled by my fault!" Even so, the Catholic penitent is exhorted, when truly sorry for his sins, to grieve, not any longer from spiritually interested motives, however good and sufficient, with the sacrament of penance, to obtain the remission of his sins, but from motives of supernatural charity. He, too, exclaims in the bitterness of his soul: "Not, O Lord, because by my sin, I have deserved thy anger; not, because by it, I have forfeited Heaven, and deserved hell; no, O Lord! but because by it, I have offended Thee, who art infinitely good, infinitely amiable in Thyself; because by my offence, I have, as far as in me lay, marred Thy infinite happiness, and caused Thee to regret that Thou didst make me; therefore do I repent, and regret from my inmost heart, that I have offended Thee, and do firmly purpose, never, oh! never again to transgress Thy holy law!" Do dispositions like these seem to encourage sin and the sinner? Or, rather, are they not the best means to eradicate sin from the soul?

But, you will answer, if this is so, how comes it, that even those Catholics who go frequently to confession, sin, and sin again;—that the swearer swears still, and the drunkard drinks again? To this question we answer, First: judge not, and you shall not be judged. Judgment without mercy to him that hath not done mercy. Secondly: do not the same phenomena occur in your system of confession? Do all those among you, who confess themselves to God in their bed-chambers, persevere in their righteousness? The real question is not, whether those who go to confession can or cannot sin again; but whether, if they do sin, they do so in virtue of confession itself? And to this we answer most emphatically, that if they sin again, they do so, not in virtue of the principles involved in confession, but in despite of them. Your objection would hold, if the principles which the Church inculcates on her children, regarding confession, led, of their own intrinsic nature, to these consequences;—but so long as these principles, on that score, point and lead to the opposite results, you must find the solution of your difficulty in other causes than those which you allege. These causes are easily found. Human nature is frail, and weak; the human heart is inconstant, the best resolves of the human soul disappear like snow melting before the sun. Passions may be checked, but they cannot be killed. Like the roots of bad weeds, they may revive, and spring up again. These evils you, as well as we, have daily to deplore; but it remains true, that whatever sinner makes a proper use of the wholesome remedy of confession, will succeed in holding these passions under due control, and in avoiding a relapse into many crimes, which, without this remedy, he would probably commit, day after day, till the end of his life.

Ask those who make the best, and the most frequent use of confession in our Church, what is their experience on this subject.

Ask that young prodigal, who, during many years of his passionate youth, lived riotously, until health and wealth were alike wasted in drunkenness and debauchery,—what has crimsoned his once haggard cheeks with the flush of health,—what has steadied his once staggering limbs,—what has made him once more an industrious, an honorable man. He will tell you, it is confession.

Ask that weeping Magdalen, once the byword of scorn in the town—the disgrace of her family, the outcast of society—whose virtue was for sale to the highest bidder, who added theft, drunkenness, and murder, to the catalogue of her crimes,—ask her, what has made her the chaste, the sober, the respectable girl, whom every one respects and honors. She will say: "I went, like my prototype, in the Scriptures, and knelt at the feet of the minister of my Master; I bathed them with my tears; I made an humble, a contrite confession of my sins, and they were forgiven me, and I was reinstated in friendship and love with God and man."

Who are the best, most honorable, and respected members of our Church? Precisely those who go frequently to confession. Whom do our separated brethren themselves, trust and respect most among us? The merchant, the lawyer, the physician, the book-keeper, the cashier, the laborer, the servant maid, who most frequently and devoutly approach the tribunal of penance.

How often have our separated friends come to us, during our ministry, to ask for a clerk or book-keeper in their store, or a servant girl for their house; adding, at the same time, "but we want a young man who belongs to the sodality, who goes every month to his confession!"

Yes, kind reader, it is mainly to the confessional that the world is indebted for the little virtue that still exists among men. How many a young man and maiden, living in the midst of corrupting influences, owe to confession the preservation of their purity and their innocence! How many a wedded couple ascribe to its wholesome influence, the peace and happiness which preside over their hearth! How many a blasphemer has there learned the proper use of his tongue, to praise and bless the name of the Lord, his God! How many a fornicator has there been taught the fearful consequences of his lust; how many an adulterer has there sworn eternal fidelity to the broken-hearted spouse of his love! How many a thief and swindler has there learned, not only to be just and honest, but, like Zaccheus, to restore his ill-gotten goods to their lawful owner, or enrich the poor with the wages of his iniquity! How often does it happen in our missions, that some citizen of the town, or some distant firm, receives unexpectedly a little note with a sum of money under the same envelope, stating that the enclosed is due to him from a certain party, whose name, for good reasons, must remain unknown! What influence sent that sum to its owner? The influence of the confessional, without which he would, very likely, never have received the welcome contents.

Who can tell all the social and personal advantages of this salutary institution! A light in darkness, a guide in doubt, a consoler in affliction, a pacifier in trouble, a harmonizer in dissension, a vivifier in death,—confession is a panacea for every moral disease, a remedy for every moral evil, a preventive against every sin. Well did the author of "Evangeline," though himself a stranger to the Church, appreciate the wholesome influence of the sacrament of penance, when he wrote:

"Fair was she to behold, that maiden of seventeen summers
. . . But a celestial brightness, a more æthereal beauty
Shone on her face, and encircled her form, when, after confession,
Homeward serenely she walked with God's benediction upon her.
When she had passed, it seemed like the ceasing of exquisite music!"

But the influence of confession is especially wholesome at the hour of death. You say, kind reader, "I confess my sins to God:" so do we; but we confess them moreover to God through his minister, whom he has appointed for that purpose. When kings and emperors, or republics, make peace with nations with whom they have been at war, they do so through their representatives, their ministers and ambassadors. The Lord of Lords and King of Kings pursues the same method. And very reasonably so. For sin being an offence against God, who knows and sees all things, is known to God the very moment it is committed. Hence, in that view, it needs no longer any confession. It likewise deserves punishment, and, as soon as it is committed, it de serves eternal shame and confusion. But this punishment, through the goodness and mercy of God, does not always immediately overtake the sinner. It is delayed in the hope that the sinner may repent. What more reasonable than that God, when He sees the sinner repent of his evil ways, should, in exchange for the eternal shame and confusion due to sin in hell, require of the repenting delinquent, that he should suffer the momentary shame and confusion, due to his crimes, at the feet of His ambassador, while he reveals to him their heinousness and deformity. But you, my friend, are left to your own judgment in this important reconciliation. Without a visible representative of the justice and mercy of Heaven, you rely upon your own convictions and feelings for the certainty of your reconciliation with your offended Master. How easy it is to be deceived in these convictions, and especially in these feelings! Hence, how many of our separated brethren have we found, who, on their conversion to the Church, acknowledged that they never felt satisfied with their repentance, and confession to God alone; that, notwithstanding their endeavor to convince themselves that it was the method of reconciliation pointed out by the Scriptures, their doubts and their fears of still abiding in God's wrath returned. This fact occurs especially at the hour of their departure hence. At that dreadful moment, when the hopes and fears of earth give place to the conflicting anticipations of the future; when time casts his vanishing shadow upon the boundless circle of eternity, then it is that sinful man needs something more solid than the educational prejudices of childhood, the imaginative convictions of youth, or the worldly-minded and self-interested views of manhood. Then, those whom mercy favors, are willing to purchase the precious pearl of the everlasting kingdom, at any price which may be asked of the buyer. Then, they call in the priests of the Church, and tremblingly exclaim: "Father! I sent for you to make my peace with Heaven before I die. In the frivolity of my youth, in the busy stir of manhood, I cared not, or neglected seriously to look into the secrets of eternity; now that I am on the brink of the fearful precipice, I crave the assistance of your steady hand, to guide me safely across its threatening abyss; I want o make my confession, Father, of all my evil deeds, and I beg of you, as the minister of God, that pardon which I dare not hope from Him alone, since He has appointed you His representative, and said to you: "Whosesoever sins you shall remit, they are remitted unto them; and whosesoever sins you shall retain, they are retained." Oh, how peacefully, how placidly they sleep in the Lord, after they have heard from the lips of that representative: "Many sins are forgiven thee, because thou hast loved much!"

Kind reader, were you ever present at the death-bed of a good, a truly penitent Catholic? Did you ever witness the calm composure with which he looked grim death in the face, after he had made his last confession? Did you observe that unshaken conviction which expelled all fear, that firm resignation with which he received the terrible message: "Thou must die; thou canst live no longer!" Did you hear him exclaim, like St. Aloysius Gonzaga: "We are rejoiced in the things which have been said to us; we shall enter the house of the Lord?" Whence this peace and tranquillity at the approach of the last struggle of life with death? Ah! from the certainty, the unwavering conviction, that, having done what he could, to repent for and confess his sins, they are forgiven him in Heaven, as they were forgiven him on earth, by the ministry of the Church.

Kind reader, look, oh! look seriously into this all-important matter. There is question of your soul; question of eternal woe, or eternal bliss. Remember, that one day we must all appear before the judgment-seat of our Lord Jesus Christ. Remember, that nothing is hidden from His sight; that He searcheth the very hearts and reins of man. Fear not men; but fear Him who can destroy body and soul in hell. What are the transitory shame and confusion which accompany confession of sin, compared with the eternal shame and confusion which must be endured by the unrepenting sinner?

Better to blush here, for a passing hour, than to crimson with everlasting shame. Let us conclude, in the words of Tertullian: "If (after all we have said) you still draw back, "let your mind turn to that eternal fire which confession extinguishes."

VI.

ON PURGATORY AND INDULGENCES.

"It is, therefore, a holy and wholesome thought to pray for the dead that they may be loosed from sins." 2 MACH. xii. 46.

WHILE the Church, in virtue of her belief in the Communion of Saints, honors and venerates the spirits of those who reign with Christ in glory, and prays to them to obtain through their intercession favors and blessings for her children; she, in virtue of the same faith, and from motives of true brotherly love, offers her sacrifices and prayers to God in behalf of those souls, who, on leaving this world, were not pure enough immediately to be admitted into Heaven. She prays for the souls in purgatory. On this head the Church teaches two things, which must be believed under pain of heresy: 1st, That there is a purgatory; 2d, That the souls there detained are helped by the suffrages of the faithful, but principally by the acceptable sacrifice of the altar.

It is well to remember that these two things are the only ones which are strictly of faith among us. All other questions on this subject are open to discussion. The Church obtrudes no private opinions of theologians or philosophers on the minds of her children. And although among those opinions there are some which, on account of the universality of belief, and the intrinsic worth of the arguments on which they rest, it would be rashness to gainsay or deny, yet she places none under the ban of her excommunication save those who deny the above two articles of her constant belief and practice. The Church, therefore, has not determined the location of purgatory, nor decided whether it is a determined place at all. Neither has she specified how long the souls of the departed are detained in their suffering, nor whether it is by material fire they are cleansed, or merely by a sorrow for their past sins. Nor has she defined the much disputed question of the manner in which the suffrages of the faithful are applied to their relief.

How do we prove the existence of purgatory, or a middle state in which those souls find themselves after death, who died in lesser or venial sins, or who, after having obtained the pardon of grievous sins, did not fully satisfy the divine justice as to the temporal punishments which remain due to sin after the guilt thereof and the eternal punishment have been forgiven?

Our first scriptural proof is found in the second book of Machabees, where we read the following: "And making a gathering, he [Judas Machabeus] sent twelve thousand drachms of silver to Jerusalem for sacrifice, to be offered for the sins of the dead, thinking well and religiously concerning the resurrection. (For if he had not hoped that they that were slain should rise again, it would have seemed superfluous and vain to pray for the dead.) And because he considered that they, who had fallen asleep with godliness, had great grace laid up for them. It is, therefore, a holy and wholesome thought to pray for the dead, that they may be loosed from sins. (2 Mach. xii. 43, 44, 45, 46.)

From this passage we learn that the Jews, one hundred and fifty years before Christ, were accustomed to offer sacrifices and prayers for the dead that they might be loosed from their sins; and the Holy Ghost commends the practice. But this practice could not exist without faith in purgatory. For the Jews, as well as we, believed, on the one hand, that nothing defiled can enter into Heaven; and, on the other, that out of hell there is no hope of redemption. They did not pray, therefore, for those who, on their exit from this world, deserved immediately to go and take their rest in Abraham's bosom, nor for those whose grievous sins doomed them, like Dives, to everlasting wo. But they prayed for a class of souls who were in a middle state of expiation, and who could be helped by sacrifice and prayer.

It may, be and it has been said by our separated brethren, that they do not believe in the inspiration of the books of the Machabees. To this we answer: Whose province is it to determine the authenticity and canonicity or inspiration of the Scriptures? Was this left to the arbitrary will of every individual, or to the same authority to which, as we have seen in our lecture on the Church, Christ left the power of interpreting the meaning of the Scriptures? If left to every individual, how will you settle this matter on your own responsibility? It would require years of study, a keen, discerning spirit of criticism, and much historical knowledge, to come to any reasonable conclusion, and even then your conclusion would likely incline you to our belief, or leave you in total suspense as to the real truth in the matter.

But, aside from this view of the case, it is certain, that the books of the Machabees are authentic history, and as such they record the faith and practice of the Synagogue on the subject, at a time that the Jews were still God's chosen people, and professed the true religion. It was in virtue of their religious convictions that they offered sacrifice and prayers for the dead. Now if these convictions were erroneous, it seems to us that the Saviour would have warned them against that practice, and condemned the error on which it rested. While He condemned all other errors, schisms, and innovations, that had crept in among them through the teaching of the Pharisees, Sadducees, and Essenes, He was silent on this score, and yet it was a practice which was visible to all, which engaged in its behalf the most solemn rites of the synagogue, the offering of public sacrifice and prayer. Though He often spoke to the Jews of the dead and the resurrection, He never once alluded to this practice as to an error in the faith, and never so much as insinuated that it was (what Calvin so loudly proclaims it to be) an invention of Satan, and injurious to the merits of His cross.

And though He did not give any explicit explanation of the doctrine, nor any explicit approbation of the practice (at least so far as we can ascertain by the written word), we should, with the existence of the Jewish faith and practice as a fact before us, conclude that as there was no necessity to teach what was already believed and done, He gave it His sanction by His very silence.

Moreover, our Saviour taught certain doctrines whence this belief and practice may be at least indirectly concluded.

Thus, speaking of the sin against the Holy Ghost, He tells us: "It shall be forgiven, neither in this world, neither in the world to come." (Matt. xii. 32.) Without investigating, in this place, what the Saviour, properly speaking, meant by the sin against the Holy Ghost, let us analyze the meaning of His words: First of all, remark that as our Saviour never acted, so He never spoke uselessly. All His words were life and truth, and though Heaven and earth may pass away, the word of the Lord shall not pass away; it abideth for ever and ever.

According to our Redeemer's reasoning, then,

there are some sins which are forgiven in the next world. This is evidently implied in that part of the text which says, It shall not be forgiven in the world to come. If there is no sin whatever which is forgiven in the world to come, then the Saviour would have uttered that part of His sentence uselessly, unnecessarily. To give them any meaning, you must suppose that He reasons thus: You know that there are some sins which failing to be pardoned here, may yet be forgiven hereafter, but the sin against the Holy Ghost is of so heinous a nature, that it is very difficult and next to impossible to receive pardon for it, either here or hereafter. But it was an article of faith that in the other world, no sin is forgiven in Heaven, since nothing defiled can enter it, and that out of Hell there is no redemption; it remains, therefore, that if any sin is ever forgiven in the world to come, that sin exists in a middle state, between Heaven and Hell. That state we call Purgatory; Christ then, indirectly, at least, confirmed the Jews in their belief in Purgatory.

Had it not been an article of faith among the Jews, how comes it then that they have always, even till our own day, prayed for the departed? It is a well known fact, that in their prayer, "Kadish," they implore rest to the souls of the departed.

It was to this faith in purgatory that St. Paul doubtless alluded, when, without any condemnation, he speaks of the practice of baptizing for the dead. (1 Cor. xv. 29.)

The fathers of the Church have seen another indirect proof of this doctrine, in the following passage from St. Paul's first epistle to the Corinthians (iii. 12–15): "Now if any man build upon this foundation, gold, silver, precious stones, wood, hay, stubble, every man's work shall be made manifest; for the day shall declare it, because it shall be revealed by fire. If any man's work abide, which he hath built thereon, he shall receive a reward. If any man's work shall be burned, he shall suffer loss: but he himself shall be saved; yet so as by fire." On these words Origen comments as follows: "If, on the foundation of Christ, you have built not only gold and silver and precious stones, but also wood, and hay, and stubble, what do you expect when the soul shall be separated from the body? Would you enter into Heaven, with your wood, and hay, and stubble, to defile the kingdom of God: or, on account of these encumbrances, remain without, and receive no reward for your gold and silver and precious stones? Neither is this just. It remains then that you be committed to the fire, which shall consume the light materials; for our God, to those who can comprehend heavenly things, is called a *consuming fire*. But this fire consumes not the creature, but what the creature has himself built, wood, and hay, and stubble. It is manifest that, in the first place, the fire destroys the wood of our transgressions, and then returns to us the reward of our good works." (Hom. xvi. in Jer.) In the same manner do St. Ambrose and St. Jerome comment on this passage of the Apostle.

But the most unexceptionable argument on this subject is the concurrent testimony of tradition. Calvin himself could not deny that the custom of praying for the dead existed for more than thirteen hundred years before his time. (Instit., B. 2, c. 5, § 70.)

Tertullian, as early as the second century, reckons oblations for the dead, on the anniversary day of their departure, among the Apostolical Traditions. (De Cor. Mil.) In his work on "Single Marriages," he advises a widow to pray for the soul of her departed husband, imploring for him repose, and a participation in the first resurrection, and making oblations for him on the anniversary days of his death, which, if she neglect, it may truly be said of her that, as far as in her lies, she has repudiated her husband. (Ch. x.) Tertullian, then, considered it a solemn duty, whose obligation came down from the Apostles themselves, to offer sacrifices and prayers for the souls of the departed.

St. Cyprian says: "Our predecessors prudently advised that no brother, departing this life, should nominate any churchman his executor; and should he do it, that no oblation should be made for him, nor sacrifice offered for his repose; of which we have had a late example, when no oblation was made, nor prayer, in his name, offered in the Church." (Epist. lxvi.)

St. Ambrose writes: "Why were the oratories destined to savage destruction, wherein prayers are offered up to the sovereign God; peace and pardon are implored for all men, magistrates, soldiers, kings, friends, and enemies; for those who are alive, and for those who have quitted their bodies?" (Adv. Gentes Lib. iv.)

St. Ephrem, in his "Testament," thus speaks. 'My brethren, come to me and prepare me for my departure, for my strength is wholly gone.

Accompany me in Psalms and in your prayers; and constantly make oblations for me. When the thirtieth day shall be completed, then remember me; for the dead are helped by the offerings of the living. .... If the sons of Mathathias, who celebrated their feasts in figure only, could cleanse those from guilt by their offerings, who fell in battle, how much more shall the priests of Christ aid the dead by their oblations?" (Test. xii.)

St. Augustine, as usual, states the doctrine and practice of the Church in a few, clear words: "The prayers of the Church or of good persons are heard in favor of those Christians who departed this life not so bad as to be deemed unworthy of mercy, nor so good as to be entitled to immediate happiness. So, also, at the resurrection of the dead, some will be found to whom mercy will be imparted, having gone through those pains to which the spirits of the dead are liable. It would not have been said of some, with truth, that their sin shall not be forgiven, neither *in this world, nor in the world to come*, unless some sins were forgiven in the next world." (De Civit. Dei, lib. xxiv.)

Every one knows the request which his dying mother, St. Monica, addressed to him: "This only I request of you," she said, "that you will remember me at the altar of the Lord wherever you may be." (Lib. ix. Conf. N. 27.)

It is alike curious and instructive to learn that all the leading sects of the first four or five centuries of Christianity agreed with the Church on this point. Thus we read in the liturgy of the Nestorians of Malabar: "Let us be mindful of our fathers and brethren, and of the faithful who are departed out of this world in the orthodox faith; let us pray the Lord to absolve them, to remit their sins and their transgressions, to make them worthy to partake of eternal felicity with the just, who conformed to the divine will."

The liturgy of the Chaldean Nestorians says: "Forgive the trespasses and sins of those who are dead."

The Armenians, in their liturgy, say through the deacon: "We require that mention be made in this sacrifice of all the faithful in general, men and women, young and old, who departed with faith in Jesus Christ." The choir answers: "Be mindful, O Lord, and have mercy on them." The priest alone: "Grant them repose, light, and a place among thy saints, in Thy Heavenly Kingdom."

The liturgy of the Greek Church, in Constantinople, Calabria, Apulia, Georgia, Mingrelia,

Bulgaria, and Russia, as well as at Rome, has the following: "We offer prayer to Thee, also for the repose and the pardon of Thy servant N., in a place of light, from which grief and amentation are far removed," etc.

The Coptic liturgy: "Be mindful, also, O Lord, of all those who have slept and reposed in the priesthood, and in every rank of the secular life," etc.

The Abyssinian or Ethiopian liturgy: "Have mercy, O my God, on the souls of thy servants, men and women, who have been fed with Thy body and blood, and have slept at death in Thy faith."

In the Syrian and Jacobite liturgies, the deacon says: "Again and again, we commemorate all the faithful departed, those who are departed in the true faith, from this holy altar, and from this town, and from every country.. We pray, we beseech, we entreat Christ our Lord, that through the innumerable acts of His mercy, He would render them worthy to receive the pardon of their offences, and the remission of their sins, and would bring us and them to His kingdom in Heaven."

Is it not strange that this invention of Satan, as Calvin calls prayers and sacrifices for the dead, should have been known not only in

Rome but all over the world, so that the whole of Christendom may be said to have been infected with an error so injurious to the cross of Jesus Christ?

Luther himself did not at first reject this humane and consoling doctrine. "As for me," said he, "who believe strongly, I might even venture to say more, who *know* that Purgatory exists, I can readily be persuaded that it is mentioned in the Scriptures. All that I know of Purgatory is that souls are there in a state of suffering, and may be relieved by our works and prayers." Molanus tells us that one portion of the Lutherans not only approve, but practise this kind of prayer. (Bossuet, Projet de Réunion, vol. i., 90.)

The Anglican bishop, Forbes, writes: "Let not the ancient practice of praying, and making oblations for the dead, received throughout the Universal Church of Christ, almost from the very time of the Apostles, be any more rejected by Protestants as unlawful or vain. Let them reverence the judgment of the primitive Church, and admit a practice strengthened by the uninterrupted profession of so many ages; and let them, as well in public as in private, observe this rite, not as absolutely commanded by the divine law, yet as lawful, and likewise profitable, and as always approved by the Universal Church, that by this means, at length, a peace, so earnestly desired by all learned and honest men, may be restored to the Christian world." (Discourse on Purgatory.) He furthermore holds, with St. Chrysostom, that this practice is derived, probably, from the institution of the Apostles.

In the epitaph composed for himself by the Bishop of St. Asaph's, Isaac Barrow, we find, among other things, this sentence: "O all ye that pass by into the house of the Lord, the house of prayer, pray for your fellow-servant, that he may find mercy in the day of the Lord!" And in that of Thorndike, prebendary of Collegiate Church, we find, "Do thou, reader, implore for him rest, and a happy resurrection in Christ."

Many other learned divines of the Anglican Church, such as Archbishop Sheldon and Bishops Blandford, Taylor, etc., believed the same doctrine.

And reasonably so. For, does not reason, enlightened by faith, naturally lead us to the conclusion, that there is such a state as we call purgatory. We are told by the Apostle of the Gentiles, that "God will render to every man according to his works" (Rom. ii. 6); and

Christ himself says, "Every idle word that men shall speak, they shall render an account for it in the day of judgment." (Matt. xii. 36.) And we are convinced, too, that we know not the day nor the hour when the Son of Man cometh.

Suppose, then, that you were surprised by death, the very moment you should have uttered an idle word, without having had the time to repent, would you think yourself guilty of everlasting punishment in hell, on account of that idle word? And yet, you would be called into judgment for it by your Saviour. If it is amenable to His dread sentence, it is something that deserves punishment. On your principle, that after death all go immediately either to Heaven or to Hell, where would you go with your idle word?

There is a distinction between sin and sin, and, consequently, between punishment and punishment. The distinction is evident, from the Scriptures: "I say to you, that whosoever is angry with his brother, shall be in danger of the judgment. And whosoever shall say to his brother, Raca, shall be in danger of the council. And whoever shall say: Thou fool, shall be guilty of hell fire." (Matt. v. 22.) St. John speaks of a sin that is not to death, and of a sin that is to death. (1 John, v. 16, 17.) Our Saviour said, that he who had betrayed Him hath a greater sin than Pilate, who condemned Him. (John xix. 11.) If as you assert, there is no such distinction, how comes it that you allow your courts of justice, your codes of criminal laws, to make one in practice? How comes it, that all punishment is not capital; that there is such a distinction as grand and petit larceny; murder in the first, second, and third degree? Would you consider that your child is equally guilty before God, when he is a little stubborn or disobedient, as when he would plunge a deadly weapon into your heart? On what do nations and individuals ground these practical distinctions in daily life, if not on the principles of eternal law, and justice, which emanate from God Himself? God, then, makes the very same distinctions. He is offended more by one than another transgression of His law, and the one deserves greater punishment than the other. He will, therefore, punish the unbeliever and blasphemer, the thief and adulterer, more severely than him who utters an idle word, or takes a slight pleasure in a thought of self-complacency, or vanity. The murderer or perjurer will experience the weight of his wrath to a greater extent than the man who gave way to a slight impulse of impatience. The drunkard will fare worse than he who, while he observed the laws of temperance, drank his coffee or his tea not for the glory of God, as the Apostle bids us do, but because it pleases the palate, and gratifies the appetite. The woman who stands before the looking-glass to make her toilet, and, with a slight touch of vanity, inwardly admires at once her own beauty and the nice fit of her dress, does not commit the crime of those who, by their nudity, would entice others to sin and corruption.

Suppose, my friends, that you were present at the death-bed of your mother. We will suppose, that she was a good woman, a virtuous wife, a loving mother, a devout Christian, after her own views, and ways of piety, and godliness. But, like most people, she had her faults. Perhaps she was a little hasty—slightly vain, inclined to worldly-mindedness in dress or furniture, not so, however, as to exceed her means, or her rank in life. She had, at times, bewailed these peccadillos, and been pardoned their guilt. But now, as she draws nearer to the portals of eternity, and a burning fever is about to take away her reason, without return, she gives way to a moment's impatience; and, before she has time to repent, she loses the use of her faculties, and dies. Have you the heart to say of that mother: She died in a slight act of impatience, and she is gone to hell? And yet, you know that repentance is not to be had beyond the grave—that the time of probation is passed. No, your heart, on that occasion, as on most others, would instinctively show its Catholicity. You would drop on your knees, and exclaim, "O Lord, have mercy on the soul of my mother. Receive her spirit in mercy, and in peace!" And if you could pray thus immediately upon her departure hence, why not afterwards, as well? Why not, on the third day, or in the third week, month, or year?

Now, we repeat again, and insist upon the case: Is it not probable, that many thus guilty of these minor faults, are surprised by death before they have time to repent for them, and consequently, to obtain the pardon of them? And if they do thus die, whither do their spirits go? To Heaven? Impossible; for they are still defiled; and nothing that is defiled can enter there. To hell, eternal hell, eternal punishment? That seems contrary to the mercy of Him whose mercies are above all His works. But they will be cleansed by the merits of the blood of the Lamb. When? After they are dead? And how? Without repenting; without grieving; without suffering for their faults, and transgressions? Then hell ceases to be a hell, and becomes a purgatory, a place of expiation, and not of reprobation; for, then the greatest sinner has the same hope laid up in his bosom as the greatest saint. He, too, has a strong claim on the merits of the blood of the Redeemer, and, as Luther taught, a greater claim, because Christ came to seek and save the sinner, and not the just; and consequently, his claims on Christ increase in proportion to the number, and the heinousness of his iniquities. Who does not see that such doctrine is injurious to the cross of Christ, destructive of all virtue and morality, yea, of faith itself?

Besides those who die in minor sins, there are others who die absolved of their sins, whether mortal or venial, but who, at the moment of their death, have not fully satisfied divine justice as to the temporal punishments which remain due to them, after the guilt, and, in the case of mortal sins, the eternal punishment, have been forgiven. Three things are to be distinguished in every deadly sin: First, the guilt, properly so called, or the affront, the insult, which the sinner offers the Lawgiver, whose law he transgresses, the Creator to whom he owes love and obedience. Hence, God said to the Jews, "If I be a Father, where is my honor? And if I be a Master, where is my fear?" (Matt. i. 6.) Second, The eternal punishment which every mortal sin deserves. Christ, the Judge, will condemn all unrepenting sinners, who have committed deadly crimes, to everlasting fire. Lastly, the temporal punishment which is due to every sin. Sin is committed in time by those who journey on towards the shoreless ocean of eternity. Immediate death of body and soul does not always follow the commission of crime. Yet, iniquity of its very nature cries for punishment, at the very moment it is committed. The eternal punishment is, through mercy, delayed. The sinner, then, who would postpone his repentance till the moment of his death, would escape all punishment due to sin, if there were no other than an eternal punishment in hell. For, on the hypothesis that he repents at his death, he would immediately enter upon the joys of Heaven. The justice of God and the nature of sin require, that he should suffer a temporal punishment for his wickedness. But these punishments may be so numerous, and so great, on account of the many and heinous sins committed, that perfect atonement has not been made by the sinner, at the moment he expires. In such a case he does not go to hell, for he has repented, and the guilt of sin and its eternal punishment have been forgiven; nor can ne go to Heaven, for some of the consequences of his sin still remain unexpiated. In that case, he goes to purgatory, there, by temporal punishments, to make satisfaction for the consequences of his sin. And, since on earth we are allowed to pray for each other, and the petition of the just man availeth much before God, in behalf of his fellow-men, so, even after death, the prayers of the Church, and her children, avail much in behalf of the poor souls who undergo the punishment of their sins in their temporary state of suffering and expiation. That such punishments are inflicted by God, upon the sinner, even after his sins have been forgiven, is evident, from the Scriptures, and daily experience. We all know, that God forgave our repentant parents the guilt and eternal punishment due to their disobedience, and yet left them to undergo temporal punishments.

We read, that David repented of his double sin of adultery and murder, and that God forgave them both, through His prophet, Nathan; yet, the child that was born to him was doomed to a premature death. In vain did David weep, and implore the mercy of the Lord; in vain did he keep a fast, and prostrate himself upon the ground, that the child might live. "It came to pass, on the seventh day, that the child died." (2 Kings, xii. 14–18.) When, through vanity, David had numbered his people, his heart was struck with remorse, he confessed his sin, and prayed for pardon; yet, notwithstanding his repentance, he was punished, and the prophet gave him his choice of one of three temporal punishments, war, famine, or pestilence. He chose the last; and there died of the people, seventy thousand, that day. (Ib. xxiv.)

Do we not witness the same in every-day life? When your child is regenerated by the waters of baptism, and its sin is cleansed, are all the consequences of that sin removed, together with its guilt, and exclusion from the kingdom of Heaven? Does it not weep, and wail; is it not subject to disease, and suffering, and death, as well as before? Can a just God punish without cause? When you have repented of your sins, do you escape all the punishments, the afflictions of life? Yet, your sins are forgiven you. You trust in the saving blood of your Redeemer, that all is well with you. And yet, you fail in business; your crops are destroyed by a hailstorm; your houses and barns, with all they contain, become a prey to the fury of the flames; your wife, your dearest child, are taken away from your embrace. Are not all these punishments willed or permitted by an all-just Providence? They are, therefore, due to your sins, even after you have been forgiven. Return, once more, to our first hypothesis. Suppose, that at the moment of your death, your indebtedness is not fully cancelled, does not Divine justice require that you should go to that prison, whence none shall go forth, till the last farthing has been paid? That prison we call purgatory.

Cannot the ruler of a people remit a greater, and inflict a less punishment, on the offender against the law? Does not this happen almost daily? Is not capital punishment often commuted into imprisonment for life, or for a stated term of years? And, even when the punishment is commuted, cannot the same ruler leave to his subjects the privilege of interceding in behalf of the prisoner, and of obtaining of him a dimunition of, or entire release from punishment? Why should not God's mercy and justice prompt Him to proceed in a similar way? When, by the prayers of priest and people, a hardened sinner has at length been brought to repentance; when, through the merits of the saving blood of Christ, his sin, and the eternal punishment due to it, have been forgiven; when, instead of these, a certain amount of temporal punishment is inflicted, why cannot God allow His Church and her members to come to the aid of the suffering, and helpless prisoner, and by their prayers and oblations, addressed to the throne of mercy, obtain for him a partial, or a total release from his imprisonment?

How such practice can be considered injurious to the Cross and blood of Christ, we are at a loss to perceive. Is it injurious to the Cross or blood of Christ for a minister of the Gospel to pray for the President and the people; for the happiness and prosperity, temporal and spiritual, of his fellow-worshippers; to beg God that He would avert from us the ravages of bloody war, the scourge of pestilence, and all other calamities, which God inflicts upon a nation in His anger? And how then can that same prayer become injurious to Christ, when it is addressed for those, who, having departed this life, undergo other punishments due to their sins? Nor can we see sufficient reason for the violent opposition which our separated brethren make to this wholesome doctrine. What more comforting to the poor sinner than to believe that however displeasing sin is to His Maker, and insulting to His Redeemer, He who knows our frame, who knows what is in frail man, who wills not the death of the sinner, but that he should be converted and live, makes a distinction between sin and sin, malice and malice, iniquity and iniquity, punishment and punishment, and that He observes this law not with regard to the living only, but even with regard to the departed! Without encouraging the sinner in his sins, it stimulates his gratitude and his love to greater fidelity in the service of His Master, and preserves him from that fearful despair, which is the almost inevitable consequence of the contrary doctrine. For, convinced as every one must be by his own sad experience, that even the just man falleth seven times, and that whoever saith he hath no sin deceiveth himself, and the truth is not in him; knowing that every one of us is bound daily to say: forgive us our trespasses,—how can any Christian hope to escape hell, if he believes that every sin, however small, deserves eternal punish ments? How can he hope to be so pure at the hour of his death, as not to deserve that horrible retribution? How consoling, on the contrary, to know that, even if God should find some stain, which deserves punishment, He will not be angry with him forever! How consoling the doctrine of prayers and sacrifices for the dead, to surviving relatives and friends! To know that the flame of our love for the departed is not necessarily quenched in the darkness of the grave; to know that we can still extend a helping hand to those for whom we would have sacrificed our very lives, is a conviction, which soothes the pangs of the loss we sustain in their departure, and dries up a portion, at least, of those otherwise unavailing tears, which friendship sheds over their mouldering remains. No wonder, therefore, that such men as Molanus, the Anglican bishops before mentioned, and Dr. Johnson, should have borne their testimony to the reasonableness of this doctrine, and that the latter should have prayed for the repose of his beloved mother's soul.

After establishing the scriptural, traditional, and rational grounds for our doctrine on purgatory, we hope it is not necessary to refute the objection that it was gradually introduced into the Church for the sake of making money by masses said for the departed. The dishonest motive attributed to the priests of the Church needs, however, a brief reply. It is calumnious to assert that priests exact money for masses, as masses. They are paid for their time and their service; but masses, as sacred and holy property, are not made venal any more than the sacraments. Priests receive money in no other sense than that which the Apostle implies when he writes (1 Cor. ix. 13): "Know ye not that they who work in the holy place, eat the things that are of the holy place; and they that serve the altar, partake with the altar. So also the Lord ordained, that they who preach the Gospel, should live of the Gospel." Surely, it would be considered slander, if we should reason thus with regard to our separated friends: "You receive two or three thousand a year for preaching to your congregation; hence, you sell the Gospel at that price." A priest has, to say the least, as much right as any minister of the sects, and a much greater right than the minister's wife and children, who scarcely can be said to preach the Gospel, to the support of his people; for he does more for them than does a minister for his own; and to pay his services and time for saying masses, is one of the means of supporting him, just as to be paid for baptizing and marrying is one of the means of supporting the minister and his family.

We now pass to the Church's doctrine on indulgences, which is closely connected with her doctrine on confession and purgatory. The Council of Trent declares: "As the power of granting indulgences was given by Christ to the Church (Matt. xvi. 19; xviii. 18; John, xx. 22, 23), and she has exercised it in the most ancient times, this holy Synod teaches and commands that the use of them, as being wholesome to the Christian people, and approved by the authority of Councils, shall be retained, and anathematizes those who say that they are useless, or deny to the Church the power of granting them; but in this grant the Synod wishes, that moderation, agreeably to the ancient and approved practice of the Church, be exercised; lest by too great facility ecclesiastical discipline be weakened." (Sess xxv. De Indulg.) The Church, therefore, teaches two things: 1st, That she has received power from Christ to grant indulgences; and 2d, That the use of them is wholesome and beneficial.

Before proving these truths, we must first

understand what the Church means by an indulgence. An indulgence is a total or partial remission of the temporal punishments which remain due to sin, after the guilt and eternal punishment have been forgiven. We have already seen that there are three things to be considered in every deadly sin. 1st, Its guilt; 2d, its eternal, and 3d, its temporal punishment. The first and second are forgiven by the sacraments of baptism and penance, as the ordinary channels of pardon; the latter is expiated by our sufferings, and our penances, or by remission or commutation through an indulgence.

An indulgence, therefore, has, properly speaking, nothing to do with the guilt of, and the eternal punisment due to mortal sin, nor does an indulgence forgive venial sin. Much less is it a permission for the commission of future sins, as the adversaries of the Church have calumniously asserted. An indulgence regards temporal punishment only. Many of our separated brethren do not sufficiently understand the nature of an indulgence, and hence arises their misrepresentation of the doctrine. Many imagine that it forgives sin, and many more, that it is a permission to sin. They represent a man who gains a full, or plenary indulgence, as one who for a certain sum of money, to be given to the pope, bishop, or priest, obtains absolution from all his crimes, without any sorrow or repentance of heart, and, at the same time, a kind of permit, to sin as much as he pleases, in the future. Once more, therefore, an indulgence has nothing whatsoever to do with the guilt of past sins, nor their eternal punishment, much less with sins to come. And if some of the bulls or briefs, regarding the grant of indulgences, speak in that strain, they are either falsified by our enemies, or else must be understood in the only Catholic sense, namely the remission of the temporal punishments which sin deserves. Indeed, how could any honest and sensible man think the Church so silly as to contradict herself on this score? She teaches most positively that in order to obtain the pardon of sins committed after baptism, the *only ordinary* means instituted by Jesus Christ is the sacrament of penance, as we have proved in a preceding lecture; and now, she is made to say, by the mouth and pen of our adversaries, that the sacrament of penance is by no means the only ordinary means, but that indulgences without any repentance whatsoever, will answer just as well. She says in her doctrine on confession that sorrow for sin, including a firm purpose of amendment, so firm that one should be resolved to die rather than offend Almighty God by any deadly sin, is an absolutely necessary condition of pardon for sin; and in her doctrine on indulgences she is made to say, by our adversaries, that any one can, on paying a certain sum of money, purchase not only pardon for sins already committed, but for such as he has a mind to commit in the future. (See Abominations of Popery, by De Cœtlogon, p. 13; Strictures on Female Education, by Mrs. Hannah More, vol. ii., p. 239.)

We prove that the Church has power to grant indulgences, first from these words of the Saviour to St. Peter: "Thou art Peter [a rock], and upon this rock I will build My Church, and the gates of hell shall not prevail against it. And I will give to thee the keys of the kingdom of Heaven. And whatsoever thou shalt bind upon earth, it shall be bound also in Heaven, and whatsoever thou shalt loose on earth, it shall be loosed also in Heaven." (Matt. xvi. 18, 19.) Here, besides the primacy of power and jurisdiction given to St. Peter and his lawful successors, which power is symbolized by the delivery of the keys of the kingdom of Heaven, St. Peter receives the fulness of power to bind and loose the spiritual bonds of his spiritual subjects. These spiritual bonds are sin and the consequences of sin. Now, among the consequences of sin must be reckoned the temporal punishments which (as we have proved before) every sin deserves. Peter and his successors, therefore, have received the fulness of spiritual power to inflict or to remove whatever temporal punishment the sins of their subjects deserve. But this is the same as to say that the Church has the power to grant indulgences. Therefore, the Church possesses the power of granting the total or partial remission of the temporal punishments which sin deserves. This same power, was afterwards communicated to the other Apostles, so however, that the fulness thereof should descend to Peter's successors only, from whose jurisdiction the descendants of the Apostles, the bishops of the Church, should derive such a share as the head, the source of power, might be willing to communicate to them. Hence, in practice, as well as in right, the Pontiffs of Rome alone exercise this power, and the Bishops dependently upon the faculties which they receive from them. Nor is there any thing so very strange in this doctrine. Socially speaking there must be such a power for the well-being of the members of the social body. What kind of government would that be whose ruler should not be allowed the power of inflicting punishment for transgressions of the law, or of releasing those who repent, reform, and promise to do better? Our government exercises this power daily both through the head of the federal government of all the states, and through the governor, or ruler of every state separately. Suppose you have had the misfortune of committing a crime against the state, and are condemned to death. Your friends who know you well, and love you dearly, touched with sympathy for your person, meet together, draw up a petition to the governor, in which they testify to the honesty of your character previously to the commission of your deplorable deed, assure him of your repentance, and stake their credit and reputation on your good behavior in the future. The governor grants the petition, and releases the prisoner. What power has he exercised in your regard? The power of absolution from the sentence of capital punishment, and the power of indulgence, remitting to you, in full, all the temporal punishments which you deserved. Or, suppose you were sentenced to imprisonment during ten years, and that a similar petition should obtain the abridgment of that term by five years; the governor would in that instance grant you an indulgence of five years' temporal punishment.

The same power exists in every community which has a ruler, in every school, academy college, and university, and in every family.

The Church is an organized society; it has a ruler, a sovereign, or supreme head. The members of this society are liable to sin, they can violate the laws of that society, and, therefore, become amenable to punishment. The head will, therefore, be obliged at times to inflict spiritual punishments; and, if occasion requires, he must be empowered to remove spiritual punishments already inflicted.

That this power was exercised, is evident from St. Paul's epistles to the Corinthians. (1 Cor. v.; and 2 Cor. ii.) St. Paul hearing that one of the Corinthian Christians had married his father's wife, writes:

"For I verily, as absent in body, but present in spirit, have judged already as though I was present, concerning him that hath so done this deed. In the name of our Lord Jesus Christ, when ye are. gathered together, and my spirit, with the power of our Lord Jesus Christ, to deliver such an one unto Satan for the destruction of the flesh, that the spirit may be saved in the day of the Lord Jesus Christ."

Observe here that St. Paul exercises the right of judgment in the case of the incestuous man; that he orders the brethren to deliver him over to Satan, yet only for a time and in the flesh, and that he exercises this power in the name of Jesus Christ, the invisible head of the Church.

When the subject of this temporary punishment repented, the Apostle, with the same power with which he had inflicted the punishment, removes it. In his second epistle, he writes: "Sufficient to such a man is this punishment, which was inflicted of many. So that, contrariwise, you ought rather to forgive him, and comfort him, lest perhaps such a one should be swallowed up with overmuch sorrow, wherefore I beseech you that you would confirm your love toward him. To whom ye forgive any thing, I forgive also: for if I forgave any thing, to whom I forgave it, for your sakes forgave I it in the person of Christ."

St. Paul was evidently the first to inflict the punishment, and the first to remove it ("for if I forgave any thing, to whom I forgave it"), and then orders the assembly, the Church of Corinth, to forgive, so that he may be restored to all the former privileges of church membership.

The Church, in all ages, has claimed and exercised this power. In the first general Council of Nice, held in 325, we read: "In certain cases, they who have given signs of true repentance must undergo a course of penitential works. But, in all cases, the disposition and character of repentance must be considered. For they who by fear, by tears, by patience, and by good works, manifest a sincere conversion, when they shall have passed over a certain time, and begun to communicate with the faithful in prayer, to these the bishops may show more indulgence, but to those who manifest indifference, and think it enough that they are allowed to enter the Church, these must complete the whole period of penance." (Can. xii.) In this canon the power of inflicting certain temporal punishments, and removing the same, is evidently asserted. Every one who is acquainted with ecclesiastical history, knows how rigorous and severe were the so-called canonical penances, inflicted upon certain classes of sinners, how often the guilty party implored the aid of the martyrs to be released from these punishments, and how the Church, at the request of these heroes of the cross, imparted to those who were worthy, either a total or partial remission of these punishments. These canonical penances have ceased, but the power to inflict them or to dispense with them, or to commute them into other works of penance, has not been abrogated. The regulation of the nature and duration of the punishments and the conditions of remission, necessarily belongs to the institution that has received the power. To her judgment must it be left to determine whatever is to be done or observed in this matter. The same government may, according to times and circumstances, modify, alter, or even annul certain penalties or punishments, which other times and circumstances made it necessary to inflict for the well-being of the nation. Even so it is with the government of the Church in matters of discipline. The suspension of the exercise, or the change of manner in the exercise, does not destroy the power itself. One only thing can be asked of her, namely, that she preserve the spirit of the power which alters, commutes, or even annuls certain punishments. To this the Church has always been true. Hence, though no longer so severe in inflicting certain outward punishments on public crimes, and more lenient than in the days of paganism, in exacting conditions for the application of her indulging power, she yet preserves the essential spirit of those days by making true sorrow, repentance, and confession of sin, together with the worthy reception of holy communion, fasting, almsgiving, or the visiting of a certain church with sentiments of true devotion and piety, the necessary conditions for gaining an indulgence. It is, therefore, a calumny to say that indulgences take the place of repentance and good works, for these are inseparably connected with them.

Moreover, the disposition of the person has not a little to do with the reception of the indulgence. As in all applications of the moral law, this disposition may be favorable or unfavorable to the application of the benefit.

Thus, St. Gregory VII. grants indulgences to the Bishop of Lincoln, "On condition," as he writes, "that applying yourself to good works and bewailing your sins, you make of your body a pure temple to God."

Pope Gelasius II. approves the principle which says: "Each one receives the value of indulgences in proportion to his penance and good works."

Innocent IV. writes: "Although indulgences are generally granted to labors, perils, and devout exercises, some, nevertheless, receive more benefit from them than others, according as they dispose themselves for them with greater devotion."

"The man," says Boniface VIII., "who visits the Church of the Apostles most frequently and with the greatest devotion, deserves and receives the most from indulgences."

When Pope Urban VIII. proclaimed the ordinary jubilee, he thus addressed himself to the patriarchs, metropolitans, and bishops: "Instruct your people, that in vain will they expect to derive any benefit from the sacred treasure of indulgences, if they do not prepare themselves by a contrite and humble heart, and do not exercise themselves in works of Christian piety."

The share, then, which Catholics have in plenary or partial indulgences depends not only on the power of the indulgences, and the fact that they are given, but on the disposition of their own heart, and the manner in which they fulfil the conditions attached to them.

What shall we say in answer to the objection, that indulgences are sold, and that the income thus derived, fills the purses of popes and bishops, who sell them through their subordinates.

We deny that indulgences were ever sold by the Church. We admit, that one of the conditions to gain an indulgence was not unfrequently the giving of an alms, either to the poor, for the propagation of the faith, or to build up or adorn the temples of the living God. We also admit, that the gatherers or collectors of these alms, not unfrequently abused their office, and thus, indirectly at least, brought odium on the indulgences themselves. But the Church never approved or connived at these abuses. Thus, the General Council of Lateran, held in the year 1215, to obviate similar abuses, ordained, that in future the receivers of these alms should be nominated by the Holy See, or by the diocesan bishops. "Many of those who receive alms have given themselves out falsely for other persons, and have advanced certain objectionable propositions in their sermons; we, therefore, forbid any to be admitted as collectors, who shall not have been authorized thereto by authentic letters from the Holy See or the diocesan bishops. And then it shall not be lawful for them to propose any thing but what shall be granted in their letters."

The Council of Vienne, in the year 1311, ordered that all collectors of alms who abuse their trust or power, be immediately punished by the bishops of the diocese where they are found.

The Council of Trent seeing that these abuses had, unfortunately, not yet been eradicated, suppressed the office, and abolished the very name of Questor, or collector.

You have frequently read, or heard Catholics speak of a jubilee, a plenary indulgence, and a partial indulgence, *v. g.*, of seven or ten years, of forty days, and the like, and you would perhaps wish to know the meaning of these expressions. Allow us, in conclusion, to explain the nature of these indulgences.

The word jubilee comes from the Hebrew word, *jobel*, and means joy, cheerfulness, and, by extension, remission, liberty. Among the Jews the jubilee took place every fifty years, and its privileges were, that all the lands returned to their former owners, all debts were canceled, and freedom was restored to slaves. Among Catholics it is an extraordinary plenary indulgence, granted by the successors of St. Peter, to the whole Church; and its special advantages are in the extraordinary powers which the pontiff gives to all approved confessors, to absolve their penitents from certain reserved cases of conscience, and to commute simple vows

A plenary indulgence is the entire remission of all the temporal punishments which remained due to sin, after the guilt and the eternal punishments had been forgiven by contrition, confession, and absolution; so that whoever should fulfil all the conditions required to gain a plenary indulgence, would, the moment he gains it, be free from all the consequences of his sins, and were he to die at that moment, would immediately go to Heaven.

A partial indulgence is the remission of a part only of our temporary indebtedness to divine justice for our past sins.

An indulgence of so many years, or days, means not only a remission of so many years or days of public canonical penances, but the remission of as much temporary indebtedness as would have been gained by a faithful submisssion to, and compliance with, the canonical penances of the primitive Church. The better to understand this view, you should remember, that during the first ages of the Church, she was accustomed to impose long and rigorous penances upon her delinquent children. Thus, if any one performed unnecessarily any servile work on Sunday, the individual was condemned to a fast of three years, on bread and water. A ten days' fast was imposed on those who talked in the Church during divine service. Whoever was wanting in respect to his parents was condemned to do penance during three years, and during seven if he struck them. Backbiting was punished by a fast of seven days, on bread and water; to bear false witness against one's neighbor, by a penance of seven years' duration. Usurers had three years' penance, during the first of which they were to fast on bread and water. Adultery was visited with seven or ten, and incest with twelve years' penance. Revolts against spiritual or temporal rulers were punished with life-long penance; and homicide with standing at the Church-door during divine service, for life, and privation of holy communion till the hour of death. When the charity of those heroic times passed away, much of this disciplinary rigor gradually passed away with it, and other penitential works were enjoined and annexed, as conditions to the indulgences, which the Church granted to her children. You read, also, of quarantine indulgences. They mean indulgences of forty days, and have reference to the same canonical penances of the first ages of the Church. When those indulgences are applied to the souls in purgatory, they signify a remission of so much temporal indebtedness or sufferings incurred by them, as would have been removed by the corresponding canonical penances in the primitive Church.

Indulgences are sometimes *local*, when they are attached to a certain place, such as a church, or oratory; *personal*, when granted to certain communities, confraternities, or pious associations and persons only. Finally, *real* indulgences are those attached to things, or objects of piety, such as crosses, images, beads, medals, and the like.

How tender and compassionate the care of Mother Church for her children! Her watchful eye is on them, her loving heart is with them, from the day that she begets them unto Christ, till she sees them enter triumphantly into Heaven. By her baptism she brings them forth unto Christ, and the hope of salvation; by confirmation she strengthens the weakness of their new birth, and prepares them for the fearful struggle of a life beset, on all sides, with innumerable dangers; by the sacrament of penance she heals their bruises, binds up their wounds, and restores them to life again. By holy communion she feeds their hungry souls, and quenches the thirst of their feverish concupiscences. By holy orders she preserves them from heresy, schism, discord, and anarchy among themselves. By marriage she bur-

monizes carnal with spiritual love, and continues to bring forth spiritual subjects of her spiritual kingdom. Finally, by her sacrament of extreme unction, she disarms death of its sting, and the grave of its indestructible power. To these blessings she adds others. In the fulness of her power, and the deep affection of her love, she not only pardons the shortcomings of their ignorance and weakness, and the follies of their passions, when they truly sorrow for their crimes, but she washes them daily more and more, in the laver of Christ's saving blood, by applying to them the superabundant merits of her Heavenly Spouse, through her manifold indulgences. And she assists them by these indulgences, by her sacrifices, and her prayers, when they themselves are no longer able, save through sufferings, to expiate the consequences of their sinfulness. Would to heaven, that our separated brethren would open their eyes to these blessings and benefits that are to be found in the Church of Rome alone. Would that they were to pray God earnestly, and frequently, to make them worthy of a share in all these graces and favors! "Ask and you shall receive, seek and you shall find, knock and it shall be opened unto you, for every one that asketh receiveth." (Matt. vii. 7.)

VII.

ON THE REAL PRESENCE.

"The chalice of benediction which we bless, is it not the communion of the blood of Christ? And the bread which we break, is it not the partaking of the body of the Lord?" 1 Cor. x. 16.

[The authorized Protestant version reads as follows:
"The cup of blessing which we bless, is it not the communion of the blood of Christ? The bread which we break, is it not the communion of the body of Christ?"]

This question of the Apostle St. Paul, to the Corinthians, it is our intention to answer in the present lecture. Read the question again, so that you may understand its meaning. The Apostle asks, whether the cup of blessing, which, in those days, as in our own, was blessed by the ministers of God, is, or is not, truly, verily, substantially, the blood of Christ, so that whoever receives that cup, receives the blood of Christ; and whether the bread which is broken, is, or is not, verily and substantially, the body of the Lord; so that, whoever receives that consecrated bread, receives the body of the Lord, the very same body and blood, that were conceived of the Holy Ghost, in the Virgin's womb; the same body that suffered, and the same blood that was shed for us, from the garden to Calvary. The question here put by the Apostle, is put oratorically. There is this difference between a question, properly so called, and the figure of speech called interrogation, that the former always implies or expresses real doubt in the mind of the questioner, whereas an interrogation expressed in a negative form, supposes not only the interrogator, but the interrogated to be thoroughly convinced of the truth or the principle, concerning which they are interrogated. This manner of impressing certain ulterior conclusions upon the mind of man, is not confined to the orator and logician. It is in daily use among all. Thus, for instance, suppose, you have laid down the principle for your children, that they shall never stay out after sunset, and it happens that one of them returns home at ten o'clock, or midnight. What more natural for you, than to address your child as follows: Did not I tell you, my son, that every one of the children should be home at sunset? Do you ask your son this question by way of doubt? By no means; you appeal, by way of interrogation, to the conviction of his mind concerning the well-known truth, in order that you may the better impress upon him the grievousness of his offence, and the necessity of avoiding it for the future.

It was, evidently, in this sense that the Apostle St. Paul, put the question to the Corinthians. He knew full well, that they were convinced of the truth of the real presence, as explained by him, in the next chapter; he knew that they believed, as we still do, that by the words of blessing, or consecration, spoken by the priest of God, the substance of bread becomes the flesh, and the substance of wine the blood of Christ; so that, after the words of consecration, there are no longer present real bread and wine, but only the appearances of bread and wine,—there are present, truly, substantially, and really, the body and blood, together with the soul and divinity, of Jesus Christ; the same that was born of the Virgin Mary, suffered under Pontius Pilate, was crucified, died, and was buried; the same that rose again from the dead, ascended into Heaven, is there seated at the right hand of His Father, and shall thence come again, to judge the living and the dead. But, the Apostle's object was to draw from this well-known truth some practical inferences for the Corinthians. Thence he inferred, in the first place, the necessity of their abstaining from things which were offered in sacrifice to idols; for, he concludes, " you cannot drink the chalice of the Lord and the chalice of devils; you cannot be partakers of the table of the Lord, and of the table of devils." (Ibid. x. 20, 21.) Secondly, he desired to show them (as is evident from the next chapter) the sinfulness of the abuse which some of them made of their Agapes, or love-feasts, in connection with the reception of the body and blood of Christ.

" When you come, therefore, together in one place, it is not now to eat the Lord's supper. For every one taketh before his own supper to eat. And one indeed is hungry, and another is drunk."

And he concludes: " If any man be hungry, let him eat at home; that you come not together unto judgment."

It is in a similar sense that we ask and answer this question for ourselves personally, and our Catholic friends; but for the sake of our separated brethren, who deny the real presence, we ask it in doubt: and we pledge ourselves, to the best of our limited ability, to clear up their doubt, and to convince them that the doctrine of the Real Presence was always believed in the Roman Catholic Church, is clearly taught by the Scriptures, and by the fathers and doctors of Christianity throughout the Christian ages.

The Scriptural argument may be brought under three several heads.

First, Christ promised to institute the Sacrament of His body and blood.

Secondly, He instituted it.

Thirdly, St. Paul testifies to the truth of that institution.

In the first place: Our Saviour promised, in the plainest and most unmistakable terms, to institute the Sacrament of His body and blood. This promise is found in St. John's Gospel, the sixth chapter.

Before entering upon a detailed proof of this proposition, it may not be amiss to remark with his eminence Cardinal Wiseman, that "it was a practice with our Saviour, to adapt His discourse to the circumstances in which he was placed, and, more especially, to draw them from the miracles which He had wrought." If this was His practice, He could not have a "more appropriate and favorable opportunity to propound the doctrine of the Real Presence, than the miracle which He had just wrought, of feeding five thousand men, without counting the women and children, with five barley loaves, and after sating the cravings of their hunger, gathering twelve basketfuls of fragments. But before He introduces the topic of the Real Presence, He calls their attention to the necessity of believing in Him. Indeed, the doctrine of the Real Presence is of its own nature so mysterious, so impervious to human sense, that without faith in Christ, who promises and institutes it, no one could possibly accept it as an article of belief necessary unto salvation. Hence He concludes that portion of His discourse by saying: "Amen, amen, I say unto you, he that believeth in Me, hath everlasting life."

After establishing the absolute necessity of faith in Him, as the unerring Truth, who can neither be deceived Himself, nor lead others into error, He continues (vi. 48.), "I am the bread of life."

The Jews, during Christ's discourse on faith in Him, had said to Him: "What sign, therefore, dost Thou show that we may see and believe Thee! What dost Thou work? Our Fathers did eat manna in the desert, as it is written, *He gave them bread from heaven to eat.* Then Jesus said to them :"Amen, amen, I say unto you, Moses gave you not bread from Heaven, but My Father giveth you the true bread from Heaven." (Ibid 30, 32.)

Now, which is that true bread which cometh down from Heaven, and giveth life to the world? Listen: "*I* am the bread of life."

V. 49. "Your Fathers did eat manna in the desert, and they are dead."

50. "This is the bread which cometh down from Heaven, that if any man eat of it, he may not die."

51. "I am the *living* bread which came down from Heaven."

But, Lord, why hold us any longer in suspense? What meanest Thou by, "*I* am the bread of life," and again, "I am the *living* bread which came down from Heaven." We see Thee standing before the Jews, a true, a veritable man, made up of flesh and blood and a living soul; tell us what Thou meanest when Thou sayest, *I* am the bread of life, *I* am the *living* bread. Look at Jesus again, look at Him, as He stands there, the Son of man, the Son of Mary, with His real flesh, and His real blood, His real soul, truly God, though His divinity is hidden under His humanity, truly God as well as man; and listen:

52. "And *the bread* that *I* will give, is *my*

flesh for the life of the world." It is no figurative, no symbolical flesh, it is His flesh, the very flesh, the *personal* flesh of the God-man, Jesus,—"My flesh."

And well did the Jews understand Him to speak of His own, His real, His substantial, His personal flesh. For, turning Protestants at once, they strove among themselves, saying: "How can *this* man give us *His* flesh to eat?" Notice the emphasis—*this* man, the man who speaks, the man who stands before us—the man of whom they had said, a while before, "is not this Jesus, the son of Joseph, whose father and mother we know?" (42.) How can He give us *His* flesh, His own, identical flesh, the flesh which we see, which is within the reach of our touch—how can *this* man give us his flesh to eat?

We Catholics understand the words of Christ, so far as the reality of the identical flesh of Jesus is concerned, in precisely the same way. Our separated brethren understand them in a figurative or symbolical sense. Which of us is right? Let us listen to the answer of the Saviour.

Previously, however, it is well to remark, after Cardinal Wiseman, and other controversialists, "that whenever our Lord's hearers found difficulties, or raised objections to His words, from taking them in their literal sense, while He intended them to be taken figuratively, His constant practice was to explain them instantly, in a figurative manner, even though no great error could result from their being misunderstood." Thus, when Nicodemus conversed with Christ, the latter, among other things, told him: "Amen, amen, I say to thee, unless a man be *born again*, he cannot enter the kingdom of God." Nicodemus understood Christ *literally;* hence he said: "How *can* a man be born when he is old?" Our Saviour continues to explain His words in a figurative meaning, by repeating them with such a modification as could leave no further doubt of the sense in which He spoke them. "Amen, amen, I say to thee, unless a man be born again of *water* and the *Holy Ghost*, he cannot enter the kingdom of God." (John, iii. 3–5. See other examples, Matt. xvi. 6; xix. 24; John, xv. 23; xi. 11; viii. 21; v. 32; v. 40; vi. 33.)

On the other hand, when His words were *rightly* understood in their literal sense, and they objected to the *doctrine* contained under the literal sense, it was His custom to stand to His words, and repeat again the very sentiment which had given offence. Thus, on a certain occasion, our Lord said; "Abraham, your Father, rejoiced that he might see my day; he saw it, and was glad." His hearers understood Him to say what He meant,—that He was as old as Abraham; and murmuring, they said: "Thou art not yet fifty years old, and hast Thou seen Abraham?" The Saviour, because they understood His words rightly in their literal sense, repeats the same, saying: "Amen, amen, I say unto you, before Abraham was made, I am." (John, viii. 57, 58. See other examples, Matt. ix. 2; John, vi. 42.)

Assuming these facts, as the rules for interpreting the sense of the words of Christ, in His answer, to the objection of the Jews: "How can this man give us His flesh to eat?" let us carefully analyze the text which follows. We shall take the text of the authorized Protestant version:

"54. Then Jesus said unto them, Amen, amen, I say unto you, except you eat the flesh of the Son of man, and drink His blood, you shall not have life in you."

Does this look like a figurative presence? "Except you eat *the flesh of the Son of man*, and drink *His* blood."

Again: "Whoso eateth My flesh, and drinketh

My blood, hath eternal life; and I will raise him up at the last day; for My flesh is meat (food) indeed, and My blood is drink indeed."

How can it be food *indeed*, and drink *indeed*, if it be figurative only? Surely, symbolical or figurative flesh and blood were never food and drink *indeed!*

"57. He that eateth My flesh, and drinketh My blood, dwelleth in Me and I in him."

Could there be any thing stronger than this *indwelling* of Jesus in man, and of man in Jesus?

"As the living Father hath sent Me, and I live by the Father: so he that eateth Me, even he shall live by Me."

We know that the Son lives by the Father in the oneness of their nature, the identity of their essence; so, in a similar manner, as far as human nature can become one with the divine nature, he who eats the flesh, and drinks the blood of Christ, becomes one with Christ, and Christ one with him. This strong expression evidently says much more than the mere moral or spiritual union, which would result from a figurative eating of the flesh, and drinking of the blood of Christ.

The fact is, the language of our separated brethren is grammatically, as well as theologically, unintelligible. They tell us, that in the

Lord's Supper, the flesh of Christ is eaten figuratively by faith, which takes hold of the real body and blood of the Redeemer, through the medium of their symbols, or signs, the bread and wine. But, who ever heard of eating or drinking any real substance, figuratively, or by faith? Suppose you invite me to a dinner-party, the meats of which, you announce to me, will consist of roast veal and mutton. I accept the invitation; but, behold, when I am seated at the table, I find only a piece of bread. You beg me to eat my veal, and mutton. I look around in astonishment, and my searching eye seems to ask the question: "But, where are they?" And you answer me, seriously, and without a smile: "They lie before you, sir. The bread which is on your plate, is your veal, and mutton—only remember, that in eating the bread, you must make up your mind, by faith, that it is meat you eat, not bread merely." Could you invent so absurd a farce as this, without laughing or smiling at your own silliness? Yet this very same thing, you tell me, the Saviour of the world did, when, by promise, and even threat, He invited and pressed us to eat His flesh, and drink His blood, which He tells us, are food and drink, *indeed.* Could any thing be more absurd, than to put a figurative construction on words, so frequently, so emphatically repeated, which, of their own nature, and from the circumstances under which they are spoken, convey no other than a literal sense to the hearer and the reader?

Let us, for a moment, suppose, that Christ spoke figuratively—how, then, should we read His answer to the Jews? Our Scriptural comment would, mentally, be the following:

Verily, verily I say unto you: except ye eat (figuratively) the (figurative) flesh of the Son of Man, and drink (figuratively) His (figurative) blood, ye have no (figurative) life in you.

Whoso eateth (figuratively) My (figurative) flesh, and drinketh (figuratively) My (figurative) blood, hath eternal life (of course, figuratively).

For My (figurative) flesh is (figurative) meat, indeed (figuratively), and My (figurative) blood is (figurative) drink, indeed (figuratively). He that eateth (figuratively) My (figurative) flesh, and drinketh (figuratively) My (figurative) blood, dwelleth (figuratively) in Me (figurative), and I (figurative) in him (figurative).

As the living Father hath sent Me (why not add, with the Socinians, figuratively!) and I live (also, according to them, figuratively): so, he that eateth Me (figurative, figuratively) even he shall live (figuratively) by Me (figurative).

May we not conclude with Horace, on another topic of absurdity, "*Risum teneatis amici*"?

Which of you, my friends, on reading your own comment on the text of St. John's Gospel, concerning the promise of the Real Presence, can help smiling at its palpable silliness?

Still, many among you, we fear, will do as the Jews did in the synagogue at Capharnaum. Unwilling to believe, although you plainly understand the doctrine of the Saviour, your only answer is: "This is a hard saying, and who can hear it?"

Does this saying cause the Redeemer, finally, to explain Himself, in a figurative, rather than a literal sense? By no means. When He knew in Himself, that His disciples murmured at it, "He said unto them, doth this offend you? What, and if ye shall see the Son of Man ascend up where He was before?" As though He were to say: "If now, while I am personally before you, while you can see My flesh and blood, and touch it with your hands, you are unwilling to believe Me and My words; how much more difficult will it be, when you will see Me no more; when I shall hide My flesh and blood under the appearances of bread and wine; when your sight, your taste, your touch, when all your bodily senses will be at a loss to discover the reality of My Presence; when I shall be seated at the right hand of My Father, in My Heavenly Kingdom? 'It is the spirit that quickeneth, the flesh profiteth nothing.' You Jews understand My words in the literal sense in which you should understand them, so far as the reality of the flesh and blood, which I am to give you, is concerned; but you blend your carnal views with this spiritual and heavenly doctrine. You imagine that it is dead flesh and clotted gore, such as you buy in the shambles of the meat-market, which I am to give you, and that it is to be eaten, after the same carnal manner, in which the cannibal devours human flesh: you are mistaken. It is the spirit which quickeneth that flesh: I shall be there, the living Christ, as you see Me now—the God-man, whom I proved Myself to be by My miracles; the flesh alone profiteth nothing. It is My soul, My Divinity, together with My flesh, which are to quicken you, which are to raise you up, on the last day, and give you life eternal; understood in this sense, 'the words that I spake unto you, are spirit and life.'" (Ibid. 64.)

In vain does our Saviour endeavor to enlighten their darkened intellects, and to move their stubborn hearts. They reject His grace, and "from that time many of His disciples went back, and walked no more with Him.' (Ibid. 67.)

Was it not then, at least, high time for the Teacher of all truth, to undeceive His own disciples, if they had really misunderstood His words? Did He not owe it to Himself, to His credit, as a plain, straightforward, outspoken evangelist of the new revelation, to call them back, and to speak to them after some such fashion: "See here, my friends, you have misunderstood my meaning: you think that I meant to say, that I am about to give you, and the world that will believe in Me, My real flesh to eat, and My real blood to drink. Not so. All I wished to say was, that I shall give you a morsel of bread, and a sip of wine, which will be commemorative, symbolical, figurative of My real flesh, and My real blood, which no man shall ever eat or drink, indeed, but only by faith, in a sign, a symbol." Is He honest enough to do so? It would seem not; for, instead of calling back His sceptical disciples, He turns to the Twelve, whom He had chosen to be the columns of His Church, the apostles, the messengers, the evangelists of His new doctrine, and He says unto them: "Will you, also, go away?" (Ibid. 68) That is to say: "Rather than change a word of what I have said; rather than sacrifice the least tittle of the truth which I have just now taught you, I am willing to sacrifice even you, and to choose others in your place, who will believe My doctrine, and My words."

Then it was, that Simon Peter, who was destined to be the head of those Apostles, the immovable rock on which Christ was to build His Church, against which the gates of hell should never prevail, anticipating the expression of the faith of his colleagues, and, as we may piously suppose, dropping on his knees, adoring that same flesh and blood, now visible before his eyes, but soon to be hidden under the mystic veils of bread and wine, exclaimed: "Lord, to whom shall we go? Thou hast the words of eternal life." (Ibid. 69.)

Peter believed. He, no more than the rest, could fathom the depths of this stupendous mystery—he, no more than the Jews, could explain the *how*, the *manner* of the Real Presence. But, it was enough for him, that Incarnate Wisdom had spoken: he knew that, in believing Christ, he could not be deceived, though sense should fail to see, and reason to comprehend, the intrinsic nature of the mystery. Blessed wert thou, Simon Barjona; for flesh and blood hath not revealed these things to thee, but the Father of that same Christ, who is in Heaven. Blessed still, all they, who, like Peter, have not seen, and have yet believed.

What the Saviour so clearly and solemnly promised, He, with equal accuracy and solemnity, fulfilled.

It was the eve of His cruel passion. The gloom of Gethsemani and Calvary was already upon His soul. He spoke of His being betrayed by one of His disciples; of His not drinking of the fruit of the vine till He should drink it new in the kingdom of His Father. He had eaten the Passover, the Paschal lamb, with His Apostles. He had washed their feet, and now, seated once more at table, "while they were at supper, Jesus took bread, and blessed and broke, and gave to His disciples, and said: Take ye and eat. *This is My body.* And taking the chalice, He gave thanks, and have to them, saying: Drink ye all of this; *for this is My blood* of the new Testament, which shall be shed for many, for the remission of sins." (Matt. xxvi. 26–28.)

How shall we construct an argument on these words of the Saviour? They are so plain, so simple, they carry their own conviction with them in the bare reading, for all those who are not wilfully blind, and incorrigibly obstinate. Recall the fact that the Apostles had heard the full explanation of the words of the promise. They had remained faithful. When others refused to believe, they, through Peter, had made an open profession of their belief in the future institution of the Eucharist; all they expected was the fulfilment of the promise, that their Master would give them His flesh to eat, and His blood to drink. That Master is now on the eve of His death. He is about to make His last will, or testament. It was now no time to speak in figures or in parables. A dying man does not busy himself with the language of poetry or rhetoric. If ever, it is then he speaks in plain, unvarnished prose, which every one can understand. Moreover, those who hear the Saviour on this solemn occasion, are simple, uneducated fishermen. They can scarcely understand the commonest expressions of their own language. Their reason, like their speech, is untutored, and uncultivated. They would scarcely think of such nice distinctions as the difference, in a given instance, between a figurative and a literal expression of speech. How much less were they capable of nicely sifting out the certainly concealed figurative expression of Christ's thought, which our separated brethren appear to have discovered in the text. If what we have premised seems plausible, then I ask you, how, think you, did the Apostles understand the words of Christ above cited? Think you they understood them to mean what they obviously, and on first hearing of them, convey to the mind, or the very opposite? If the former, then they believed Christ to have changed the bread, which He broke, into the real, substantial flesh of His own personal body, and the wine, which He blessed, into His own real and personal blood; and, consequently, they believed in what we call transubstantiation, and the Real Presence. And how could they believe otherwise? They had heard Him say that He would give them His flesh *to eat*, and His blood *to drink;* for that His flesh was food indeed, and His blood was drink indeed. Now they hear Him say—take ye, *eat ye;* this is *My body. Drink ye* all of this: this is *My blood.* True, they had heard from His lips— I am the door, the vine; the field is the world; and the like figurative expressions; but what resemblance could they discover between those obviously metaphorical sayings, and the words: this is My body; this is My blood? To do so they must have been immediately struck with the perfect parallelism not only of the words, but of the things. Where is that similarity? Not surely in the fact that bread was a well known type or figure of the human body; for who ever heard that bread was assumed as an object of similarity or resemblance with the human body? Certainly, Christ's body did not in any imaginable way resemble bread— nor could bread in any possible way represent His body. Christ's words were, therefore, understood by the Apostles in their literal sense.

Moreover, Christ, as St. Luke says, added to the words "this is My body" which is delivered for you," "this is My blood which shall be shed for you." (Luke, xxii. 19, 20.) Did not Christ give His real, substantial flesh, shed his real, substantial, personal blood for us? And yet it is that flesh, of which He says: "Take ye, and eat;" it is that blood, of which he says: "Drink ye all of it."

Let us illustrate the whole argument by an example. Suppose you are father of a family, and about to die. You wish to make your last will in behalf of your children. In the presence of the notary public and two witnesses, you dictate as follows: "To my daughter Mary, I leave this house with all its appurtenances. To my daughter Sarah, I leave the block of houses situated on Verona street. To my son John, I leave my farm of 150 acres, and all the improvements on the same." Suppose further that you are dead, and that your children go to the Probate Court to settle the question of their inheritance. There they are told by the judge: "Well, Mary, you doubtless imagine that your father left you the real, substantial brick-and-mortar house in which he died?" "Most certainly, your honor," replies the girl. "Yet, I am sorry to say," returns the judge, " that you are mistaken. The words of the last will of your father mean, that sometime before he fell sick, he had a photograph taken of his house, which must be somewhere hanging or lying in a room, and that is the portion of your inheritance." "As to your share, Sarah, he left you a birdseye-view of the block of houses mentioned in the codicil, which, upon diligent search, you will probably find somewhere in the house." "To you, John, he left a landscape-view of the farm and its scenery, which you will find in some corner of the attic or the garret." Now, suppose these children go home in search of their respective heirlooms, and hug them to their bosoms, as a rich fortune left them by their departed father; would you not say, that both the judge and the children, had lost their senses? Yet this is what our good friends have done. During sixteen hundred years the Church of Rome had never ceased to transmit to her dear children the legacy which she herself had received on the eve of the death of her divine spouse; His flesh as food, His blood as drink for their hungry souls. Then come Carlstadt and Zwingle, and tell these children: " Your mother and you are mistaken: Christ, her spouse, did not leave her or you His real flesh, as food, nor His real blood, as drink; but only a piece of bread and a sip of wine, as the images, the signs, the symbols, the figures of His real flesh and blood." Which, think you, is right, the Church or the sacramentarians; Rome or Zwingle?

Our separated brethren cannot but admit, that, whether real or figurative, Christ instituted a new rite; propounded, on that occasion a new law; inculcated a new practice, to be kept by the faithful throughout all time. But, it would be unreasonable to suppose, that a wise and prudent lawgiver would make use of terms which would be open to cavil, on account of their vagueness or ambiguity. That is contrary to all experience; much less could that be supposed of our Saviour, on so important a subject, and on so solemn an occasion. Now, t is evident, that the whole terminology of the Redeemer, from the words of the promise to those of the institution, as related by the several evangelists, favors the Roman Catholic, rather than the Protestant interpretation; so, that nothing less than the most ingenious sophistry could possibly construct an argument on those words, which would incline us to think that He spoke figuratively, rather than literally. Nor did our Divine Saviour, as on other occasions, when He was misunderstood, vouchsafe an explanation, which could induce His Apostles to believe the words in any other than the literal and obvious sense, which they, at first sight, convey. Every reason, therefore, compels us to believe, that Christ, at the Last Supper, gave His Apostles His real flesh to eat, and His real blood to drink.

Nor did He stop here. He, moreover, added: "Do this for a commemoration of me." (Luke, xxii. 19.) Our Lord, then, commanded His Apostles to do the very same thing that they had seen Himself do. What had He done? He had taken bread, and blessed it, and in the blessing, made it His own body, and given it as food to them. In the same manner, He had taken the chalice, blessed it, and made it His blood, giving it to them as drink; He commands them to do the very same. *This*, namely, that you have seen Me do, do ye, for a commemoration of Me. In what that commemoration was chiefly to consist, we are told by the Apostle St. Paul, who writes: "for as often as you shall eat this bread, and drink the chalice, you shall show the death of the Lord, until He come." (1 Cor. xii. 26.) The unbloody presence of Christ in the sacrament, under the appearances of bread and wine, was, then, to be a memorial, commemorative of the bloody presence of Jesus on the cross; and the invisible reality of the one, the memorial of the visible reality of the other.

We now proceed to the testimony of St. Paul, who, though he was present neither at the promise nor at the institution of the sacrament, bears the most striking evidence in the case. Besides the text which we have already quoted, in which he says: "the cup of blessing which we bless, is it not the communion of the blood of Christ; and the bread which we break, is it not the communion of the body of

Christ?" he writes as follows, in the eleventh chapter:

"For I have received of the Lord, that which also I delivered unto you, that the Lord Jesus, the same night in which He was betrayed took bread,

"And giving thanks, broke, and said: Take ye and eat: this is My body, which shall be delivered for you; this do for the commemoration of Me.

"In like manner, also, the chalice, after He had supped, saying: This chalice is the new Testament in My blood: this do ye, as often as you shall drink, for the commemoration of Me.

"For as often as you shall eat this bread, and drink the chalice, you shall show the death of the Lord, until He come.

"Therefore, whosoever shall eat this bread, or drink the chalice of the Lord unworthily, shall be guilty of the body and of the blood of the Lord.

"But, let a man prove himself; and so let him eat of that bread, and drink of the chalice.

"For, he that eateth and drinketh unworthily, eateth and drinketh judgment [Protestant version, damnation] to himself, not discerning the body of the Lord." (1 Cor. xi. 23-29.)

Observe, first, that Saint Paul repeats the formula of the institution, in nearly the very same words in which it is recorded by the Evangelists. If St. Paul had understood those words in a figurative sense, how comes it, that he does not give a turn to his phraseology which would express that figurative sense? Did not honesty require him to do it; the more so, as he was instructing a promiscuous multitude of church-members, many of whom were, perhaps, less capable of finding a figurative sense under these words, than were the Apostles themselves? Moreover, he wrote after the descent of the Holy Spirit upon the Apostles, and he himself was imbued with the same Spirit, so that his understanding, now, at least, was fully opened to the real sense of the doctrines of Christ.

But how will you explain in a figurative sense, the following strong language of the Apostle to the Corinthians? "Therefore, whosoever shall eat this bread or drink the chalice of the Lord unworthily, shall be guilty of the body and of the blood of the Lord." How can any one be guilty of the body and blood of the Lord, if there are no such body and blood, as our separated brethren teach? It is true, there would still be the symbols, the signs, the im ages; but will any one say that whoever is guilty of an outrage or assault upon a portrait or image of the king, is really and actually guilty of an assault upon his person? Yet this is the strength of St. Paul's expression, which cannot possibly be understood, except on the Catholic ground, that under the appearances of bread and wine, Christ's body and blood are really, substantially and personally present.

The same must be said of the following: " For he that eateth and drinketh unworthily, eateth and drinketh damnation to himself, not discerning the body of the Lord." (Ibid. 29.) What more fearful punishment could be inflicted in consequence of any crime than eternal damnation? The crime, then, of eating and drinking unworthily, must be an exceedingly outrageous one. But this extraordinary degree of guilt can scarcely be incurred in profaning the mere symbols or signs of Christ's body; for then there would have been the same reason for punishing the Jews, if they had eaten the Paschal lamb or manna unworthily, since both these were types and symbols, even more striking and impressive, than those which the Saviour instituted. The only way, therefore, to account for this severity, is the reason given by the Apostle: because those who eat and drink unworthily, do not discern the body of the Lord: that is, they profane the body of the Lord, really present in the sacrament. It is true, that the Apostle mentions the words bread and wine in connection with the subject, but that fact is easily accounted for; first, because this form of language is familiar to the penmen of Holy Writ. Thus the rod of Aaron was still called rod after it had been changed into a serpent (Exod. vii. 12), and in the New Testament the *blind* are said to *see*. Men are called blind after sight is restored to them (Matt. xi. 5; Luke, viii. 22.) Secondly, we often name things by appearances, the shape, and color, which they present. Thus, angels are often called *men*, in the Scriptures. (Gen. xviii. 2; Josh. v. 13; Dan. ix. 21; Acts, i. 10.) These modes of expression are adopted in order to avoid a repetition of the same phraseology; thus, in verse 27, the Apostle would have written: Therefore, whosoever shall eat this body or drink this blood of the Lord, shall be guilty of the body and the blood of the Lord. Nor was there any longer the same danger, as at the institution, of being misunderstood. The doctrine of the Real Presence was already established; its practice had been in existence for twenty-four years, so that the faithful fully understood the sense in which the Apostle used the words bread and wine, in connection with this mystery.

It now remains for us briefly to show how this doctrine has been uniformly taught and believed throughout the Catholic Church ever since the commencement of Christianity. St. Ignatius, the Martyr, who was a disciple of St. John the Evangelist, and bishop of Antioch, speaking of the Gnostics of his time, writes: "They abstain from the Eucharist, because they do not acknowledge it to be the flesh of our Saviour, Jesus Christ, which suffered for our sins, and which the Father, by His goodness, resuscitated. (Epis. ad Smyrn.)

According to this Father of the Church, it was a heresy, an error, not to believe in the Real Presence.

St. Justin, the Philosopher, suffered martyrdom at Rome, about the year 166. He says: "As Jesus Christ, made man by the word of God, took flesh for our salvation, in the same manner, we have been taught that the food which has been blessed by the prayer of the words that He spoke, and by which our blood and flesh, in the change, are nourished, *is the flesh and blood of that Jesus incarnate.* (Apol. i., ad imper. Anton.) St. Justin does not look upon the fact which he sets forth in his Apol ogy as a mere opinion, but as a real dogma of the Church: "We have been taught." What that dogma was, is too plain to need any comment.

St. Irenæus, expostulating with the heretics of his day, says: "How can they prove that the bread, over which the words of thanksgiving have been pronounced, is *the body of their Lord*, and the cup *His blood*," while they do not admit that He is the Son; that is, the Word of the Creator of the world? (Advers. Hær., lib. iv.)

How could these men, St. Ignatius at Antioch, Justin at Rome, Irenæus at Lyons, agree so accurately on the same doctrine, if it was not the doctrine of the Universal Church!

St. Hilary, bishop of Poitiers, in the fourth century, writes:

"There is no room to doubt the truth of Christ's flesh and blood; for now, by the profession of the Lord Himself, and according to our belief, it is truly flesh and truly blood." (De Trin., lib. viii.)

St. Ephrem, of Edessa, says: "*His body*, by a new method, is mixed with our bodies, and *His most pure blood* is transfused into our veins. *He is wholly incorporated with us.*" (Hymn xxxiv., de Virginitate.)

And again: "Believe, then, and with a firm faith receive *the body and blood of our Lord*. Abraham placed earthly food before the celestial spirits, of which they ate. This was wonderful. But what Christ has done for us greatly exceeds this, and transcends all speech and all conception. To us that are in the flesh, He has given *to eat His body and blood*." (De Nat. Dei, tom. iii.)

But nothing could be clearer than the testimonies of St. Cyril, of Jerusalem, in his catechetical explanations on this subject:

"The bread and wine, which, before the invocation of the adorable Trinity, were nothing but bread and wine, become, after this invocation, the body and blood of Christ." (Cat. Mystag., i., N. iii.) "The Eucharistic bread, after the invocation of the Holy Spirit, is no longer common bread, but the body of Christ." (Ibid., Cat. iii., N. iii.)

"The doctrine of the blessed Paul alone is sufficient to give certain proof of the truth of the divine mysteries; and you, being deemed worthy of them, are become one body and one blood with Christ. For this great Apostle says: That our Lord, in the same night wherein He was delivered, having taken bread, and given thanks, broke it, and gave it to His disciples, saying to them—take and eat, this is My body. Afterwards He took the cup, and said: take and drink, this is My blood. As then Christ, speaking of the bread, declared, and said: *'This is My body;' who shall dare to doubt it?* And, as speaking of the wine, He positively assured us, and said: *'This is My blood;' who shall doubt it, and say that it is not His blood?*" (Cat. Mystag., iv., N. i.)

How beautifully and forcibly the same holy Father refutes the objection, which the unbeliever and those who deny this Christian doctrine make to the possibility of this mystery, may be learned from the following passage:

"Jesus Christ, at Cana, of Galilee, once changed water into wine by His will only; and shall we think Him less worthy of credit, when He changes wine into blood? Invited to an earthly marriage, He wrought that miracle; and shall we hesitate to confess, that He has given to His children His body to eat, and His blood to drink? Wherefore, with all confidence, let us take the body and blood of Christ. For in the type or figure of bread His body is given to thee; and in the type or figure of wine His blood is given; that so being made partakers of the body and blood of Christ, you may become one body and one blood with

Him. Thus, the body and blood of Christ being distributed in our members, we become *christophori*, that is, we carry Christ with us; and thus, as St. Peter says, we are made partakers of the divine nature." (Ibid., N. iii.)

"Wherefore I conjure you, my brethren, not to consider them [bread and wine] any more as common bread and wine, since they are the body and blood of Jesus Christ, according to His words; and although your sense may suggest that to you, let faith confirm you. Judge not of the thing by your taste, but, by faith; assure yourself, without the least doubt, that you are honored with the body and blood of Christ. This knowing, and of this being assured, that what appears to be bread, is not bread, though it be taken for bread by the taste, but is the body of Christ; and that which appears to be wine, is not wine, though the taste will have it so, but is the blood of Christ." (Ibid., N. iv., v., vi., ix.)

Could human language be stronger or clearer to prove to neophytes, to those who have just been received into the Church by baptism, the reality of Christ's flesh and blood in the Eucharist? Remember, such was the faith of the whole Christian Church during the fourth century. Who, then, are the innovators, the

Catholics, or the so-called reformers of the sixteenth century? Instead of believing as the latter did, that Christ's body is present figuratively, typically, in real bread, and His blood figuratively and typically in real wine, those Christians were taught that Christ's real body was present in typical bread, and His blood in typical wine, because they believed, that after the words of blessing, or, as we generally express it, after the consecration, the substance of the bread and wine has become the body and blood of Jesus Christ, so that the appearances only of bread and wine remain.

Add to these testimonies, a well-known fact, in the history of the first four centuries of Christianity; namely, the discipline of secrecy (*disciplina arcani*), which was practised by the Church in the celebration of her mysteries, especially the mystery of the Eucharist. What reason or motive could the primitive Church have had for celebrating, with closed doors, the mysteries of the altar, if she had not believed in the Real Presence? Why should her writers have been so careful in speaking of this mystery in such of their works as were destined to be made public? Why were catechumens and unbelievers forbidden to remain in the houses of assembly, when the mystic offering was about to commence? Why did the Apologists of the Catholic religion abstain from plainly and openly stating the nature of these mysteries? Why did they allege, as a reason for their not divulging them, the command of their Master, that pearls should not be cast before dogs and swine? Why did, even, the martyrs, when they were put to the rack for practising in private cruel and bloody crimes, such as feasting upon the flesh of a new-born babe, content themselves with denying the accusation, without explaining the real nature of the practice for which they were condemned? Can you account for these facts on the supposition, that they believed in the figurative presence only? What was there so mysterious, so sacred, in the practice of eating a bit of bread, and drinking a sip of wine, in remembrance of the Saviour, who had, Himself, done so on the eve of His death, and ordered His followers to do the same? Was there any danger of ridicule or calumny on that score, from their most bitter and inveterate enemies? Was there any danger of persecution unto death for following a doctrine and a practice which had nothing in it contradicting sense? No, my friends; this secrecy, so stubbornly maintained in the midst of the jeers of infidel writers; in the midst of the most cruel persecutions of tyrants, can be accounted for only on the hypothesis, that the first Christians believed in the real presence, whose sublime doctrines were too profound for carnal-minded men; whose nature was too sacred and holy to be exposed to the impious sneers of godless antagonists.

To suppose, as some of our adversaries have done, that the doctrine of the Real Presence was gradually introduced into the Church of Rome, is a hypothesis opposed alike to fact and reason. That it is opposed to fact, we have already proved, by citing the testimonies of the leading writers of the first ages of Christianity. Nor is there any reason for admitting such a supposition.

But, if the Church of Rome had introduced this doctrine into her creed, how comes it that her enemies not only never objected this fact to her, but retained the same doctrine when they left her bosom? How comes it that Nestorius, who apostatized from Rome in the fourth century, carried with him the doctrines and practices of the Church concerning the Real Presence? How do you account for its existence among the Eutychians, Jacobites, Copts, or Syrians? Why did not the Greek schismatics, who quarreled with Rome about trifles, remonstrate with her on the score of the Real Presence ? How will you make this universal agreement of all the churches, during one thousand years, tally with your assumption, that it was gradually introduced into the Church ?

To introduce a new doctrine into the Church, especially a doctrine which, according to our adversaries themselves, is too deep for human wit, and impervious to human sense, would require more ingenuity and craft than the keenest intellect is capable of. By what process of sophistry could any individual, or individuals, however gifted, have convinced millions of Christians, that bread could, by a few words spoken over it, become the flesh, and wine the blood of the Son of God? No matter how gross the ignorance of the multitude, no matter how dark the age in which they lived, can we believe that there would have been no opposition made, no remonstrance uttered against the novelty! Ignorance favors self-interest, passion, sensuality, ambition; but, what was ignorance to gain by the doctrine of the Real Presence? A hidden God not only to be adored, but to be received in the Eucharist, humbles human pride, because it confounds human reason; requires the sacrifice of pride and sensuality, as a necessary disposition, to receive Him worthily. Moreover, universal ignorance is a chimera. There never was an age, there can be none, so entirely dark as not to possess any light at all. This is certainly true of the successive ages of the Christian era. Would no one see—no one expose the novelty? When other heresies sprang up, the learned doctors of the Church arose at once, and, with prolific pens, asserted the majesty and power of the ancient truth, against the abject slavery and weakness of error; and was there none to wield that same pen against the daring innovator, who, for the first time since the foundation of Christianity, taught the mysterious doctrine of the Real Presence? No, not one; or if there was, let his name be given—his arguments made known. On the contrary, no sooner did Berengarius, in the eleventh century, deny the doctrine of the Real Presence, than the whole Christian Church rose up to refute and condemn his innovation. Learned bishops and doctors, like Lanfranc, Quitmond, Algerus, and others, overwhelmed him with argument, and no fewer than fifteen Councils, solemnly anathematized him. The uninterrupted and undisturbed possession, therefore, of this doctrine by the Church of Rome during sixteen centuries, previous to the so-called

Reformation, is a demonstrative argument, that the doctrine is a doctrine of Christ; and that, therefore, it forms a part of that creed which it is necessary to believe unto salvation.

Luther himself, eagerly as he desired to do away with this doctrine, never denied the Real Presence, yea, denounced, with his usual violence and vulgarity, the Zwinglians, who taught the figurative presence. "I clearly saw," says he, "how much I should thereby" (viz., by overthrowing the Real Presence) "injure Popery; but I found myself caught, without any way of escaping; for, the text of this Gospel was too plain for this purpose." (Epist. ad Argent.) Of the Zwinglians, he writes: "The devil seems to have mocked those to whom he has suggested a heresy so ridiculous, and contrary to Scripture, as that of the Zwinglians." And, speaking of their comments on the words, "this is My body, this is My blood," he remarks, that "their translations and glosses on these texts have as much sense, as if one should translate the first words of Genesis: '*In the beginning God created Heaven and earth*'— *In the beginning the cuckoo eat the sparrow and his feathers.*" (Def. Verb. Dom.)

Furthermore, he calls those who deny the

Real Presence, "a reprobate sect, lying heretics, bread-breakers, wine-drinkers, and soul-destroyers." (In Parv. Cat.) "They are indevilized and superdevilized"—they have the devil in them, and above them. Finally, he devotes them all to the flames of hell.

The authorized Catechism of the Church of England, declares that, "the body and blood of Christ are *verily* and *indeed* taken"—and received by the faithful in the Lord's Supper. But it may be said: We have changed all this; we no longer believe as did Luther, or such lights of the Establishment as Ridley, Hooker, Andrew, Casaubon, Montague, Belson, Taylor, Forbes, Cosin, Samuel Parker, and others. And yet it is certain, my friends, that the truth of Christ's religion changeth not. "Heaven and earth shall pass away, but My word shall not pass away." "Christ—yesterday, to-day, and the same for ever." You must needs conclude, that either Luther, and the Anglican Church, were wrong when they taught the Real Presence, or else, that you yourselves are wrong, in denying it. And, in either instance, your Reformation was not, and could not be, the work of God; nor your pretended Christianity, the Christianity of Christ; for Christianity knows no change.

Here we might, strictly speaking, leave the matter. For, writing as we do, for Christians, we have appealed to such proofs of the Real Presence, as they, in virtue of their own principles, are bound to receive as conclusive evidence in the case. According to our separated brethren, the Bible is the only rule of the Christian's faith. We have appealed to that Bible for any evidence of a figurative presence in the Eucharist. In strict logic, the question is here at an end. Consistently with their own principles, they cannot claim a change of ground in the argumentation. But consistency is a jewel, whose precious worth our adversaries do not always properly value. Defeated in their encounter on the field of the Scriptures, they retreat into the byways of infidelity—into the haunts of sense, and the dark rocks of solitary reason. Conquered by the sword of the Spirit, they grasp the dagger of the impious. Abandoning Saints Matthew, Mark, Luke, John, and Paul, they appeal to Hobbes, Paine, Voltaire, Diderot, Rousseau, Bretscheider, and Wegschneider, for weapons of attack against the Church, and her doctrine of the Real Presence.

Boasting no longer of the Bible as their only guide to faith, they set up reason and the senses as the sole judges competent to decide the question of the Eucharist, and with greater pomp of speech than show of reason, they object to our doctrine as follows:

"The phenomenal only can lead us to the knowledge of the real; but the phenomena of the Eucharist present only bread and wine; therefore, the Eucharist contains but bread and wine."

Stripping the objection of all the accoutrements of language, they mean to say: "Nothing is true to us but what we know by the aid of the senses; but by the aid of the senses, we discover in the Eucharist only bread and wine; therefore, in truth, there are but bread and wine in the Eucharist."

If our adversaries are really convinced of the truth of the principle laid down in the above premises, then I fear that logic will lead them further than they imagine or wish.

Is it true, that we are not capable of coming to the knowledge of truth save by the aid of our bodily senses; that is to say, unless we see, hear, taste, touch, or smell, the objects of our knowledge? If so, my friends, then you must deny not only the doctrine of the Real Presence, but the very first and fundamental doctrines of Christianity itself; then you must not only borrow arguments from, but take side with the infidel against the Christian religion and its doctrines. Are you a Trinitarian, that is, do you believe in one God and three persons? By the aid of which of your five bodily senses have you come to know that mystery? Have you ever seen, heard, tasted, smelled, or touched the triune nature of the Deity? If not, then, according to your own showing, you must deny the Trinity and become a Deist. Do you believe in the Divinity of Jesus Christ? Have you ever seen, heard, tasted, smelled, or touched the mystery of His incarnation? If not, then renounce His Divinity, and take your stand on the platform of the Socinian. Do you believe in baptism as the sacrament of regeneration, by which, from children of wrath, we become the children of God,—by which we pass from the state of sin to that of righteousness? Has any one of your senses penetrated the mystery of that regeneration? Not your eyes, for they saw at most the effusion of a certain quantity of water upon the body, and not the interior cleansing or purification of the soul from sin. Much less did you discover that mystery by any one of the other bodily senses. You are bound to go further still, in virtue of your principle. Have you ever seen

God? Have you ever heard Him, tasted Him, smelled Him, touched Him? If not, then farewell not only to Christianity, but to Deism, and profess yourself, at once, an Atheist. Hail infidelity, with all its fearful consequences for time and for eternity!

When or where did Christ teach that our senses are to be the guides to our faith? Did He not rebuke Thomas Didymus, because he made those senses the conditions of his faith in the resurrection? "Except I shall *see* in His hands the print of the nails, and *put my finger* into the place of the nails, and *put my hand* into His side, I will not believe." (Jo. xx. 25.) And when our Saviour had allowed him the privilege of seeing and touching the prints of the nails and the wound of the side, what does He add: "Because thou hast seen Me, Thomas, thou hast believed: *blessed are they that have not seen, and have believed.*" (Ibid. 29.)

Our friends confound faith with knowledge. We are not asked to know, either in virtue of the testimony of our senses, or the intuitions or argumentative processes of reason, the nature of any mystery or doctrine of religion; but we are commanded to receive their truth upon the unerring testimony of the God-man, who can neither be deceived Himself, nor deceive us. The mysteries of faith are to be believed by us not on the evidence of the senses or of reason, but on the evidence of the fact of their revelation. We must not ask, "Can I see?" or even "Can I understand what I am asked to believe?" but, "*is it revealed?*" It is a fact that Jesus Christ has taught those mysteries. When I have convinced myself of that fact, I follow the example of St. Peter: I bow my stubborn neck under the sweet yoke of faith, and I exclaim: "Lord, I believe: for to whom shall we go if not to Thee, who hast the words of eternal life?"

"But my senses are deceived in this mystery. I see, taste, and touch only bread and wine; and I am made to believe that there is neither bread nor wine, but the body and blood of Christ."

Suppose, for argument's sake, that your senses are deceived. It would not be the first, nor probably the last time in your life and experience. Are there no instances in which the bare testimony of your senses must be corrected by the dictates of your reason, enlightened by science? When you judge that the oar of the boatman is not bent, as it appears to be, under the water, do you rely for your judgment on the testimony of your sight only? Witnessing the setting of the sun, you would say that the king of day descends in a line with your eyes, while philosophy teaches you that he has sunk already several degrees below the horizon.

Instances of the deception of the senses are numerous in the Scriptures. When Abraham entertained the three angels in the Vale of Mambre, and gave them to eat, were not his eyes deceived concerning their real nature? (Gen. xviii.) When Jacob wrestled with the angel who touched the sinew of his thigh, were not both his sight and touch deceived concerning the real substance of the spirit? (Gen. xxxii.) When, in the field of the city of Jericho, Josue saw a man standing over against him with a drawn sword, was he to believe the testimony of his eyes only, and refuse to believe that it was an angel? How, guided by his senses of sight or hearing only, could he fall on his face to the ground, and worshipping say: "What saith my Lord to his servant?" (Josue, v. 13, 15). Were the Jews excusable for not believing in the divinity of Jesus Christ, when their senses reported Him only as the carpenter's son, the son of Joseph and Mary? Were not the eyes of the disciples bound, so that they should not know Jesus, when they were going to Emmaus? Did their ears perceive by the sound of His voice that it was He, while "He expounded to them, in all the scriptures, the things that were concerning Him?" (Luke, xxiv. 27.) Did not Mary Magdalene see Jesus standing at the sepulchre, and yet knew not that it was Jesus, but believed Him to be the gardener? (Jo. xx. 15.)

In all these instances the manner of appearing was evidently different from His usual, His natural way, so that, till He resumed His natural appearance, voice, etc., they did not recognize Him by the aid of their senses. And yet during all that time, He was substantially the same Jesus, who walked among them, who spoke to them, on other occasions. You are all acquainted with the Saviour's transfiguration on mount Thabor. Suppose that the Apostles Peter, John, and James, had not accompanied their Master on that occasion, but, without any previous knowledge of His presence, had come to the mountain, while His garments were white like snow, and His countenance shone like the sun; is it probable that they would have recognized Him? And yet, if they had been told then to make an act of faith in the reality of His presence on the mountain, could they have refused to do so with impunity, merely because their eyes did not see Jesus in His usual natural form? Why, then, should you or I refuse to believe Him really present, under the appearances of bread and wine, when we are plainly told by Him that He is really and truly present under the accidents or appearances of bread and wine? Is not Jesus now seated at the right hand of His Heavenly Father—the same Jesus who was born of the Virgin, and died upon the cross? Are you not bound to believe this truth as an article of the Christian faith? Yet, every one of your bodily senses fails to prove it—faith, in this case, as in the case of the real presence in the sacrament, supplies the defect of the senses.

But you tell me, human reason cannot understand how it is possible, that bread and wine should be changed into the body and blood of Jesus. Do you mean to say, that we are to believe only what reason can comprehend and fathom? Then, why do you believe any mystery of religion at all? Can your reason understand *how* there are three distinct persons, Father, Son, and Holy Ghost, in one and the same undivided and indivisible Godhead; so that the Father is not the Son, nor the Son the Holy Ghost, nor the Holy Ghost the Father or the Son, and yet all three are God, and have one and the same identical essence? Is it more easy for reason, to understand, *how* God drew all existing substances out of nothing, than how He changes one substance into another? Can you explain the miraculous change of water into wine, at the feast of Cana in Galilee, more clearly and definitely than the change of bread into flesh, or wine into blood? How do you account for the mystery of the incarnation, of the union of two distinct natures and wills, in one and the same hypostasis, or person? How do you account for the action of justifying grace in the human soul; yea more, how do you account for the actions of the soul on the human body? Are not all these secrets, which it is not given to the human mind to discover? And indeed, where would be the merit of our faith, if we could fathom all its objects, by the aid, either of our bodily senses, or the faculties of our mind? We should no longer believe, but know; and knowledge, as such, was never required unto salvation; but faith, which, as the Apostle says, is "the substance of things to be hoped for; the evidence of things that appear not." (Heb. xi. 1.)

Our separated brethren forget that, in their anxiety to refute the doctrine of the Real Presence, they furnish their own coreligionists with weapons which, like a two-edged sword, cut both ways, and prove as fatal in causing them to reject all other mysteries of faith, as to reject the Real Presence. We acknowledge that the testimony of the senses, applied to their proper objects, in a proper way, is an infallible criterion of truth; and that reason, within her sphere, can decide with infallible certitude, upon all truths that belong to that sphere; but we deny that either of them was intended as the infallible criterion or judge of all truth. There are many things in Heaven and on earth, which man has not dreamed of in his philosophy; many, with the nature, the manner of which, he will never be acquainted, until the veil is withdrawn; until faith is changed into vision.

Nor are our senses, properly speaking, deceived in relation to the Real Presence. The senses of men are the organs of their rational soul, and receive those impressions only, of which, by their nature, they are capable. The eye sees the shape, color, form; the taste relishes the sweetness, etc., of the bread and wine; and they convey those impressions to the mind. Ordinarily speaking, the mind would thence infer that the sensations received from the external qualities, must lead her to judge the substances to be bread and wine; but instructed by faith, she corrects her judgment, and pronounces them, what they really are, the body and blood of Christ. Thus both have done their naturally appointed duty; the senses have reported the outward appearances, and outward qualities of the substance, and the mind yielding to the higher authority of faith, has pronounced the substance flesh and blood.

It would be ridiculous to argue from the exception to a general conclusion, as some of our adversaries do: If this is so, they tell us, with regard to the Eucharist, then we can *never* trust our senses nor our reason. You might as well say, that if you believe that Christ raised Lazarus from the dead, all the dead will rise from their graves and repeople the earth. Exceptions do not destroy, but strengthen the general rule, by the very contrast which they present.

Equally impertinent is the question, "How can the body of Christ be present in so small a space as is occupied by a wafer, and in so many different wafers, at the same time?"

Natural philosophers might answer you, that all the matter contained in the universe might be reduced to an indefinitely smaller space, and according to Newton, to no more than a cubic inch; but we forbear recurring to the known laws of matter, to prove a mystery, for the truth of which the word of God alone is and ought to be sufficient evidence. When we speak of the Real Presence of the body and blood of Jesus Christ, under the sacramental veil of bread and wine, we speak not of a natural, but a miraculous, a preternatural presence, with which the laws of nature have, simply, nothing to do. The physical impossibility cannot certainly be greater than would be the moral impossibility, that Jesus Christ should tell a lie, as He most evidently did, if we are to take His words to mean what they plainly signify to the mind. Nor is it necessary to allege the authority of certain modern writers, such as Robert Dale Owen, and others, to prove that bilocation, or the presence of the same individual in two places, at the same time, is not only possible, but is proved to have been a fact; suffice it to say, that the state and conditions of a spiritualized, or glorified body, such as Christ's is after His resurrection, cannot be adequately judged of by the knowledge we have of the conditions of a body in its natural state. Certain it is, as every Bible reader admits, that the same Jesus, who remains for ever seated at the right hand of His Father, appeared, at the same time, to St. Paul, on the road to Damascus, and stood by him, in the castle of Jerusalem. (Acts, ix. 17; xxiii. 11.) What has happened before, is not impossible now, and may happen in the same or another form, again.

"But, to say the least, you do not carry out the whole doctrine of the Real Presence, as propounded by its divine Author, and you shamefully wrong the people, by withholding from them the cup—administering the sacrament under the appearance of bread only."

To this we answer, that, when the Saviour instituted this wonderful sacrament, none but His Apostles were present at the Supper, and none but they received the Holy Communion. It is true, they received under both species, and were ordered to receive under both species. But this was natural and reasonable. For, by the words which He subjoined to the formula of consecration: "Do this for a commemoration of Me" (Luke, xxii. 19), He made them priests for ever, according to the order of Melchisedec, and commanded them to offer the same unbloody sacrifice, in the same manner, in which they had seen Him offer. As priests, and therefore, as sacrificators, it was necessary that their sacrificial act should show the nature of real sacrifice. Now, sacrifice is defined to be the offering of a sensible thing, which, with mystic rites, is consecrated, and changed, by a lawful minister, and made to God alone, thereby to acknowledge His supreme dominion over all things. Hence, to represent, in this commemorative sacrifice, the real and bloody immolation of Jesus upon the cross, it was meet, that by a separate consecration and reception of the species of bread and wine, the real separation which had preceded, should be reproduced by the priest of Christ. Not so with the faithful. For, since the resurrection of Christ, His body, is impassible, and His blood can no longer be *really* separated from His flesh, so that, wherever His flesh is, there, also, is His blood; and *vice versa*, wherever His blood is, there also is His flesh. Hence, whoever receives either species, receives as much as he who receives both; and no wrong is done the laity, by refusing them the cup, or the species of wine. A familiar comparison may help to illustrate this doctrine. Suppose a mother distributes a certain quantity of bread and wine to her children. To one of them she gives it in a cup; to the other, in bread soaked in wine. Would the latter have a reasonable complaint against the mother on the supposition that the same quantity was not given to both? The comparison needs no application. He that receives the blood in the flesh, receives as much as he who would receive it apart from the flesh, and neither could possibly complain of wrong, or injustice.

Our divine Saviour promised, indeed, that He would give us His flesh to eat, and his blood to drink; but He did not determine the manner in which He would do so. Hence, the same Jesus who said: "unless you eat the flesh of the Son of Man and drink His blood, you shall not have life in you" (John vi. 54), also said: "he that shall eat of this bread, he shall live for ever." (Ibid. 59.) And He that said, "whoso eateth My flesh, and drinketh My blood, hath everlasting life," also said: "the bread which I will give is My flesh, for the life of the world." Finally, He that said: "he who eateth My flesh, and drinketh My blood, abideth in Me, and I in him," also said: "he that eateth Me, the same also shall live by Me." (*Vide* John, vi., *passim*.) And the Apostle St. Paul writes (according to the Greek version, which our separated brethren have corrupted in their English translation), "Whosoever shall eat this bread, *or* drink the chalice of the Lord unworthily, shall be guilty of the body and the blood of the Lord."

In the Acts of the Apostles, chapter ii., 42, we read that they "were persevering in the doctrine of the Apostles, and in the communication of the breaking of bread and prayer,"—and in chapter xx., 7, "And on the first day of the week, when the disciples came together to break bread" . . .

Yea, our Saviour Himself broke bread only in the castle of Emmaus, when seated at table, before His two disciples. (Luke, xxiv. 30, 31.) This much must be conceded, that, in none of these instances the cup is mentioned.

Luther himself reproaches his disciple Carlstadt, for having introduced the practice of *communicating under both kinds*. (Epist. ad Gasp. Gustol.) And, on another occasion (says Dr. Milner), he writes: "If a council did ordain or permit both kinds, in spite of the council, we would take but *one*, or take neither, and curse those who should take both." (Form. Miss. tom. ii., p. 384–386, apud Milner.)

The same Reformer writes (Epist. ad Boh.): "Although it may be well to use both kinds in the sacrament, yet Christ has commanded nothing on the subject." And again: "They sin not, who use but one kind, Christ having left this to the choice of each one." (Capt. Bab.)

Several Anglican bishops, such as Montague, Forbes, White, and others, held the doctrine that it was not essential to the sacrament to receive under both kinds.

The Calvinists of France, in their synod at Poitiers, in 1560, decreed thus: " The *bread* of our Lord's Supper ought to be administered to *those who cannot drink wine*, on their making a protestation that they do not refrain through contempt." (On the Lord's Supper, c. iii., p. 7., ibid.)

Lastly, by separate acts of that Parliament, and that king, who established the Protestant religion in England, and, by name, communion in both kinds, it is provided that the latter should only be *commonly so delivered and ministered*, and an exception is made, in case necessity did otherwise require. (Burnet's Hist. of Reform. v. ii., p. 41; Heylin, Hist. of Reform., p. 58.) It is clear, therefore, that our separated brethren did not always believe that communion under both kinds is an essential part of the sacrament.

There are natural reasons also, which must induce every sensible man to believe it not essential.

First, Christ knew that it would, in many

instances, be very difficult to obtain as much wine as would be necessary for distribution. There are countries, where the culture of the grape is impossible, and whither, for want of easy access, especially in days gone by, commerce would scarcely venture with this article.

Secondly, This species is more exposed than bread, to the influences of the atmosphere, and, therefore, less easily preserved in that condition which is necessary for the respect due to this sublime mystery.

Thirdly, It is more exposed to the wilful or involuntary irreverence of the receiver. It is more apt to spill, than bread is to crumble, or fall to the ground.

Fourthly, It is more difficult to carry it to sick persons.

Fifthly, There are not a few who are by nature so averse to wine, that they cannot possibly receive it.

Finally, The Church, which, from the beginning, taught the nature of this sacrament, must certainly also have known the manner of its reception. Now, her teaching and her practice are such, as clearly to prove that she never looked upon communion under both kinds, as essential to the sacrament, but merely as a matter of discipline, which might vary in local

Churches, and in different times and circumstances. Her ecclesiastical historians tell us that, to the sick, she administered the sacrament under the species of bread only, as in the case of the venerable old man Serapion, who, according to Eusebius (Hist. Eccl., c. 44), received from the hands of the priest the sacred food under the species of bread only.

We are told the same by St. Paulinus, of St. Ambrose.

We know likewise from history, that holy communion was administered, during a certain period of the Church, to infants newly baptized, and they received the species of wine only.

In the days of persecution, when it was death to assemble for the purpose of celebrating the divine mysteries, the faithful were permitted to carry with them the blessed sacrament to their houses. But the historians of the time observe, that they carried with them the species of bread only. So did the hermits and monks in the desert receive under one species only, whenever the communion was brought to them from a distance.

"But is it not unworthy the majesty of the God-man to lie concealed under the appearances of bread and wine; to be exposed to the neglect and contempt, railleries and insults of men; yea, to see himself trodden under foot, stabbed with dirks, and profaned by the very animals themselves!"

These sentiments of seeming respect for the dignity and sublimity of Christ's human nature would almost cause us to applaud the authors of them, were it not that they fall from lips which are the first to insult and sneer at that dignity in the sacrament. To draw an argument against the Real Presence from the possible indignities to which it may be exposed, is to assail the reality of the Incarnation and Redemption itself. Was it not unworthy the majesty of a God to *debase* Himself to the lowliness of a slave; to hide both his Divinity and Humanity, during nine long months, in a Virgin's womb; to be born in a stable; to be insulted by Scribe and Pharisee; to be scourged, crowned with thorns, to be nailed to an ignominious cross? Was it not possible, that the blood which He shed, at the pillar, or along the way to Calvary; that the flesh which was torn piece-meal from His limbs, should be trampled under the feet of His impious persecutors, or even lapped up by the tongue of vile animals? Did He on that account interrupt the course of His cruel sufferings? Ah, no! When he loved His own, He loved them till the end. So far from deeming these indignities unworthy of His nature, He foretold them in detail by His prophets, and loved to speak of them to His Apostles. What greater outrage could He receive in His very sacrament, than He received from one of His own disciples, who, at the very moment that he partook of the sacred species from the hands of His Master, was planning the means of betraying Him into the hands of His cruel enemies?

Finally, our adversaries charge us with idolatry in worshipping and adoring a wafer, as they contemptuously call the Blessed Sacrament.

To this Protestant objection let a Protestant answer. Jeremy Taylor, of the Anglican Church, writes as follows: " Idolatry is a forsaking of the true God, and giving divine worship to a creature, or to an idol, that is, to an imaginary God, who had no foundation in essence, or existence, and this is that kind of superstition, which by divines is called the superstition of an undue object. Now, it is evident that the object of the Catholic's adoration (that which is represented to them in their minds, their thoughts, their purposes and by which God principally, if not solely, takes estimate of human actions), in the Blessed

Sacrament, is the only True and Eternal God, hypostatically joined with His Holy Humanity, which humanity they believe actually present under the veil of sacramental signs; and if they thought Him not present, they are so far from worshipping the bread in that case, that they themselves profess it idolatry to do so, which is a demonstration that their soul hath nothing in it that is idolatrical." (Liberty of Prophesying, sect. 20, N. 16.) Our separated brethren, in their objection, forget the real nature of our doctrine. They forget that by the words of consecration we believe the substance of the bread and wine to be changed into the real body and blood of Jesus Christ, which, united—as these to His Soul and Divinity—form the sole object of their worship and adoration. Is it idolatry to adore Jesus Christ, true God and true man?

Nor is it an objection, that He is hidden under the sacramental veils, for was not Jesus as worthy of worship during the nine months that He lay hidden in the Virgin's womb, as He was when lying in the manger? Was He less worthy of adoration when the cloud took Him out of the disciples' view, than when He walked with them to the mountain of Olivet?

Moreover, this charge of idolatry implies

more than our objectors intend to express. If the adoration of the Blessed Sacrament is really an act of idolatry, then has the Church of Christ been idolatrous from the very days of the Apostles, and "Christ has dealt with His Church in a manner very unbecoming His goodness, which was to leave her, for fifteen hundred years together, in such an error and idolatry, and that occasioned by His own words, as was never seen nor heard of in the world." (Coster's Discourse.)

Can you believe that the Son of God should have come on earth only to exchange one error for another, one kind of idolatry for another? It is blasphemy to entertain the thought.

After all that has been said, our separated brethren may now, perhaps, understand what before seemed to them unintelligible, if not ridiculous. First of all, the difference between our, and their own public worship. When a Catholic enters any one of our churches, he has scarcely passed the threshold, ere the eye of his faith directs the eyes of his body to the altar, and the tabernacle, in which his Lord and Master dwells. His first act is a genuflection, by which he adores his Lord and God. On entering his pew, he does not immediately seat himself and glance from worshipper to worshipper, to discover which of his friends or acquaintances have come to church; much less to discover the peculiar fashions which make their appearance on the occasion, but devoutly kneeling, he continues to adore the sole object of his love. Hence the profound stillness, interrupted only by the solemn chant of the priest or choir, during the celebration of the tremendous mysteries. Hence the pomp and grandeur of the liturgical rites, the richness of the sacerdotal robes, the splendor of gold, the beauty of precious stones, the fragrance of flowers and of incense.

Hence the celibacy of our clergy. Do you see that manly, noble, reverential form which stands at the foot of the altar, dressed in all the splendor of sacerdotal apparel? He is the son of a merchant-prince, the heir of millions. Scarcely had he finished his academic course, when, one bright morning, in anguish, he remained, after mass was over, kneeling in his pew, as if wrapped in ecstasy, and burning with charity. "Dear, sweet Jesus," whispered the youth, "Thou hast given me a heart to love. I feel the genial warmth of its flame. But, oh! the objects that surround me, in the world, and which would gain my heart, are loathing and disgusting to me. I cannot love flesh which is doomed to undergo the process of corruption; I cannot cherish blood which boils with the heat of unhallowed concupiscence. And yet, my youthful heart loves and yearns to love. But it would love Thee alone. Sweet Jesus, oh, that Thou wouldst allow me to espouse Thee, as the only object worthy of my love! Would that I might satisfy my desire, by daily standing at Thy altar, there to become united, in that most pure, chaste, and intimate manner, in which flesh can become united with flesh and blood with blood; grant me to minister within Thy sanctuary—make me, sweet Jesus, the dispenser of Thy mysteries, make me Thy priest forever, according to the order of Melchisedec." His prayer is heard, his vow is recorded in Heaven. Jesus has espoused the noble youth as His own forever. No, the love of Jesus in this sacrament cannot allow the blending of the profane, carnal, with His holy, virginal love, in the ministers of this august, this thrice Holy Sacrament.

It is at the foot of the blessed Sacrament that our young maidens learned to devote themselves, by the most solemn and binding vows of chastity, poverty, and obedience, to the service and imitation of their beloved Spouse. What has taught that beautiful, uni versally loved, and admired daughter of a Senator to go and shut herself up within the narrow confines of a convent-cell, to breathe away the fragrance of her youth in solitary contemplation and prayer! Desolate, afflicted mother, what brought that sister of charity by your side, at the moment your noble, patriotic boy, was pressing his farewell kisses on your tearful cheeks—what was it made her say, in her own gentle way: "Be comforted, weeping mother—behold, here am I to act a mother's part. I shall follow your noble boy to the field of battle; I too shall be found upon the hard-contested field. And should a fatal bullet be sped from hostile gun, into his patriotic heart, I shall be there to extract the deadly missile, or close his dimming eyes in death. Under the open heavens—in the fetid atmosphere of the hospital—whatever fate betide him, I shall be there to wipe away his tears, to staunch his bleeding wounds, or prepare his soul for Heaven." Where has she learned this heroic fortitude—this spirit of sacrifice? At the foot of her convent-altar—at the holy table where her soul fed so often on the bread of strength, on the wine of virgins. Far away from that altar, exposed to danger, with only a blanket to wrap around her weary frame,—like the soldier, on half rations—she regrets not the simple, yet soothing, comforts of home. The only loss she feels, is the absence of the daily sacrifice, and the frequent communions to which she was accustomed in her convent home.

Tell me, what inspired the master-mind of that architect, who raised yonder lofty temple to the name and glory of the God of Hosts? Who taught him to fling those vaulted arches, as if in rivalry with the Architect of the Universe, aloft in air? Whence did he learn to flute and hoist those towering columns, to crown them with their rich and varied foliage, in speaking stone and marble? From Him, who, however concealed, is to be present in the magnificent sanctuary of that temple, and to make it His dwelling-place among the children of men.

Tell me, thou thousand-tongued organ, and ye thousand chorists, who blend your varied voices in perfect harmony with that instrument of magic sounds, who trained your author's and master's mind to this strange soul-ravishing melody? Who taught your Mozarts, your Haydns, your Cherubinis, your Le Sueurs, and your Lambillottes, the secret of their wondrous art? He who, although mute and silent in His earthy temple, sent the musical winds upon their noisy tour—who caused the stars to sing together—who filled the pine forest with the dirge-like notes of the plaintive winds—who caused the zephyrs to whisper to the flowers, and the rivulets to murmur to the rocks—who blent with all, as in a mighty fugue, the roar of the cataract, and the peal of the thunder!

To conclude: Who can tell all that our separated brethren have lost in losing the Real Presence? The food of their hungry souls—the drink of their thirsting hearts—their real comfort in affliction—their light in darkness—their counsellor in doubt—their strength in weakness—their shield and armor of defence, in danger—their hope in despondency—their life in death—their Jesus—their all. Oh! that they, like ourselves, could take once more this bread from Heaven—and know how sweet is the Lord; and having been their delight during life, oh! might it prove to them the sure pledge of everlasting life in Heaven!

VIII.

HONOR AND INVOCATION OF SAINTS, VENERATION OF IMAGES AND RELICS.

"Render, therefore, to all their dues; tribute, to whom tribute is due: custom to whom custom: fear to whom fear: honor to whom honor." Rom. xiii. 7.

Why do we honor the saints? To answer this question, we must first reply to another. What are saints? Saints are the spirits of the departed, who reign with Christ in glory. Are there any such? Who can doubt it? If our separated brethren should doubt this fact, then, according to their principles, all those who die go to hell. For, according to them, there are but two places whither the spirits of the departed can go, after death,—Heaven and Hell. If none go to Heaven, then all go to Hell. This they will not and do not say. Hence they believe with us, that there are saints: for nothing that is defiled can enter Heaven, and those who are not defiled with any sin or remnant of sin, are just, righteous, holy,—saints.

Now the question is, should we honor these saints? Who dares deny it? Are we not bound to honor the just and holy ones of earth? Is not the child bound to honor its parents? Does not the Apostle write to the Romans: "Loving one another with brotherly love; in honor preventing one another?" (Rom. xii. 10.) But this honor which is due to others, is due mainly to their spirit, and terminates on the spirit rather than the body of those we honor. Thus we honor dignity, superiority, genius, talent, virtue,—all of which are qualities of, or referred to, the soul of man. Why then should we cease to honor those same spirits when they have departed this life, and entered upon the joys of life eternal? Does difference of situation, of place, take away the obligation, or, at least, the permission? On what principle?

Moreover, why should we not be allowed to do what God Himself does? God honored His friends exceedingly, and never more, than when He translates them from this valley of tears to His own beautiful Paradise. Why should we be bound to honor our parents, for instance, while they are with us in the flesh, and be obliged to cease honoring them, when as we hope, they are with God in Heaven? On what ground have they lost their right and we the privilege, if not the obligation?

"But you, Catholics, do more than honor them. You invoke them; you pray to them."

So we do, and should we not? Are we allowed to ask one another's prayers here below? Is a son allowed to say to his Christian father: Father, please pray for me? Is a daughter allowed to ask her mother's prayers? May a member of any sect go to his minister, and beg of him to pray to God in his behalf? You answer: "Most undoubtedly, and good Christians do so." Well, then, suppose that father, mother, minister die, and go to Heaven, why could you no longer ask them the same thing? Surely, the difference is not in the principle, but only in the circumstance of location. You tell me that if the saints could pray for us, they would interfere with the Mediatorship of Jesus Christ, of whom St. Paul writes: "For there is one God, and one Mediator of God and men; the man Christ Jesus." (1 Tim. ii. 5.) But pray, why then do you ask your father, mother, and minister to intercede for you, while they and you are living? Is the nature of their petition different, in principle, while they are living, from that which they address to God when they are dead? If their intercession interferes not with the only Mediatorship and advocacy of Jesus with the Father, while they are sinful sojourners in this vale of tears, why should it interfere in Heaven? Study the case in its true light. There you are—here is your minister,—yonder in Heaven is Jesus Christ, seated at the right hand of His Father. You say to your minister: "Reverend sir, please pray to God for me that I may be a true, a pious Christian." Your minister accepts your request. Standing between you and your Heavenly Father, he presents your petition to the throne of grace, and, as you hope, his prayer in your behalf is heard. Has he interfered with the only Mediatorship of Jesus Christ? If not, then take the other view of the case. The minister is now dead, and say that he is in Heaven. You are still on earth, and, addressing yourself to his departed spirit, you make to him the same petition. Where is the difference in the principle? If he could pray for you, while you were both on earth, without interfering with the sole Mediatorship of Christ, why can he not do so yet, now that his spirit is in Heaven?

"True," you say, "but the case, however, is different. My father, mother, and minister, while on earth, can hear me, but I have no certainty that they can hear me, when they are in Heaven. For, in order to hear those who pray to them on earth, they should, like God, be present everywhere, and that would be absurd to suppose."

So then, you shift the ground of your objection from the principle which you said was involved in it, to extrinsic circumstances, which have, properly speaking, not the slightest connection with the principle? For it is one question, to ask how the saints can hear us pray, and quite another, to ask whether we are allowed to pray to the saints, and they for us. Before we answer this new difficulty, you must indulge us in a further explanation of the principle itself.

Our separated brethren do not distinguish a twofold mediatorship, which, however, really exists. There is a mediatorship of redemption and salvation which belongs to Christ alone, and cannot possibly be shared by angel or saint. It is on this account that the Apostle St. Paul immediately subjoins to the words already cited,- "There is one God, and one Mediator of God and men, the man Christ Jesus, who gave Himself *a redemption* for all." Christ is our only Redeemer, and our only Mediator of redemption and salvation.

But besides the mediatorship of redemption and salvation, there is another of prayer or intercession, which belongs to all just men on earth, and the Angels and Saints in Heaven, in virtue of which it is allowed them to offer up their prayers to God for men, as the Council of Trent expresses it; and consequently "it is good and useful, suppliantly to invoke them, and to have recourse to their *prayers*, help and assistance, to obtain favors from God, *through His Son Jesus Christ, who is alone our Redeemer and Saviour.*" (Conc. Tr., sess. 25, De Invoc.)

Nor can we see how the prayers of the saints interfere with, or are injurious to the mediatorship of Jesus Christ. If we believed that the saints have any virtue or power of their own, apart from that of Jesus Christ, in granting us what we petition for, then the objection would stand. But we do not believe so. We believe that Jesus alone is the Giver of all good gifts, and that all the saints can do, is to ask Him for those which we request them to ask for. Yea, it seems to us that, in so doing, we doubly honor the Mediatorship of the Saviour. For, besides our own acknowledgment, we employ the Saint to profess, by His petition to the throne of grace, that Jesus is our only Mediator and Redeemer, that He alone can give what we asked.

Suppose that you desired to obtain a certain

situation in the service of the government, which, it is in the power of the president alone to give; but that, in order to obtain it, instead of applying personally and directly to the president, you call upon a friend of yours, who is likewise the friend of the president, and you beg that mutual friend to intercede for you. Do you underrate the power, or even the goodness of the president, in employing that friend as intercessor? By no means. Rather you pay double honor to that power and its possessor. First, you acknowledge that the benefit you seek for can be bestowed by the president only, and you cause your friend to own it with you, when he shall lay your petition at his feet. The case is perfectly similar with regard to prayers addressed to the saints and by the saints to God.

That the saints do pray for us is evinced from the Apocalypse (ch. v. 8), where we read: "The four and twenty ancients fell down before the Lamb, having every one of them harps, and golden vials full of odors, which are the prayers of the saints." And (ch. viii. 4): "The smoke of the incense of the prayers of the Saints ascended up before God, from the hand of the Angel."

Judas Machabeus, relating a certain vision

with which he was favored, says: "Now, the vision was in this manner: Onias, who had been highpriest . . . holding up his hands, prayed for all the people of the Jews . . . And after this there appeared also another man . . . and Onias, answering, said . . . This is he that prayeth much for the people, and for all the holy city, Jeremias the prophet of God." (2 Machab. xv. 12, 14.) And why should they not? If Dives could call upon Abraham from the depth of hell in behalf of his brethren, why should not the Saints of Heaven be allowed to call upon their Lord in behalf of their clients? Again, if the Angels of Heaven enjoy that privilege as is evident from Zacharias (i. 12), where the prophet heard an Angel praying for Jerusalem and the cities of Juda, saying: "O Lord of hosts, how long wilt thou not have mercy on Jerusalem, and on the cities of Judah, with which thou hast been angry," why should it not be a privilege shared by the spirits of the departed just, to do the same for their brethren in the flesh? The more so that we are told by our Saviour, that such spirits shall be like the Angels of God, not in nature surely, for the nature of a human spirit will never be changed into the angelic, but in some, if not all their qualities and privileges. And, indeed, reason enlightened by faith, cannot refuse to accept this doctrine. Is not Heaven the possession and fruition of all real happiness, to its inhabitants. And is it not a pure, unalloyed happiness, without any mixture of imperfection here on earth, for a mother to pray for her child, a friend to petition for a friend, and to know that these prayers are acceptable to God, and wholesome to those who are prayed for? Is that mother's spirit to be deprived of that pure happiness immediately on her entrance into the Paradise of bliss?

Furthermore, are we not told that while faith and hope shall be absorbed in vision and fruition (1 Cor. xiii. 8, 13), charity, which is greater than these, never falleth away? Has not that charity a twofold phase or aspect here below? Is not the second commandment: "Thou shalt love thy neighbor as thyself," equal to the first: "Thou shalt love the Lord thy God with thy whole heart, and with thy whole soul, and with thy whole mind?" (Matt. xxii. 37, 39.) And is not charity proved by works, is it not kind? (1 Cor. xiii. 4.) How could the Saint prove his charity, if not by praying for those whom he was bound to love here on earth; or those who call upon him for help and assistance? Nay, since charity is perfect in Heaven, its works must prove that greater perfection by an increase of interest in our behalf.

Add to this that death, though it severs the bonds of the flesh, does not sever those of the spirit. Here upon earth these saints were united to us in a holy fellowship of good works and prayers. They were members of the same mystical body of Christ, His Church, of which He is, and will continue to be, the invisible head; and is it not natural that these members should be "mutually careful one for another?" And that "the comely parts," which "have no need," should endeavour to procure for those that want a "more abundant honor?" (1 Cor. xii. 23, 24, 25, 27.) Their change of state and place has not changed their fellowship with us. Otherwise, why do the creeds of nearly all religions profess a "Communion of Saints?" Does that communion exist on earth only, or rather are not its golden links drawn closer when sanctity is crowned with its eternal reward in Heaven? Has the laureled martyr no sympathy with the struggling combatant? Does the triumphant confessor feel no longer any interest in the still imprisoned soldier of the Cross? Hath the lily-crowned virgin, who is admitted to the nuptials of the bridegroom, no fellow-feeling for them that stand still knocking at the door of the banquet hall?

We now proceed to the objection, that these Saints cannot hear us.

The objection supposes something which is absurd, namely, that there is in Heaven no other than physical hearing. If it does really suppose that, then, how can God hear our prayers? For we have always supposed that God has no material body, and consequently no physical hearing.

How do the Angels hear us? Not with any bodily ears, and yet we are taught that they are acquainted with the concerns of mortals here below.

It is certain, that they knew the persons and individuals to whom they were sent. The angels that visited Abraham, Lot, Jacob, Josue, Daniel, Tobias, Mary, Joseph, and St. Peter, doubtless knew how to distinguish those individuals and their necessities from other persons and individuals. Moreover, every guardian angel must needs know his client, and it is a general belief, grounded on the Scriptures, that every man that cometh into this world, has a heavenly spirit appointed him as his inseparable companion and protector.

The only question at issue, then, is whether the saints, like the angels, can become acquainted with the fact that we address our prayers to them, and crave their intercession.

Did not Almighty God communicate, at times, to His friends on earth, a degree of knowledge which, naturally speaking, they could not have nor acquire? What was the knowledge of prophecy? Could they lift the veil from futurity and peer into the events of years to come, without a miraculously infused communication from Heaven? Was Eliseus present when he saw the ambush prepared for the king of Israel? (4 Kings, vi. 9.) Why, then, cannot God manifest to His friends in Heaven the wishes of their friends on earth?

Besides, we are told by our Saviour, that there is joy before the angels of God upon one sinner that doeth penance (Luke, xv. 10.); and that the departed in Heaven shall be like unto the angels of God: why then should not the latter be able to know what occurs on earth as well as the former? We are told by the Apostle St. Paul (1 Cor. iv. 9), speaking of himself and his fellow Apostles: "We are made a spectacle to the world, and to *angels*, and to men." How are they a spectacle, if the angels do not see or know them, and what concerns them? In like manner, how would the departed be like to the angels, if they shared not this privilege with the angels?

How do the souls of "them that were slain for the word of God, and for the testimony which they held," cry out with a loud voice: "How long, O Lord (holy and true), dost thou not judge and revenge our blood on them that dwell *on the earth*" (Apoc. vi. 9, 10), if they were not conscious of the fact that their persecutors remained still unpunished? And if they were made acquainted with the fact, why not with our prayers? If to him that shall overcome and keep Christ's words unto the end (that evidently means death), He will give power over the nations, "and he shall rule them with a rod of iron; and as the vessel of the potter they shall be broken, even as I have received from my Father" (Apoc. ii. 26–28); doubtless he must know the nations and the punishments which they deserve; and if such power is given them for inflicting punishment, why should not power be given them to benefit those who call upon them?

Are we to question the power of God in this matter? Does it exceed the limits of His omnipotence, or is it derogatory to any of His attributes, to communicate such knowledge to His friends?

Is there no happiness in the study of nature and man? Why, then, does the astronomer watch through weary nights the course of the stars? Why does the geologist undertake such painful and dangerous journeys to become acquainted with the structure of the earth; why does the psychologist task his brain with the difficult process of analyzing the nature of the human soul? And why may it not enter into the ways of God to reward His faithful servants in His Heavenly palace, with a knowledge of these things proportioned to their merits? Is it no happiness to the mother to hear and know about her absent child? Why less in Heaven than on earth?

And even if we could not satisfactorily account for the manner in which God communicates that knowledge, would it follow thence, that He does not or cannot communicate it at all? This it were presumption and blasphemy to assert.

But even the manner may be conceived to a certain extent. We are told by St. Paul (1 Cor. xiii. 12): "We see now through a glass in an obscure manner, but then face to face. Now I know in part, but then I shall know even as

I am known." And St. John says: "That when He (God) shall appear, we shall be like to Him, because we shall see Him as He is." (1 Jo. iii. 2.) Our knowledge then in Heaven shall be perfect, with that perfection of which the human mind is capable, and we shall see God as He is. But God, as He is, is everywhere, and in all things, and all things subsist in Him. The atom that plays in the sunbeam, the rippling wave that catches it in its fold, all created things subsist in God, and God is in all things, as the Apostle says to the Athenians: "For in Him we live, and we move, and we are." (Acts, xiv. 28.) If then the saints see God as He is, they see Him in us, and us in Him, since in Him we live, move, and are. What prevents them, therefore, from seeing the motions of our hearts and lips in prayer, and that everywhere, since God is everywhere. But whatever the manner may be in which God communicates to His saints the power of hearing our petitions, we know that he does so in fact. It is not for us to be searchers of majesty, lest we be overwhelmed by glory. (Prov. xxv. 27.)

Remember that "great is the power of God—and seek not things that are too high for thee, and search not into things above thy ability: but the things that God hath commanded thee, think on them always, and in many of His works be not curious; for it is not necessary for thee to see with thy eyes those things that are hid. And the suspicion of them hath deceived many and hath detained their minds in vanity." (Eccl. iii. 21–23, 26.)

"But is there no danger of idolatry in honoring and invoking the saints? Does such practice not resemble that of the heathen, who called upon numberless inferior deities, from whom they expected benefits and favors?"

We have already defined the nature of idolatry in our lecture on the Real Presence. Idolatry consists in giving to a creature the worship which is due to God alone. Do we do this? With regard to the honor which is given by us to the saints, our catechism teaches: "We are to honor saints and angels as God's special friends and servants, but not with the honor which belongs to God." And with regard to the prayers we address to them, the catechism of the Council of Trent, published in virtue of its decree, by order of Pope Pius V., says: "God and the saints are not to be prayed to in the same manner; for we pray to God that *He Himself would give us good things, and deliver us from evil things;* but we beg of the saints because they are pleasing to God, *that they would be our advocates,* and *obtain from God* what we stand in need of." (Part iv.)

Hence our forms of prayer differ. We say to God: "Have mercy on us," "deliver us," "grant us," "save us;" to the saints we say: "Pray for us," "intercede for us." And if, at times, the forms of prayer are identical, the faith which offers them is quite different. These forms, when addressed to God, mean, in the minds of those who address them, that He is the only source of all the favors and graces which are asked; that He possesses in himself the benefits and blessings that are prayed for; whereas, addressed to a saint, they mean only that, while these have them not themselves, as of their own, they may, as the special friends of God, obtain them by their prayers, through Jesus Christ, who alone is our Saviour and Redeemer.

This made Hallam, a Protestant writer, say: "The invocation of saints as held and explained by that Church [the Roman Catholic] in the Council of Trent, is surely not idolatrous." (Constitutional Hist.)

It was not thus the heathens honored and prayed to their inferior deities. Their worship terminated on the idol as a Deity, and they expected from the very deity they addressed, the benefits they asked for.

Finally, observe that the Church does not teach that it is necessary unto salvation to pray to the saints. All she says is, "That it is *good* and *useful*" suppliantly to invoke them, and to have recourse to their prayers. And although it would show a disposition adverse to the spirit of the Church not to do so, we may be true members of the Church, without conforming to this good and useful practice.

With regard to pictures and images of Christ and of the saints, the Church teaches as follows: "The images of Christ, of the Virgin mother of God, and the other saints, are to be kept and retained, particularly in the churches, and due honor and veneration is to be paid them, not that we believe there is any divinity or power in them, for which we respect them, or that any thing is to be asked of them, or that trust is to be placed in them, as the heathens of old trusted in their idols, . . . but the honor which we pay to images is referred to the originals whom they represent; so that, by means of images which we kiss, and before which we kneel, we adore Jesus Christ, and venerate His saints." (Council of Trent, Sess. 25.)

Notwithstanding this plainest and clearest posssible statement of our doctrine, on the respect and honor due to pictures and images, our separated brethren have, from the beginning of the so-called Reformation till this day, never ceased to misrepresent it in their books and from their pulpits. It is objected by them, that it is forbidden by the second (first, they should say) Commandment to make any images or pictures: "Thou shalt not make to thyself a graven thing, nor the likeness of any thing that is in heaven above, or in the earth beneath, nor of those things that are in the waters under the earth." (Exod. xx. 4.)

We can hardly think that our separated brethren believe their own objections. If they mean to say, that by these words Almighty God forbids the making every and any kind of pictures and images, how will they reconcile one scripture with another? For it is certain that the same Jehovah who gave this commandment, through his servant Moses, ordered the same Moses to make two cherubim of gold on both sides of the mercy-seat (Exod. xxxvii. 7.) And also, "the Lord said to him" (Moses): "Make a brazen serpent, and set it up for a sign; whosoever being struck shall look upon it, shall live. (Numb. xxi. 8.)

Solomon, who, by the order of Heaven, built a magnificent temple to the Lord, "carved all the walls of the temple round about with carved figures of cherubim and palm-trees, and open flowers within and without." (3 Kings, vi. 32, etc.)

And so he did with the doors. (Ibid. vii.) And he made a molten sea (ibid. 23), and it stood upon twelve oxen (ibid. 25); and on the borders that were between the ledges were lions, oxen, and cherubim. (Ibid. 29.)

It is rather strange that God should forbid the making of any likeness in heaven or on earth, and yet allow so many of them in His very temple?

But do our brethren themselves observe this commandment? Let the traveller who has visited London answer this question, with regard, for instance, to Westminster Abbey, St. Paul's, and other churches. If our separated brethren have not all an image of the cross on their steeples, there are not a few who place the changeable weathercock in its stead. And surely, it is as much forbidden to make the image of a weathercock, as to make that of the cross itself. Enter their parlors and drawing-rooms. Are there no pictures on the wall? none on the mantelpiece or the centre-table? Open their purses. Are there no graven things therein? Is there a family, whose members scruple to have their likenesses taken by a painter or a photographer? are there any who think it a sin, to keep and retain them in their houses, to carry them about, to hang them on their breasts, to wear them in their finger-rings?

It cannot be, therefore, that they believe that God forbade, absolutely and unconditionally, the making or engraving of any image or likeness. What, then, *did* He forbid? To make them our gods, our idols, and to adore them, and serve them. Hence the commandment says: "Thou shalt not adore them, nor serve them." (Exod. xx. 5.)

"But you Catholics adore them; for you kiss them, bow your heads to them, take off your hats; you kneel to them; you pray to them."

We never kneel or pray *to* any picture, image, or likeness whatsoever, but *before* them. To kneel and pray *to* an image would suppose life, energy, power, consciousness in the picture or the image, if, namely, these acts, as the preposition *to* would seem to indicate, terminates *on* the image or the likeness; but to perform these same acts *before* them, while they are expressions of respect, honor, and veneration, are not acts which terminate on the picture or likeness as such, but are, through them, referred to the originals whom they represent. Nor is this practice forbidden by the Scriptures. How, otherwise, could Joshua fall to the earth upon his face before the ark of the Lord until the eventide, he and the elders of Israel, and exclaim: "O Lord God, why wouldst thou bring this people over the river Jordan, to deliver us into the hands ot the Amorrhite?" etc. (Jos. vii. 6, 7.) Thus, God ordered Moses and Joshua to put off their shoes, because the ground on which they stood was holy. Doubtless the respect and reverence which these men of God showed to the ground on which the Lord had stood, could not be idolatry—was not an act of adoration—for then, how could God Himself have commanded it?

But do not our separated brethren fall into the same sin of which they accuse us? Who among them never kissed the portrait of his departed mother? Who, whether sitting, standing, or kneeling, in the presence of that portrait, never gave way to his feelings, and soliloquized after some such manner? "Dearest mother, oh how we regret your absence from your children! Who will restore you to your beloved?" etc. Do you deem such a burst of filial love an act of idolatry? Would you not answer, if the objection were made, "It is not that I believe the spirit of my mother dwells within this canvas, or lives in these colors; but I refer my heart to that spirit which lives, I trust, in heaven. To that spirit I breathe my prayer—to it I raise my plaintive voice." And why then do you blame the Catholic, who kneels, who weeps, who prays before the image of the Crucified, the Madonna, or his favorite Saint in heaven.

Suppose your patriotic son stood before a statue of Washington, and spoke as follows: "Father of my country, would to Heaven thou couldst return to earth once more. In these days of civil discord and bloody war, in this fierce contest of social passions, would thou wert once more the leader of our armies, the counsellor of our States, the hope of all!" Would you rush to your son, and, with a holy indignation, exclaim: "My son, O my son! Mummery, trumpery, idolatry, superstition! you are speaking to a lifeless form of marble, and you identify it with the father of your country!"

or rather, would you not admire and applaud his noble feelings, his truly patriotic spirit?

Now, suppose, on the other hand, a Catholic standing or kneeling before an image of Christ, and praying as follows: "Sweet Jesu, oh grant that the wicked, the sinful of this world, may be converted from their iniquities, and return to Thee in all the sincerity of repentance. Grant that virtue and justice may reign, where iniquity abounds!" etc. Why do you now become indignant, and vent your animosity in calling him an idolater? Has he done any thing more than did your son, whose conduct you not only approved but applauded?

And would you allow us to show any disrespect to the statues or portraits which represent the loved ones among your departed or living friends? Would not a husband resent the tearing up or burning of the portrait of his departed wife? With what eye would you look upon us, if, in our indignation against hero-worship, so common in our day, we were to break to pieces the statues of your favorite presidents or generals? What mean those national monuments, which, with statuary, and sculpture, and pompous inscriptions, adorn the public squares of the cities that witnessed the birth or death of the departed great? Are·

not these erected by the nation out of respect, gratitude, and love, and preserved from the same reasonable feelings? Are they not a part of the history of the greatness of empires, kingdoms, and republics,—a history, too, which all can read, the ignorant as well as the learned; the poor as well as the rich? They are history carved in stone, sculptured in marble, breathing on canvas.

Who has not felt the powerful influence exercised by painting and sculpture upon the human heart? Who can gaze upon the Crucifixion by Rubens, without experiencing a feeling such as came over the penitent thief, who hung beside the dying God-man, and exclaiming with Him: "Lord, remember me, when Thou shalt come into Thy kingdom!" (Luke, xxiii. 42.)

Who ever cast his eye upon the sweet face of one of Raffaele's or Murillo's Madonnas, and did not feel the worth of that spotless virginity, that priceless purity, which beams from the eyes and is wreathed in heaven-lit smiles around her lips?

On the other hand, what can the visitor of Westminster Abbey learn from the monuments, the busts, the statues, the marble tablets erected to statesmen, admirals, generals, orators, and poets, along the walls or in the side chapels of that once Catholic temple, adorned by our ancestors with memorials sacred to the sainted dead? Alas! alas! the altars of the living God, the memorials of His saints are defaced, disfigured, or stand neglected relics of things that were; and in their stead a new religion and a new priesthood have desecrated the house of the Lord, by introducing into its very sanctuary monuments and statuary raised to men and women, whose lives, whose deeds, whose writings were often a disgrace to religion and morality.

After all we have said, we deem it unnecessary to prove that Christianity has, from its earliest times, always paid a due respect and veneration to sacred images and pictures. The portraits of the Good Shepherd, represented, as Tertullian testifies (Book on Chastity, c. x.), on the chalices, the palm branch sculptured on the martyr's tomb, the statue erected to the Saviour, of which Eusebius speaks (Eccl. Hist., b. vii.), and the portraits of the Saviour, and the Apostles S. Peter and S. Paul, which were preserved till his own day, were the work of Christians in the first and second centuries, and prove that it was *the tradition of the Apostles and Holy Fathers* which led the

Council of Nice unanimously to decide and confirm, that the images of Jesus Christ, our Lord, were to be respected, in honor of Him whom they represented. The 8th General Council defined, "*According to the most ancient tradition*, that images should be placed in our temples, to the end that at the sight of these sacred representations, they who behold them may transport to their prototypes their mind, their thoughts, and desires." (2 Can. Conc., c. v., vii.)

"But do not the Catholics, especially the ignorant portion of the Church, believe that there is some life, power, or virtue in those images and statues?"

By no means; and the Catechism which every child, rich and poor, lettered and unlettered, has to learn before he is admitted to Holy Communion, plainly tells him that he is forbidden "to pray to images and pictures," "because they have neither life nor sense to hear us."

Away, then, away forever with the unjust calumny, and conclude with the Anglican bishop, Montague (Epist.), that "the pictures of Christ, of the Blessed Virgin, and of the saints, may be had in houses, and placed in churches; and respect and honor may be given them;" and with the catechism of the Council of Trent (Part iii.), "that images are prohibited only inasmuch as they may be the means of transferring the worship of God to inanimate objects, as if the adoration given them were given to so many Gods."

"But you represent God the Father under the form of an old man, and the Holy Spirit under that of a dove or fiery tongue, and the images of your Madonnas and Saints do not bear any resemblance to the subjects they represent. Is not this dangerous to the simple and unlettered believer?"

If so, then the Scriptures are equally blamable, for they represent them thus. Daniel, for instance, paints Him as "the Ancient of days seated on a throne, and before Him the books opened." Angels appear as men, eat and drink like men. And besides, is there any picture, even a daguerreotype, that always exactly resembles the original? If the Catholic thought that the exact representation of creatures is required, then, indeed, might the objection have some weight with us; but such is not the case. The object of our veneration and honor is not the perfection of the likeness, the resemblance of the picture to the original: it is its memorial nature, which, through the symbol, lifts up the soul to the person symbolized. Images are intended to recall events, to reproduce history, to stimulate imitation, etc.

Do our adversaries suppose that the triangle, representing the Trinity, does actually represent the nature of the oneness of divine essence in three divine persons? Do they imagine that the symbol of an eye shadows forth the real nature of the omniscience of God? And yet these signs or symbols are as familiar to them as crosses and crucifixes, portraits and paintings of Madonnas and saints, are to us. In fine, do they require, in order that their children may learn geography or astronomy, that the wood-cuts of mountains, seas, lakes, rivers, sun, moon, and stars, should resemble in every particular, the reality of those objects in the universe?

From the honor due to pictures and images we pass to the respect and veneration which, with still greater reason, we bestow upon the relics of the Saints who reign with God in heaven. This practice is sneeringly called honoring dead men's and women's bones. In reference to the relics of the Saints the Church teaches, "that the bodies of holy martyrs, and of others now living with Christ, which were the living members of Christ and the temple of the Holy Ghost, by him to be raised up and glorified unto everlasting life, are to be venerated by the faithful, through which many benefits are bestowed on men by God; so that they who affirm that veneration and honor are not due to the relics of Saints, or that such relics and sacred monuments are uselessly honored by the faithful, and that the places dedicated to their memories are in vain visited for the sake of impetrating their aid, are absolutely to be condemned, as the Church has long since condemned, and now also condemns them." (Council of Trent, Sess. xxv.)

In these words of the Council of Trent we find, besides the doctrines, the leading motives which induce us to honor the earthly remains of the Saints. The first motive is, that they were the living members of Christ. The Church, as we have had occasion to remark before, is a body, of which Christ, its founder, is the ever living head, and his followers the several members. As when Christ died, He did not cease to remain the head, so neither when the Saints died, did they cease to be members of that spiritual body. And as the influence of the head animates the other members of the body, so the respect which is due to the head must, with due proportion, be shown to the members. The head being God as well as man, is to be adored, but the members, being divine by adoption and participation only, while they cannot be adored, must, nevertheless, be honored and venerated according to the share which they had in the influence of the head upon the members. In the language of the Saviour Himself, "I am the vine, you the branches. Abide in me, and I in you. As the branch cannot bear fruit of itself, unless it abide in the vine, so neither can you unless you abide in Me. Without Me you can do nothing." (St. John, xv. 5, etc.) We honor, then, the relics of the Saints because of their intimate union with Jesus Christ; and the honor bestowed upon the relics of the members is bestowed for the sake of the head. This union in the Catholic is of a peculiar nature. He is a member of Christ's body, not merely through faith and the grace of justification, but he becomes united, through the Holy Communion, in that most intimate manner in which, next to the hypostatical union and that of the Incarnation, man can become united with God. Flesh with flesh, blood with blood, and concomitantly, Divinity with humanity. This union is, according to the Saviour, the principle at once of our resurrection and our glorification in heaven. It must, therefore, be the principle of the respect and honor which are due to the instrument of that union. This is no other than the body of the saint; that body, therefore, whether dead or alive, deserves to be honored for the sake of Him who honored it exceedingly, and promises to honor it by a glorious resurrection, and assumption into heaven.

The second motive is, that those bodies were the temple of the Holy Ghost: "The temple of God is holy, which you are" (1 Cor. iii. 17); "know you not," continues the same Apostle, "that your members are the temple of the Holy Ghost, who is in you, whom you have from God, and you are not your own." (1 Cor. vi. 19.) Now, if any man violates that temple, him shall God destroy. (Ibid. iii. 17.) The bodies of the Saints, then, instead of being treated with contempt, as our separated brethren would have us do, should be respected and honored, as having once been the temple of that Holy Spirit who was poured out into their hearts, helped their infirmity, prayed in the Saints and for them, with unspeakable groanings, and who bore testimony that they were the children of God.

The third motive is the future resurrection of those bodies. To raise the dead is an act of omnipotence; it is an honor God will bestow upon all, it is true, but in an especial manner upon His Saints. For while all shall rise again, not all shall be changed. Though the body of the saint "is sown in corruption, it shall rise in incorruption; it is sown in dishonor, it shall rise in glory; it is sown in weakness, it shall rise in power; it is sown an animal body, it shall rise a spiritual body." (1 Cor. xv. 42, etc.) Why should we not honor the remains of the departed, which God will so greatly honor?

The last motive, is the immense weight of glory which these bodies shall share with their spirits in the kingdom of heaven.

Nor is there any thing more natural, than that we should honor the remains of those whom once we honored and loved, while they were on earth, or who deserved our respect and love. True friendship, real love, are not confined to the living person who is the object of our love. It extends to every thing that belongs to him.

We value a watch, a ring, any object whatsoever, for the sake of the person we loved and cherished, more than for their intrinsic material worth. So we daily read of swords of generals, bullets, and balls found on a celebrated battlefield, yea, of furniture and clothing purchased at enormous rates, exhibited to visitors with peculiar delight, inspected and handled with extraordinary relish and care, and preserved with worshipful devotion. What but this in born respect and reverence for the relics of the departed, caused the Egyptian to embalm, and thus preserve till the latest posterity, the remains of his ancestors, sovereigns, relatives, or friends? What but this principle, applied in a different way, made the Greek and Roman burn the bodies of the departed, and preserve their ashes in costly and curiously wrought urns? What but this same principle causes our separated brethren to fence in the graves of their relatives, and erect monuments above their tombs? That love which dies with death is cold indeed, and scarcely deserves the name. Gratitude, like true love, survives the death of benefactors; yea, it is not unfrequently kindled only when the flame of life is gone out in the darkness of the tomb. When envy has quenched her torch, and jealousy closed her jaundiced eye, then it is that benefits bestowed appear in all their worth, and elicit those grateful feelings in the human breast, which, during the benefactor's life, were suppressed by interest or by passion.

"But, you expect favors from these relics, and attribute to them the power of miraculous cures—you imagine that the contact with, or touch of these dead bones, or of saints' garments, can restore health to the sick, sight to the blind, hearing to the deaf, yea, life to the dead. And is not this superstition?"

We believe, indeed, that through their instrumentality God, whose power is infinite, can, often did, and still does bestow such blessings and favors. I say, through their instrumentality. For, of themselves they have no such virtue or power. He who would believe that any relic of any saint has such virtue of itself, that is to say, as bone or garment, would do wrong, and deserve the censure and condemnation which you yourself pronounce upon him. We believe the same of relics as we do of images—that they have no special virtue or efficacy of their own, but, that God, at times, makes use of them as means and instruments to bestow favors and graces. It was in this spirit that Eliseus smote the waters of the Jordan with the mantle of Elias, and they parted, and the prophet passed over. (4 Kings, ii. 14.) It was with this faith that a dead man was let down into the sepulchre of Eliseus, and no sooner did he touch the bones of the prophet than he revived, and stood up on his feet. (Ibid. xiii. 21.)

With the same faith did the woman in the Gospel (Matt. ix. 20-22), who was troubled with an issue of blood for twelve years, come behind the Saviour and touch the hem of His garment. "For she said within herself: If I shall but touch His garment, I shall be healed. But Jesus, turning about, and seeing her, said: Take courage, daughter, thy faith hath made thee whole. And the woman was made whole from that hour." Observe, that the object of the woman's hope of being cured, was Christ's garment; on it, as on the instrument of her cure, did she fix the eye of her faith. She might, like the blind man along the way, have called aloud upon Jesus to bless her; but no, her faith is centred on the hem of His garment, as the instrument of the desired cure. What peculiar virtue was there in the hem of that garment, as such? None whatever, save what He who wore it gave to it, as to a medium or an instrument to heal diseases.

"What would you think," said we, on one of our missions, to an intelligent young Protestant, who expressed to us his abhorrence of his mother-in-law's superstition, in believing that the relics of the Holy Cross and Saints could be of service in the healing of diseases, "what would you think, sir, if any of the faithful should come with handkerchiefs and aprons, to touch the living body, or garments, of a holy minister of Christ's Church, with a full conviction, and unwavering confidence, that if these handkerchiefs and aprons were laid on a sick child, it might, through their instrumentality, be cured?" "Why, sir," was his answer, "I would think it gross and ignorant superstition." "Have you read your Bible, friend?" was our next question. "I have, sir," was the reply. "Well, then, please read it again, especially Acts, xix. 11, 12, where you find it stated: 'And God, wrought special miracles by the hand of Paul, so that even there were brought from his body to the sick, handkerchiefs and aprons, and the diseases departed from them, and the wicked spirits went out of them.' Again, my friend, what would you think of the Christian, who, seeing a holy minister of his Church coming up the street, would run into his house, to carry his sick babe, on a couch, into the street, so that the saintly man's shadow might cover the babe; and the babe be healed?" "I would judge it superstition still more silly." "Well, friend, turn back to the Acts of the Apostles (ch. v. 14–16): 'And the multitude of men and women that believed in the Lord was more increased; insomuch that they brought out the sick into the streets and laid them on beds and couches, that when Peter came, *his shadow*, at the least, might overshadow any of them, and they might be delivered from their infirmities; . . . who were all healed.'"

Is there any more power in the empty shadow of a saint passing through the street, than in his bones or garments? Observe that this superstition, as some are pleased to call it, was practised not by the heathen nor the Jews, but by *the multitude that believed in the Lord.* And so far from rebuking them for it, St. Paul and St. Peter allow it without any resistance, and Heaven approves their faith and practice by astounding miracles. Miracles belong to divine power, and when wrought in approbation of the faith of the believer, are irresistible proofs of the truth of that faith, and of the practices dictated by it. For since the power of working miracles must come from God, when it is exercised in approbation of any practice of faith, God so sanctions that practice, that we cannot condemn *it* without condemning *Him* who sanctions it.

Nor did this faith and these practices of the

Catholic Christians cease with the death of the Apostles. Our divine Saviour had promised that they that believed in Him, the works that He did they also should do, and greater than these should they do, because He was to go to the Father. (John, xiv. 12.) Not that every man who believes would work miracles at his choice, for this would be tempting God, but that in His true Church there would always be chosen souls, by whom, when need was, God would Himself display His miraculous power, and that not during life only, but even after death.

Hence ecclesiastical history, like the Bible, is full of evidences of respect shown to, and of miracles wrought by, the mediation of holy men and women, and their relics.

Giving an account of the martyrdom of St. Polycarp, who was the disciple of St. John the Evangelist, the members of the Church of Smyrna write: "And so we afterwards gathered up his bones, more valued than stones of much price, and purer than fine gold, and laid them in a fitting treasure-house. Thus, assembling as we may in joy and triumph, the Lord shall grant us to celebrate the birthday of his martyrdom, both to the remembering of them who wrestled before in the cause, and the training and preparing of those that shall come after." (Euseb. Eccl. Hist., b. iv., ch. xv.)

"The holy blood of the martyrs is everywhere received," says St. Hilary, "and their venerable bones daily bear witness; while before them devils tremble, maladies are expelled, and wonders wrought." (Contr. Const. Imp., n. 8.)

St. Cyril of Jerusalem writes: "And let us not foolishly disbelieve, as though this had not happened; for if handkerchiefs and aprons, which are external, when they touched the bodies of the sick, raised up the infirm, how much more should the body of the prophet raise the dead!" (Catech. xviii., n. 16.)

St. Ephrem teaches that "God dwells in the relics of the saints; thence are they able to work every kind of miracle." (Vita B. Abra.)

But it is useless to multiply testimonies on this head. Let us conclude the subject by regretting, from our hearts, that our separated brethren should have rejected so good, so profitable, so holy and instructive a doctrine and practice. What has become among them of that beautiful article of the creed: "I believe in the Communion of Saints?" Can you believe that death severs all the relations that ever existed on earth between man and man, Christian and Christian? Can you believe, mothers, that your feelings of sympathy and affection, and the external expression of them for your dearly loved but departed children, if they are in heaven, are without an echo in the other world? Can you believe that, when in your distracted grief you cling to the dead, the inanimate form of your fondly loved child; when you call upon it with many sobs and sighs; when you address it as your own, dear, sweet, innocent, darling, little angel, that your angel is indifferent to your affectionate sympathy and sorrow? Do you believe, my friends, that all the ties of love and kindred are severed by the hand of inexorable death, so that when the loved husband of your choice, and the dear wife of your affection, take their seats in the kingdom of bliss, there is suddenly a veil drawn over their knowledge, which makes it impossible for them to see or hear you in spirit? Ah, no! We are too well acquainted with the heart of man to believe that it really admits the existence of so cruel a law of separation and unmitigated divorce. Oh, tell us not, whatever else may be your creed, that on this point, at least, your heart is not naturally Catholic, as well as Christian. Alas! to what absurdities has not the contrary doctrine logically led! Instead of the moral, spiritualizing, and elevating intercourse between the departed and the living, such as we read of in the written word of God and the pages of tradition, we hear and read of a heaven which is all material, and as immoral as the Olympus of the ancient Greeks and Romans. The highest conception of the communion of the saints in heaven, with those on earth, is found in the theories of the demonologists of old; and our new demigods, in the modern heavens, amuse themselves and their friends here below by overturning sofas and bedsteads, rapping on tables, and playing on guitars and banjos. According to the last development of these theories, we must conceive the inhabitants of the heavenly paradise as pursuing the same avocations there as they did here below, as tilling their spiritual farms, running their spiritual saw and grist mills, making spiritual butter, and drinking spiritual buttermilk. (Judge Edmonds, vol. ii., p. 134, 135.)

Oh! all ye blessed Angels and Saints of heaven, intercede for us and for our separated brethren. Obtain for us an increase of love and respect for your holiness of life, veneration for your pictures, images, and relics, and for them that light which is necessary to open their eyes to the beauty of sanctity, and the power of your intercession in heaven. Amen.

IX.

ON THE HONOR AND INVOCATION OF THE BLESSED VIRGIN MARY.

"Behold! from henceforth all generations shall call me blessed." LUKE, i. 48.

Is it pride, madness, or inspiration, which makes a young maiden, scarcely sixteen years of age, the descendant of a royal but fallen family, the inhabitant of an obscure town, exclaim, in the bold language of the text above cited, "Behold! from henceforth all generations shall call me blessed?"

Pride or presumption it cannot be, for the words which precede the text give the Virgin's humility as the reason of her bold language. "Because He hath regarded the humility of His handmaid. Behold! from henceforth all generations shall call me blessed!" Much less was it madness; for who dares blasphemously assert that the infinite Wisdom of the Father should have chosen a woman that was crazed for His beloved mother? It was, then, the voice of inspiration, the voice of the Holy

Spirit, the voice of the Most High, which made her exclaim: "Behold! from henceforth all generations shall call me blessed." As the voice of inspiration, we must examine the meaning of the prophecy. The sense is plain and obvious. Mary prophesies that from that very day, onward through the ages, all generations shall call her blessed. To call one blessed, is the outward expression of inward respect, honor, veneration, which the person deserves. Mary, then, foretells that from the day on which she became the mother of Christ, all generations should continue to respect, honor, and venerate her as she deserves. The objective reason of this respect, honor, and veneration was evidently her divine maternity,—the fact that she had become the mother of Christ.

Hence, we may infer, without doing any violence to the text, that the full meaning of the prophecy is as follows: Behold, from this day, on which I am the mother of Christ, true God and true man, all Christian generations shall call me blessed. There was then to be a succession of Christian men and women, in all ages, among all nations, who from the commencement of Christianity till the end of time, should, in the self-same manner, show Mary that respect, honor, and love which her dignity, as mother of the Redeemer, entitled her to, from that very day. Now, where are those Christian generations? To what Christian association or church do they belong? Which among all the so-called Christian churches, has existed ever since the birth of Christianity, throughout all ages, and among all nations, and consistently and uniformly honored the Blessed Virgin as she deserves to be honored? The voice of history unhesitatingly answers: The Church of Rome. She, among all other churches, is the first and the last which till now has fulfilled that prophecy: she was the only one that could fulfill it. Born with the rise of Christianity, she alone has existed among all generations, for she alone was always Catholic or Universal. Hers was the only spiritual empire upon which the sun never set, and she is the only one which has always honored Mary according to her dignity and the excellence of her sublime office. Even those churches which rose up afterwards, and retained, as some of them did, a certain degree of respect and love for Mary, could not fulfil the prophecy, merely because they came too late.

Take Simon Magus, Diotrephes, Ebion, Cerinthus, Hermogenes, the Nicolaites, though they founded their sects and churches in the very days of the Apostles, they came too late, if it were only one year, to fulfil a prophecy whose fulfilment was to commence with the very birth of Christ. Much less could the Encratites, Marcionites, Carpocratians, and the Gnostics of the second, the Elcesaites, Sabellians, the Aquatics, or Manicheans of the third century, fulfil this prophecy. Moreover, none of those churches continued to exist throughout all ages, and none of them existed among all nations, even in their short-lived day. None of them were Catholic or Universal. With much more force does this reasoning apply to our separated brethren, whose churches were founded only three hundred or two hundred years ago. Even on the hypothesis that some of them have a due regard for the Immaculate Mother of their Redeemer, they came much too late to fulfill the prophecy of the Virgin. Sixteen centuries had passed by, before their particular Christian churches could begin to fulfill the prophecy. Nor can any one of them even now fulfill it; for none of them exist among all generations now living on the surface of the earth. All are of their nature either national, or confined to a portion only of the wide world. Yea, what is stranger still, most of the modern Christian churches oppugn the honor which is due to Mary, and rank it among the superstitious and idolatrous practices of heathendom. The Roman Catholic Church alone, therefore, has fulfilled Mary's prophecy, which was inspired by the Holy Ghost, and so far, at least, proves herself the true Church of the Bible, and therefore of Jesus Christ.

" But why do Roman Catholics make so much of Mary; why are they so prodigal of their praises in her regard? Why do they so honor and love her?"

We blush to think that such a question should have fallen from the pen or lips of those who call themselves Christians! Our answer is, because of the example the Deity itself has given us of this honor, and praise, and love; and because of the excellence and dignity of Mary as the mother of the Redeemer.

Is there any danger of superstition or idolatry in doing what the three divine persons of the most adorable Trinity themselves have done?

How could God the Father honor any woman more highly, than by choosing her, from all eternity, to become the mother of his only-begotten Son? This the Bible teaches us He did. From all eternity did He decree to make man; and when in His omniscience He foresaw that the man whom He would create in the course of time would fall, and his whole posterity with him, He likewise decreed that, to lift him up from his degradation, and to restore him to life and hope again, He would send His only-begotten Son into this world, clothe him with the garb of a slave, and in the flesh redeem the world. While decreeing this mystery of His infinite condescension, He decreed that Mary should be the fortunate woman of whose flesh His own Word would take His flesh and become the Emmanuel, the God with us. She was truly the chosen one of Heaven, among thousands and thousands of millions. Hence it stands written, at the very head of the book: "I will put enmity between thee (the serpent) and the woman, and thy seed and her seed; she shall crush thy head." (Gen. iii. 15.) The woman here alluded to is no other than Mary, who, by giving birth to the Saviour, crushed the head of the serpent which had seduced Eve and brought ruin on our race. Hence He continues to honor her throughout the ages that precede the accomplishment of the great event. All the prophets who prophesy of the Messiah, either explicitly or implicitly prophesy of Mary. What honor, to prepare the world during four thousand long years for the coming of a creature who was to give birth to the Creator of the world!

But, oh! what exceedingly great honor for the Eternal Word to choose Mary as His own mother—to make her virginal bosom His lonely sanctuary during nine months, to make the flesh and blood of Mary His own, so that it is no exaggeration to say, with one of the Fathers of the Church, that the flesh of Jesus is the flesh of Mary, and the blood of Jesus the blood of Mary!

To accomplish this mystery, the Holy Ghost, in a miraculous manner, supplies the place of Joseph, the husband of Mary. In vain does the Archangel plead the cause of Heaven before this chaste, this humble Virgin. She will not consent to become the mother of her God, if it is to be with the loss of her virginity. "How shall this be done, because I know not man? Fear not, Mary, for no word shall be impossible with God." The Holy Spirit shall honor thee exceedingly. He Himself shall vouchsafe to become thy spouse; He shall come upon thee, "and the power of the Most High shall overshadow thee. And therefore, also, the Holy which shall be born of thee shall be called the Son of God." (Luke, i. 34, 35, 37.)

Again, we honor Mary on account of her dignity and excellence as the Mother of our Redeemer. "Honor to whom honor is due," says the Apostle. That honor must be proportioned to the dignity and the excellence of the person honored. But among mere creatures, none can possibly possess a dignity greater, nobler, sublimer, than that of Mother of God. Cast your eyes, we do not say over the whole world from the creation of Adam and Eve till this very day, but over the hierarchies of the heavenly spirits; which among them all can declare, rising from his throne, and standing before the Lamb: "Thou art my Son; I have brought Thee forth." Mary is the only one who can claim that privilege; Mary, alone, enjoys the title of Mother of God.

Our brethren outside of the Church seem to ignore, or to forget, the real nature of the relation in which Mary stands to Jesus. Most of them have fallen into the heresy of Nestorius, who taught, that while Mary could appropriately be called the Mother of Christ, she could not, without blasphemy, be called the Mother of God.

It will be well, therefore, to refresh our

memory on the real nature of the mystery of the Incarnation, and thence conclude to the dignity of Mary as the blessed Mother of the Saviour.

St. John the Evangelist gives us an explanation of that mystery, when, in his first chapter, he exclaims: "In the beginning was the word, and the word was with God, and the word was God. The same was in the beginning with God. All things were made by Him, and without Him was made nothing that was made. And the Word was made flesh, and dwelt among us." (1-3, 14.)

The same Word, therefore, who was begotten of the Father from all eternity, who had with Him the same divine nature—the same divine and undivided, as well as indivisible Essence—became flesh. Of whom? Of Mary. He received from her, therefore, His nature of flesh and blood—His human nature; so however, that the divine and human nature, themselves distinct, and unconfounded the one with the other, were united in one and the same divine Person, the Word of the Father; and thus Mary became, and was truly, what she is said to be, the Mother of God. "Whence is this to me," exclaimed Elizabeth, filled with the Holy Ghost, "that the Mother of my *Lord* should come to me?" (Luke, i. 43.) The Lord of Elizabeth was no other than God; and that God had come to her with her cousin, who bore Him in her virginal bosom.

It is true, that Mary did not give His divine nature to Jesus; that He held it exclusively from His heavenly Father. We do not wish to convey the idea that the divine nature and person of the Word did not exist before Mary became the Mother of the Redeemer; but we maintain, that since, at the conception of Christ, the human nature which He had from Mary became united in one and the same Divine Person of the Godhead, Mary must be, and is rightly styled, the Mother of God. An example will illustrate, to some extent, the truth of this mystery. When a mother gives birth to a child, she is truly and deservedly called the mother of that child; yet she did not create the soul of that child—the soul was created by God. All she formed in her bosom was the earthly part of his compound being. So, although Mary did not conceive the divine nature of the Word, yet, because at the very moment she conceived, the human nature was united in one and the same divine Person with the divine nature, she is truly the Mother of God. As such she has no rival, no equal in dignity, consequently, among mere creatures; no rival in the honor, love, and veneration which are due to her on that account.

Hence the universal belief of the Church on this subject, till Nestorius disturbed it by his heresy. In the liturgy of St. James, which, if not composed by the Apostle, is certainly very ancient, we read this invocation: "Most Holy, most Glorious, Immaculate, etc., *Mother of God*, and ever Virgin."

In the liturgy of St. Mark the Evangelist, we find: "Most Holy, Immaculate, and Blessed *Mother of God*, and ever Virgin Mary."

In those of St. Basil, of Alexandria, and Rome, she receives the same appellation.

St. Athanasius exclaims: "Queen and *Mother of God* intercede for us." (Serm. in Annunt.)

St. Ephrem prays thus: "We fly to Thy patronage, Holy Mother of God." (Serm. de Laud. B. M. V.)

St. Augustine says, similarly, "Holy and Immaculate Virgin Mary, Mother of God our Saviour Jesus Christ, deign to intercede in my behalf before Him whose temple Thou hast deserved to be." (Med. ch. xl.)

Mary, then, occupies a special position of dignity and office among all other creatures, hence the special honor which is due to her, and which she receives from us.

Her character, her virtues, her holiness, were undoubtedly in keeping with her prerogative. And these constitute a new claim to our respect and veneration. The title of maternity is of itself a claim to the respect and filial piety of a mother's children, but when to these she adds genius, or talent, virtue, and sanctity in an eminent degree, that mother's claim on the honor and love of her children increases in proportion to the perfection of these qualities. That Mary must have been pre-eminent in every prerogative of nature and of grace, we shall scarcely dare to doubt, when we reflect that she became the Mother of Him who had it in His power to bestow all these special favors. There was, among many other marks of distinction, this difference between the maternity of Mary and that of other women; that her Son was at the same time her Creator. He could, therefore, make her all she deserved to be, all He wished her to be; yes, we venture to say, He made her all she should be to be worthy of Himself. If any one of us had had it in his power to create and to make his own mother whatever he could wish her to be, what do you think he would have made her?

According to the body, beautiful and lovely among all other women; according to the spirit, endowed with the highest genius and the most upright heart. According to grace, spotless, pure, free from the shadow of sin. Do you not suppose that Jesus did all this for His mother? Hence, for instance, our firm belief in her Immaculate Conception, which does not mean, as some of our Protestant contemporaries seem to have understood our doctrine, that Mary was conceived, like her Son Jesus, without the knowledge of man, but that by a special privilege and grace of the Omnipotent God, in virtue of the merits of Jesus Christ, the Saviour of mankind, she was, at the first instant of her conception, preserved free from all stain of original sin. And, indeed, how could He, who was to take up His abode in her chaste bosom, dwell in a tabernacle, defiled by the least taint of sin? How could He who came to destroy sin, have taken flesh of sinful flesh, without in some manner contaminating His own? How could He allow Satan, whose empire on earth He came to overthrow, have it in his power to say: "The temple in which you dwelled during nine months was once my own. The flesh which you received from your mother, was once under my control. She who gave you life was once my slave." Never could Christ permit such taunts to be true. Hence, while all others came under the law, Mary alone was exempted. Like Esther, she alone was saved from the decree of death, which by sin entered into this world and made all the children of Eve, except Mary, children of wrath.

The same dignity exempted her from all actual sin. She alone had no need of saying: "Forgive us our trespasses;" she alone was not deceived, and could say, without wounding truth, that she had no sin, that unlike the rest of the just, she never fell. Who does not see that all these singular privileges entitle her to a special regard and honor, which is not due to other men or women here below.

Mary had, in her maternity, a double title to the love of her Son. In all other instances the father holds the first, and leading rank, and the love of the child is necessarily divided between the father and the mother; but in this instance, the mother alone, has a claim to the undivided love of her Son. No man shares with her the privilege. She conceived, indeed, in a supernatural manner, but she contributed, likewise, as secondary cause, to the formation of that sacred Body, which was to be immolated on the Altar of the Cross, for the sins of the world. Who can tell the secrets of their mutual love! Imagine all you have ever read of the fondness of a mother for her child, and of a child for its mother. Picture to yourself the kind words that are spoken, the loving smiles that are exchanged, the tender caresses, the embraces, that are bestowed, the fond endearments that pass between a loving child and mother, and even then you cannot form a correct idea of the affection which existed between Mary and her darling Child. No! To understand the fulness of their mutual love, you should penetrate the secret of their hearts. Mary, the purest of mothers; Jesus, the most loving of men! Oh! how those loving hearts beat together! How pulse answers to pulse, throb to throb, sigh to sigh, joy to joy, while the heart of the Son rested under the heart of His Mother. There was no sensuality, no carnal feeling in the affection of either the Son or the Mother. It was more than angelical—it was divine. In a word, it was the love of a Mother for her God, and the love of a God for His mother.

No wonder, therefore, that the incarnate Word should continue to show, by His example, the same deference to Mary, which, as the

Word of the Father, He exhibited to her, long before He chose her as His Mother.

We read of Him, that after having been found in the temple, and having returned to His earthly home, in Nazareth, He was subject to Mary, and to Joseph. Submission implies respect, honor, and obedience. Jesus therefore, respected, honored, and obeyed His mother through thirty long years. Respect is outward, as well as inward. Honor sincerely bestowed is felt inwardly. Jesus, then, respected, and honored Mary in all those ways in which inferiors love to show their respect and honor to their superiors. What forbids our supposing, that Jesus did towards His mother what dutiful children are wont to do, when they manifest their feelings of respect and deference to their parents? What forbids our supposing, that He saluted her after the fashion of the Eastern nations, by prostrating Himself before her? What forbade his giving her precedence in the presence of others; asking her consent to do those things, which good children generally do not undertake without the leave of their parents? What, if like other pious children, when occasion required, He asked His mother's blessing? Suppose an **artist**, like St. Luke, had given Him a copy of her portrait, would He indignantly have refused to accept, and keep the same? Would He have refused to kiss it with filial affection? We beg leave to differ from those, who, in their antagonism to Mary, would entertain the doubt. Jesus was the Son of Mary, and the best son that the best of mothers ever had.

Why, then, do you blame the Church, and her children, for doing what Mary's Son, according to the dictates of common sense, Himself did during His lifetime at Nazareth? Why will you not allow us to kneel before her, and ask her blessing? Why do you oppose the making, the keeping, and the honoring of her portraits, and her statues? Why do you deem it an insult to her Son, to pray to His mother, that through her intercession, we may obtain benefits and favors? Has she less power over her Son, now in Heaven, than when she was on earth? Who has never felt the influence of a mother over the hearts of her children?

We all know how great her power was on earth. You remember having read of her visit to her cousin, Elizabeth! Having learned from the Archangel Gabriel, that this holy woman had conceived a son, in her old age, Mary rose up, and went into the hill-country, with great haste, into a city of Juda, "and she entered into the house of Zachary, and saluted Elizabeth. And it came to pass, that when Elizabeth heard the salutation of Mary, the infant leaped in her womb. And Elizabeth was filled with the Holy Ghost: and she cried out with a loud voice, and said: Blessed art thou among women, and blessed is the fruit of thy womb. And whence is this to me, that the mother of my Lord should come to me? For, behold, as soon as the voice of thy salutation sounded in my ears, the infant in my womb leaped with joy." (Luke, i. 39, etc.)

According to the testimony of the Holy Ghost Himself, the first miracle in the order of grace took place through the instrumentality of Mary. For it is the opinion of many learned Fathers and Doctors of the Church, that St. John, the Baptist, was at that instant sanctified in his mother's bosom. And this seems reasonable, when we reflect that he leaped with conscious joy at the sound of Mary's salutation, at a time, when such consciousness cannot be but the result of a miraculous interposition of divine Providence.

As in the order of grace, so the first miracle in the order of nature, was wrought by the intercessory power of Mary. We are told by

St. John that "there was a marriage in Cana of Galilee, and the mother of Jesus was there. And Jesus also was invited, and his disciples, to the marriage. And the wine failing, the Mother of Jesus saith to Him: They have no wine. And Jesus saith to her: Woman, what is to Me and to thee? My hour is not yet come. His mother saith to the waiters: Whatsoever He shall say to you, do ye. Now, there were set there six waterpots of stone, according to the manner of the purifying of the Jews, containing two or three measures a piece. Jesus saith to them: Fill the waterpots with water. And they filled them up to the brim. And Jesus saith to them: Draw out now, and carry to the chief steward of the feast. And they carried it." (John, ii. 1–8.) And what did the chief steward find upon tasting the water? He found it changed to wine. At whose request? At the request of Mary the mother of Jesus. Under what circumstances? When His hour was not yet come; that is to say: when, according to the ordinary course of His divine Providence, He Himself, without the request of His mother, would not have wrought the miracle. And observe the confidence of Mary in her son's goodness and filial piety. Apparently, His answer is disrespectful. "What is to Me and to thee, woman?" He calls her woman instead of mother. But as Bloomfield, the learned Protestant commentator, remarks: "This word was a form of address which implied nothing of disrespect, and was employed by our Lord on the most affecting of all occasions, and when He especially evinced His exquisite sympathy and tender regard for this very parent." Or, as St. Augustine remarks: "To indicate to her, that in divine operations, He did not recognize maternal authority."

She understood the character of her son, despite the apparent harshness of His words, and felt confident that, for her sake, He would be willing to do, what otherwise He would not have done. Has Mary less influence over her son, now that both are in heaven, than when they were sojourners on earth? Who dares assert this paradox? What wonder is it, therefore, that Catholics, who understand the relations which Mary bears to Jesus, and who have learned their respective characters, should have such unbounded confidence in her powerful intercession?

"But you make more of her than of the redeemer. You worship her as a goddess; you call more frequently upon her than upon her

Son. In her litany you bestow extravagant titles upon her, and, in general, your orators eulogize her more frequently, and more feelingly, than they do the Saviour of the world."

God forbid that we should compare the worth of Mary with that of Jesus. We know, that however exalted she may be above all other creatures, she yet stands at an infinite distance from her divine Son. Listen to the answer which St. Epiphanius made to the Collyridians, who gave undue honor to the Virgin Mary: "Her body I own, was holy, but she was not God. She continued a virgin, but she is not proposed for our adoration; she herself adoring Him, who, having descended from heaven, and the bosom of His Father, was born of her flesh. Against this error the Gospel itself has guarded us, saying (John, *ubi supra*), "Woman, what is to thee and to Me? My hour is not yet come." He calls her woman, lest any one should imagine that she was of some superior nature. Though, therefore, she was a chosen vessel, and endowed with eminent sanctity, still she is a woman, partaking of our common nature, but deserving of the highest honors shown to the Saints of God. She stands before them all, on account of the heavenly mystery accomplished in her. But we adore no saint, and as this worship is not given to angels, much less can it be allowed to the daughter of Ann. Let Mary, therefore, be honored, but the Father, Son, and Holy Ghost, be adored. Let no one adore Mary." (Adv. Collyridianos Hær. lix.) Does this suffice to convince you that we are not Mariolaters, or Mary worshippers?

It is true that we call upon her very often; but in a different way from that in which we address her Son. We call upon Mary to intercede, to pray for us; we call upon her Son to obtain a favorable answer to our petitions. There are even natural motives for these frequent calls upon the goodness and power of Mary. The tenderness of woman's nature, the sympathy which she feels for misery, the readiness with which she succors, especially when her nature is unmarred by prejudice or passion, instinctively induce the child to have recourse to his mother for those very favors which it is only in the Father's power to bestow. Moreover, we know the influence of a virtuous woman over a virtuous man's heart. We know that she seldom, if ever, pleads in vain. Our countrymen ought to be the very last to object to this reasonable and natural practice of their Roman Catholic fellow-citizens.

What is more common among us, than to make use of woman's mediatory influence to obtain certain results, which men do not hope to realize by the means of the highest genius or talent? It is not that we doubt either the power or the good will of the Son, to grant our petitions. No, far be it from us to entertain so heretical, so blasphemous an opinion. But like the servants of the marriage feast in Cana, although they might have addressed themselves first to Jesus, we address ourselves to His Mother, as the most certain means of obtaining what we desire. We know our sinfulness and our unworthiness, we know that "the countenance of the Lord is against them that do evil things," but that "His eyes are upon the just, and His ears unto their prayers (Ps. xxxiii. 16, 17); we know that, as one of the conditions of being heard, we must abide in Jesus Christ, and His words must abide in us (John, xv. 7), that our heart must not reprehend us, in order to have confidence in God, and that whatsoever we shall ask we shall receive of Him, if we keep His commandments, and do those things which are pleasing in His sight. (1 John, iii. 20, 21.) But alas! who of us fulfills all these conditions of an efficacious prayer? We know, on the other hand, that "the continual prayer of a just man availeth much" (James, v. 16), and that Mary is full of grace, and blessed among all other women; consequently that her prayer in our behalf is certain to be heard, inasmuch as it is the prayer of Jesus' ever pure, holy and immaculate Mother.

As to the various titles which we bestow upon her in our prayers, and, in particular, in the litany recited in her honor, which of them all transcends, in praise or eulogy, that which Elizabeth by divine inspiration bestowed upon her, when she called her the Mother of her Lord, or which the Holy Ghost lavishes upon her, when He so often calls her the Mother of Jesus? Select a few specimens: "Holy Mary!" Is not she holy, whom the spirit of sanctity proclaims "full of grace?" "Mother of divine grace!" Was she not the parent of Him, whom St. John calls "full of grace?" (John, i. 14.) "Most pure Mother!" Was she not the purest of mortals, who was conceived without sin, and was she not chaste, who remained a Virgin after she had become a Mother? "Mirror of justice!" Was it not she who reflected the light of the just, the Holy one, who was born of her flesh? "Seat of wisdom!" Did not incarnate wisdom repose during nin-months in her womb? "Honorable, spiritual vessel!" Who but she carried the precious treasure beneath her mother's heart? "Vessel of devotion!" Was she not the devoted mother who followed her Son to Calvary, and heroically took her stand beneath the ignominious cross? "Mystical rose!" Was she not the root of Jesse, out of which a flower was to rise up? (Is. xi. 1.) Was she not the "Tower of David," the mother of that King who swayed the nations from the cross, and "Ark of the covenant," who bore not only the law but the lawgiver Himself? "Queen of Angels,"—by which of God's angels was it ever said: "Thou art my son; this day have I begotten thee?" Mary could say to the King of angels: "This day I have conceived Thee and brought Thee forth." "Queen of patriarchs!" After whom did they sigh, when they asked the clouds to rain down the "Just One?" Whose son did Abraham long to see, if it was not the son of Mary? "Queen of prophets!" The chief burden of their oracles was the Messiah, His coming, His suffering, death, and glorious resurrection, His spiritual power over the nations, His kingdom that would have no end; and the Virgin who would bring forth that mighty king. "Queen of Apostles!"

Was it not Mary, that gave birth to Him, who afterwards said: "All power is given to Me in heaven and on earth, going, therefore, teach all nations?" (Matt. xxviii. 18.) Was it not her free will, which chose Him for a son, who afterwards chose the twelve, and sent them that they might bring forth fruit, and that their fruit might remain? (John, xv. 16.) What made the martyr's blood so fruitful as the seed of new Christians, if not the blood of Christ, whose blood was the blood of Mary? "Queen of Virgins,"—was she indeed, who, after as before the birth of her Son, remained a Virgin. In fine, "Queen of all saints,"—who gave to the world the "Saint of saints," and opened to it the fountain-head of all sanctity.

Does not the woman blessed among all others deserve the highest eulogies and encomiums from orators, the sweetest lyrics from poets? Should not sculpture love to chisel her matchless form, and painters to portray her peerless graces? We do not wonder, therefore, that even Protestant writers should have felt inspired to sing this lovely Virgin's praise. And that in quest of the beautiful in human nature, they should have fixed upon her as their ideal, and exclaimed with the meditative Wordsworth:

> "Woman! above all women glorified!
> Our tainted nature's solitary boast!
> Purer than foam on central ocean tost,
> Fairer than Eastern skies, at sunset strewn
> With fancied roses."

No, the wonder with us is not that Catholics are so lavish of their eulogies of Mary, but that those who call themselves Christians, and own Mary as the Mother of Jesus, should be so chary of their encomiums and panegyrics, when there is question of the Virgin.

The ministers of those Christian sects love to dwell upon the characters of the women of the Old Testament. They discourse eloquently on Rachel, Rebecca, Ann, the mother of Samuel; Miriam, the sister of Moses; Ruth, Esther, and Judith. Elizabeth, Anna the prophetess, Mary Magdalen, Martha, can win their admiration, and rouse their souls to a sacred enthusiasm but when there is question of Mary, the Mother of their Saviour, their courage and their eloquence fail them, and their heart grows faint, in the fear lest every sound of praise in honor of Mary, be a reflection cast upon her Son. The audience share the scruples of the speaker. They are thrilled with horror, when from pulpit or platform they hear her name. What minister would dare salute her as Gabriel did, or, in the eloquent prayers which Sabbath after Sabbath he addresses to the throne of grace, would venture to mingle those sweet words of inspiration: "Hail, thou highly favored, the Lord is with thee, blessed art thou among women, and blessed is the fruit of thy womb?" His hearers would deem him a papist or a madman, if he attempted it. And yet these men boast of pure Christianity, and charge the Roman Catholic Church with Mariolatry, as if the Archangel Gabriel, as if inspired Elizabeth, as if the Holy Ghost, as if God Himself were abhorred and detested worshippers of Mary? Who does not see the absurdity of such hypocrisy! Suppose that you were living in the days of Mary, and were her neighbor. Suppose, further, that you knew then, as you know now, that Jesus is the Son of Mary, and she His Mother, would you have any scruple to go to her dwelling and to say to her, as follows: "Mary, Mother of my Saviour, I am a poor, a miserable sinner. I know that my course of life displeases thy beloved Son, my Redeemer. Please be so kind as to ask Him to grant me the grace of being a good, a virtuous man; a good, a holy woman." We are sure that in so doing, you would not consider yourself superstitious, nor a worshipper of Mary. Why have you any scruple to do the same now that she is in Heaven. For you doubt not but Jesus has taken Mary up to Heaven; you doubt not but He has placed her on a throne next to Himself. Would He allow any saint to have precedence of His mother? Are you afraid that she cannot hear you? We have already answered that difficulty, in our lecture on the invocation of saints. What then are you afraid of? That she is less kind, less charitable than you would suppose her to have been on earth? But charity is perfected, not diminished, in the kingdom of God. Oh! then, address yourself to Mary. If you dare not join in our prayers, salute her at least, in the words of your inspired Bible, say to her with the Archangel, "Hail, full of grace (or, Thou highly favored), the Lord is with Thee, blessed art thou among women;" and with her inspired cousin: "And blessed is the fruit of thy womb" (Jesus); and we promise you, you will love Mary as we do; and you will experience, as all of us do, her powerful intercession.

Besides the general objection to the honor and love we exhibit towards the mother of our Redeemer, some of our separated brethren take delight in underrating the excellence of Mary, by dwelling on those Scripture texts in which mention is made of the brethren and sisters of Jesus, as if the ever chaste and Immaculate Virgin had been the mother of other children besides her Only Begotten.

True, we often read of the brethren, and of the sisters of Jesus. Thus (Matt. xii. 46): "Behold, His mother and His brethren stood without." (See also, Mark, iii. 31; Luke, viii. 19.) And again: "Is not this the carpenter's Son? Is not His mother called Mary, and His brethren, James, and Joseph, and Simon, and Jude? And His sisters, are they not all with us?" (Matt. xiii. 55, 56.) They are also mentioned in John, vii. 3, 5; Acts, i. 14; 1 Cor. ix. 5; Gal. i. 19.

St. Augustine asks: "Had our Lord brethren? Did Mary bring forth other children? Far from us be the thought; for, with her the dignity of Virgins took its rise. . . . Read the Scriptures, and you will find that the uncle and sister's son are called brothers; and having this usage present to your mind, you will perceive why all the relatives of Mary are styled the brothers of Christ. . . . When you hear of the brethren of the Lord, think of the kindred of Mary, not of any children of hers: for, as in the tomb where the body of the Lord was placed, no one was laid before or afterwards, so the womb of Mary, neither before nor afterwards, conceived any thing mortal.". (Kenrick on St. John, ch. ii. and vii.)

It is well known, that the Jews and the Greeks often used the words, "brother and sister" to express relationship merely; and this is the case with the Evangelists and Apostles, when they speak of the brethren of our Lord. In St. Matt. xxvii. 56, we read of Mary Magdalen, Mary, the mother of James, and Joseph (or Joses, as St. Jerome calls him), and the mother of the sons of Zebedee. In St. Mark (xv. 40) we also read of a Mary who was the mother of James the Less, and of Joseph (Joses). In St. John (xix. 25) we read: "Now there stood by the cross of Jesus, His mother, and His mother's sister, Mary of Cleophas." James and Joseph, or Joses, were the sons of Mary of Cleophas, or Clopas. Now, as this Mary was the sister of the Mother of Jesus, James and Joses, therefore, were cousins, and from this relationship, the two latter are called the brethren of our Lord.

St. Jude the Apostle calls himself servant of Jesus Christ, and brother of James. This Jude was also called Judas Thaddeus, and is styled by St. Luke, the brother of James (vi. 16). St. Jude, then, bears the same relationship to Jesus, as is borne by his brother James of Alpheus. But Alpheus and Clopas are the same names, according to the learned commentators on the subject, such as Lightfoot, Gesenius, and others. Jude and Jesus, therefore, were first cousins, on the maternal side.

The fourth brother of the Lord is called Simon. According to Hegesippus, whose testimony is given by Eusebius (Lib. iii., Hist. G., ii.), he was another son of Clopas, or Alpheus, and of Mary, the sister of the mother of our Redeemer, and consequently, bore the same relationship to Jesus as did James, Joses, and Jude.

As to the sisters of Jesus, we are told that Salome and the Mary mentioned in Matt. xxviii. 1., were the daughters of Clopas, or Alpheus, and of Mary, the mother of James and Joses; so that they were, likewise, the cousins of Jesus.

There are other opinions among the Fathers and doctors of the Church, on the degrees of relationship existing between the so-called brethren and sisters of the Lord and our Saviour; but none, save the wicked heretic

Helvidius, and his followers, during the last three hundred years, have been so daring as to suppose that Mary had any other than her "first born Son," Jesus. (Luke, x. 7.) Some suppose that Mary, the mother of James and Joses, and Mary the mother of Jesus were not uterine sisters, but only cousins. They proceed on the supposition, that Clopas was not the husband, but the father of Mary the mother of James and Joses, and that Clopas and St. Joseph, the foster-father of Jesus, were brothers. On that hypothesis, there would be no consanguinity between them, but only a relationship, resulting from the fact, that the foster-father of Jesus was the brother of Clopas, who was the father of Mary, of James, and Joses. Whatever opinion we adopt, it will always remain proved, that Mary was a Virgin, after, as well as before she conceived and brought forth her divine Son. In conclusion, allow us to say to you, whatever you be, if you cannot, like us, love the mother of your Redeemer, cease, at least, to revile and insult her. As every mark of respect and honor shown to a parent redounds on the child, so every affront and insult offered to Mary, redounds on her Son. How can Jesus honor those who calumniate His mother? **How** can He confess them before His Father, who were ashamed to confess the dignity, the excellence, the greatness of His mother, before men!

We have a solemn duty to perform towards Mary. Next to God, next to Jesus, she has done more for us than any creature on earth, or in heaven, could possibly do. She gave us the price of our ransom; by her mediation we were delivered from sin and from hell; for she gave us Him who triumphed over both in the flesh, which He received from her. She opened to us the gates of a better paradise than that which our first mother Eve was the occasion of closing against us. O Mary, mother of Jesus, pray for us! Pray for those who sit in darkness and the shadow of death. Pray for those that hate you, that they may learn to love you as you deserve to be loved. Pray for our countrymen and countrywomen, many of whom neither know you nor the blessed fruit of your womb, Jesus. Pray for those who know and love you, that they may daily love you more and more. Pray for us, dear Mother, that we may know and love you so as to spread the love of you among all those who shall come to hear, or read your praises. Pray for us, that having fought the good fight for Jesus, your Son, and for you, His mother, we may obtain the reward, which of all others we cherish most, namely, to praise and love you and your Jesus, for ever in the Kingdom of Heaven. Amen.

THE END.

www.ingramcontent.com/pod-product-compliance
Lightning Source LLC
Chambersburg PA
CBHW051235300426
44114CB00011B/745